OPIUM ADDICTION
IN CHICAGO

PATTERSON SMITH REPRINT SERIES IN
CRIMINOLOGY, LAW ENFORCEMENT, AND SOCIAL PROBLEMS

A listing of publications in the SERIES *will be found at rear of volume*

PUBLICATION No. 126: PATTERSON SMITH REPRINT SERIES IN
CRIMINOLOGY, LAW ENFORCEMENT, AND SOCIAL PROBLEMS

OPIUM ADDICTION
IN CHICAGO

BY
BINGHAM DAI

Reprinted with the Following Additions:

Introductory Essay by Lois B. DeFleur,
CHICAGO ADDICTION IN CONTEMPORARY PERSPECTIVE

New Preface by the Author

Index

MONTCLAIR, N. J.
PATTERSON SMITH
1970

Originally published 1937
Reprinted 1970 by special arrangement with Bingham Dai
Patterson Smith Publishing Corporation
Montclair, New Jersey 07042
New material copyright © 1970 by
Patterson Smith Publishing Corporation

SBN 87585–126–6

Library of Congress Catalog Card Number: 72–124503

This book is printed on three-hundred-year acid-free paper.

CHICAGO ADDICTION IN CONTEMPORARY PERSPECTIVE

By Lois B. DeFleur

DURING the early 1930's, Bingham Dai approached the study of drug abuse in Chicago within a cultural, ecological and social-psychological perspective. At the time, such orientations represented a considerable departure from existing traditions. Problems of addiction were generally thought to be understandable mainly in medical terms or to be phenomena associated with mental illness. Not only did he bring new theoretical perspectives to the study of the illicit use of narcotics, but he brought new research methods to bear on this difficult problem. It is for these reasons that Bingham Dai's work is recognized as a classic of the "Chicago School."

More specifically, the problems Dai investigated and the methods he employed include the following. Within an historical perspective, he first undertook to trace the origin and spread of opium addiction in the United States (and in Chicago) as a cultural complex. Such an orientation defines the central problem as one of determining what groups are the recipients of the complex and how it becomes part of the behavior of the individual addict. Dai then undertook to assess the general characteristics of the addict population as it existed in Chicago. To do this he assembled basic demographic data from a variety of sources: the Cook County Psychopathic Hospital, the Federal Bureau of Narcotics, and the Narcotics Division of the Chicago Police Department. In order to understand the crucial problem of how the pattern of opium addiction is transmitted to the potential addict, Dai focused on the social and cultural situations within which this adoption process occurred. He found concentrations of addicts and noted their locations within the ecological organization of the city. He also conducted intensive interviews with selected addicts, seeking insights into the nature of their personality problems and emotional reaction patterns.

Through this multidimensional and multimethodological approach, Dai hoped to achieve new perspectives on this major social problem.

Perhaps more significantly, he sought clues as to possible ways to stop the continuing spread of opium addiction. Then, as now, the destructive impact of narcotics on the lives of their users was recognized and solutions were eagerly sought. Unfortunately, thirty years after Dai published his findings, and on the eve of the reprinting of his classic work, hope of finding means to minimize the problem remains elusive. In fact, public concern over narcotics addiction, and drug abuse more generally, has risen sharply since the 1930's. The dimensions of the drug problem itself have increased critically. In noting this increase, the President's Commission on Law Enforcement and the Administration of Justice recently reported that:

> In 1962 a White House Conference on Narcotic and Drug Abuse was convened in recognition of the fact that drug traffic and abuse were growing and critical national concerns. Large quantities of drugs were moving in illicit traffic despite the best efforts of law enforcement agencies. Addiction to the familiar opiates, especially in big-city ghettos, was widespread. New stimulant, depressant, and hallucinogenic drugs, many of them under loose legal controls, were coming into wide misuse, often by students. The informed public was becoming increasingly aware of the social and economic damage of illicit drug taking.[1]

In light of these trends, Bingham Dai's work has taken on added importance. It is hoped that a wider circulation of his findings and ideas, which will be achieved through the present reprinting of his work, will aid in stimulating further inquiry into the causes and consequences of drug abuse. Only through research on all aspects of our current drug problem can more adequate understandings be achieved.

The present reprinting is also significant for the discipline of sociology. The book is a good illustration of why the field has flowered in the United States during the last several decades. Shortly after the turn of the twentieth century, sociology was making a firm bid to establish itself in the American intellectual community. The central thrust of its teaching and research during this period was concern for a variety of social problems which were associated with industrialization and the

---

[1] President's Commission on Law Enforcement and Administration of Justice. *Task Force Report: Narcotics and Drug Abuse* (Washington, D. C.: U. S. Government Printing Office, 1967), p. 1.

urban environment. The Dai work, plus many others that focused on specific social problems in urban settings, showed that sociology could add significant dimensions to understanding these issues and could contribute to their eventual solutions.

Today's sociologists have benefited from pioneers such as Dai. For example, such efforts established a tradition of problem-oriented empirical research. This tradition is not only being continued today but it is yielding a growing accumulation of evidence from which more adequate theories can be formulated. From such early investigations have come today's perspectives on delinquency, suicide, adult crime, race relations, and many more. Furthermore, work such as that of Bingham Dai offered concrete evidence that sociology had something significant to say. Today's relatively easy access to research funds did not come about by accident. An earlier generation of sociologists made it clear to those who controlled funds that sociological research could yield relevant information on important problems.

There are other reasons why the present reprinting is sociologically noteworthy. Dai's research on opium addiction was one of the earliest to focus attention on the sociological and the social-psychological aspects of addiction. He not only examined addiction as a cultural complex which was being rapidly diffused in the United States, but he attempted to unravel the configuration of social variables that surrounded this diffusion. In addition, he investigated the personality characteristics of addicts because he felt that personal as well as social variables were important—even crucial—in the process of becoming an addict. The findings which resulted from this study are of more than historical significance; they are still relevant for current research on the addiction process. Dai's generalizations provide a sound basis for developing theories and hypotheses for the further investigation of addiction.

For students of the recent history of sociology, Dai's research on addiction provides an illustration of the type of studies that characterized sociological investigation during the 1920's and the 1930's. A number of the other studies done during this period were very similarly oriented and have attracted considerably more attention than Dai's. More widely known, for example, are the studies of suicide by Ruth S. Cavan,[2] of

[2] Ruth S. Cavan, *Suicide* (Chicago: University of Chicago Press, 1928).

delinquency by Clifford Shaw,[3] and of family disorganization by Ernest R. Mowrer[4] which have become classics in their respective areas. The principal reason for the lack of attention to Dai's work has been the fact that copies of the book were never widely distributed. All but a very few copies of Dai's book, which was originally published in Shanghai in 1937, were destroyed in the Sino-Japanese War. As a result of this misfortune, Dai's research did not receive the attention it deserved.

Chicago Sociology in the 1920's and 1930's

Bingham Dai was a student at the University of Chicago at a time when that department occupied a dominant position in American sociology. It was a department rich in professorial talent, not only in sociology, but also in a number of related disciplines such as psychology, philosophy, political science, and anthropology. Under the influence of men like Robert E. Park, Ernest W. Burgess, Ellsworth Faris, and others, the department made a number of significant contributions to the growth of the field.

It is clear that men such as Park and Burgess had a tremendous impact on their students. Robert Faris, in his book on Chicago sociology during this era, points out that morale was high. Students were hardworking, highly motivated, and enthusiastic for sociology.[5] It was with such a spirit that students carried out elaborate and significant research projects. Bingham Dai was one of these students. In the Preface to the First Edition, Dai acknowledges his indebtedness to several of these professors—Robert Park, Edward Sapir (of anthropology), Ellsworth Faris, and Herbert Blumer.

Perhaps more important at Chicago was the development of an emphasis on objectivity in sociological work coupled with a focus on urban problems. Robert Park, in particular, urged that the city of Chicago be used as a "laboratory" for study.[6] What followed was a whole series of research endeavors focusing on a number of specific topics

---

[3] Clifford R. Shaw, *Delinquency Areas* (Chicago: University of Chicago Press, 1930).

[4] Ernest R. Mowrer, *Family Disorganization* (Chicago: University of Chicago Press, 1927).

[5] Robert E. L. Faris, *Chicago Sociology 1920-1932* (San Francisco: Chandler Publishing Co., 1967), pp. 32-35.

[6] *Ibid.*, pp. 52-53.

with the aim of uncovering both the spatial structure of the city and the social processes operating within it. Many of these studies focused on problem-aspects of the city, such as crime, homelessness, suicide, and addiction, as part of the attempt to better understand urban life in the United States. Largely because of these emphases, the study of *urban* social problems became a major concern in American sociology.

One of the principal accomplishments of Chicago sociologists of this period was the formulation of a comprehensive theory of social change and social problems. This became known as the "social disorganization" or "social pathology" approach.[7] It stressed the fact that in areas where the usual community processes of social control, social solidarity, and socialization are disrupted for various reasons, social problems, such as addiction, would be generated. Burgess and Bogue point out that:

> On the one hand, individuals are incompletely or differentially socialized and on the other hand social solidarity and social control are weakened, so that both personal and social disorganization results. This theory was found to be highly useful in explaining many urban social problems.[8]

Thus, concepts such as personal and social disorganization were prominent in most of the conceptual schemes of the time.

Today, methodological techniques used in these early urban studies would be regarded as rather simple and descriptive; however, as was indicated above, most of the studies were regarded as complex and theoretical at that time. Of course, the level of quantitative sophistication varied from researcher to researcher, and perhaps more important, from topic to topic. The types of techniques used included ecological rates, percentages, prolonged interviews, life-histories, participant observation, and the analysis of documents.[9]

Overall, *Opium Addiction in Chicago* is rather typical of the urban research conducted in the 1930's in the sense that the conceptual framework is primarily personal and social disorganization. Also, it is typical in that the research makes use of techniques that were under development at the time.

[7] Ernest W. Burgess and Donald J. Bogue, *Contributions to Urban Society* (Chicago: University of Chicago Press, 1964), p. 488.

[8] *Ibid.*, p. 488.

[9] See Chapter 5, "Urban Behavior Research," in R. E. Faris, *op. cit.*, pp. 64-87.

Dai's Findings in Contemporary Perspective

Chapter 3 of Dai's book is devoted to an extensive discussion of the characteristics of Chicago opium addicts. The author presents various data summarizing many social and demographic features of his addict sample. Dai's findings on these issues can be compared and contrasted with the characteristics of addicts from more contemporary research. The recent data discussed below have been gleaned from a variety of sources and do not necessarily pertain solely to Chicago addicts. Nevertheless, it is important to try to place Dai's generalizations into such a perspective. The following discussion will be organized around both similarities and differences; that is, around characteristics of addicts that apparently have changed since Dai's approach and those that have seemed to remain stable over a thirty-year span.

The most striking changes in the addict population have occurred with respect to age, race, nationality, and type of drug used. A recent article by John Ball emphasizes these changes:

> Evidence from the present study and a review of the literature support the thesis that two quite distinct patterns of narcotic drug addiction exist in the United States at the present time. One addiction pattern is followed by young heroin users who come predominantly from metropolitan centers and are engaged in illegal endeavors. The other pattern is typified by the middle-aged southern white who uses morphine or paregoric and obtains his drugs through legal or quasi-legal means. The heroin pattern of addiction has increased markedly since World War II and is currently associated with minority group status. The second type of addiction preceded the passage of the Harrison Act in 1914 and has, in the subsequent years, decreased materially.[10]

Specifically, in terms of age, Dai found that, "Chicago drug addiction is mainly a problem of the adult population, the most common age group among these addicts being between 30 and 34.[11] This would suggest a median of approximately 32 years. Ball's recent study of over 3,000 addict patients discharged from the U. S. Public Health Service

[10] John C. Ball, "Two Patterns of Narcotic Drug Addiction in the United States," *Journal of Criminal Law, Criminology and Police Science,* 56, no. 2 (1965): 203.

[11] See p. 45.

Hospitals during 1962 found a median age of approximately 30 years. However, more comparable figures are Dai's percentage of slightly more than 24 per cent who were under 30, as contrasted with just over 49 per cent who were under 30 in Ball's study.[12] Other studies indicate the same trend—drug abuse is more and more becoming a problem of the young.

Other characteristics of addicts that have changed are race and nationality. Bingham Dai summarized his findings as follows:

> . . . the majority of Chicago's drug addicts of this period were members of the white majority. But compared with their respective incidences in the general population of the city the number of Negro and Chinese addicts did appear disproportionately large.[13]

Ball's study found that addict patients who had been in the federal hospitals were less often members of the white majority and more often members of minority groups. Ball notes:

> What has occurred since the 1920's is the increased use of heroin among addicts and the concentration of this type of addiction among Negro, Puerto Rican, and Mexican youth in metropolitan slum areas.[14]

A large-scale study of addicts in Chicago, now in the data-gathering stage (which will be discussed in a later section), also indicates a predominance of minority group offenders.

Finally, in terms of the type of drug most commonly used by addicts, Dai found that morphine was by far the most popular drug in Chicago in the 1930's. However, he did note that the use of heroin seemed to be increasing.[15] This contrasts sharply with the current situation reported by Ball:

> First, there has been a decrease in the use of morphine and a corresponding increase in the use of opium derivatives or synthetic analgesics. Second, the use of the underworld drug of choice— heroin—has increased until it is now the principal addicting opiate in the United States.[16]

[12] John C. Ball, op. cit., p. 208.
[13] Bingham Dai, "Opium Addiction: A Sociopsychiatric Approach," in Burgess and Bogue, op. cit., p. 646.
[14] Ball, op. cit., p. 209.   [15] See pp. 60-61.   [16] Ball, op. cit., p. 206.

There are two other areas in which notable changes have occurred since Dai's study. It now appears that proportionately fewer females are involved and that the link between addiction and crime has become more firmly established. In the 1930's Dai reported that the sex ratio among addicts was approximately 3 to 1.[17] At present in the United States, male addicts outnumber female addicts by about 4 or 5 to 1.[18] The relationship between drug addiction and crime has been a source of continuing debate. Dai gathered data on this issue and a number of subsequent studies have also been addressed to the same problem. O'Donnell recently reported the results of a follow-up study of 266 white Kentucky addicts and related his findings to a number of previous studies, including that of Bingham Dai:

> Only one-third of the men in this sample and less than ten per cent of the women had any arrests before they became addicted. The proportion with a prior record, however, increased steadily with the recency of addiction. Ninety-five per cent of the men addicted before 1920 had no prior record, and this percentage dropped to 53 for the men who became addicted in the 1950's. The finding that the proportion with prior criminal records has changed over time is consistent with the low percentage of prior records reported by Dai and Pescor, whose samples were collected in about 1930 and 1936 respectively.[19]

Thus, it appears that crime and addiction have become increasingly related over the last thirty years.

There are several characteristics of addicts which apparently have not undergone much change since the time of Dai's study. In particular, more recent research indicates little change in marital status and family ties, or in occupational characteristics, educational background, and general intelligence of addicts. For example, Dai found that over half of the male addicts were single. A number had experienced broken marriages. Very few of the addicts had children.[20] In his study of white Kentucky addicts, O'Donnell found much the same situation—many of

[17] See p. 46.
[18] John A. O'Donnell and John C. Ball, eds., *Narcotic Addiction* (New York: Harper and Row, 1966), p. 10.
[19] John A. O'Donnell, "Narcotic Addiction and Crime," *Social Problems,* 13, no. 4 (1966): 382.
[20] See pp. 55-56.

his male subjects had never married; many marriages had ended in divorce or separation; and the subjects had very few children.[21]

In terms of employment and occupational pursuits, Dai found that the addicts he studied were characterized by a great deal of irregularity in employment. When they were employed a large number of them were in domestic and personal service jobs or other low status occupations.[22] More recent studies also indicate that most addicts are unemployed a substantial part of the time, or they are engaged in lower status jobs.[23] Finally, Dai pointed out that the education of drug addicts was not particularly deficient compared to the general population and that limited data on intelligence indicated that over 50 per cent were normal or above normal.[24] O'Donnell and Ball also note that addicts are similar to their respective base populations in education and intelligence.[25]

These various findings are generally confirmed in a recent study of the characteristics of long-term drug offenders.[26] Thus, while there have been a number of very important changes in the personal and social characteristics of addict populations, many of their attributes, such as marital and occupational status, have remained much the same.

Currently, the present writer is conducting a comprehensive study of addiction patterns in Chicago over a thirty-year span.[27] When completed, this inquiry should offer many more points of comparison with Dai's work. In fact, it will supply information from the time period immediately following the Dai investigation up to the present. Briefly, the project is designed to locate spatial concentrations of drug abuse in Chicago from 1940 through 1969. It will analyze clusters of social, economic, and cultural variables which are and have been associated with high and low rates of addiction in specific areas of the city. One source of data is Chicago admissions to the Clinical Research Centers

---

[21] John A. O'Donnell, "Marital History of Narcotics Addicts," *The International Journal of the Addictions,* 2, no. 1 (1967): 21-38.

[22] See pp. 51-55.

[23] O'Donnell and Ball, *op. cit.,* p. 10.

[24] See pp. 51 and 58.

[25] O'Donnell and Ball, *op. cit.,* p. 10.

[26] Lois B. DeFleur, John C. Ball, and Richard W. Snarr, "Long-Term Social Correlates of Opiate Addiction," *Social Problems,* 17, no. 2 (1969): 225-234.

[27] NIMH Grant No. 16332-01, "Long-Term Ecological Patterns of Drug Addiction."

(U.S. Public Health Service Hospitals) in Lexington and Fort Worth. Over 11,000 admissions from Chicago for the years 1940–1969 have been assembled. In addition, samples of arrest data from the Narcotics Division of the Chicago Police Department for 1942–1969 are being gathered. It is anticipated that over 20,000 additional cases will be obtained from this source. Once the data-gathering has been completed, attention will be devoted to extensive analyses of addiction rates, Chicago census data, and other information on the city of Chicago. Through the use of graphics, multivariate techniques, trend-surface analyses, and other procedures, temporal sequences in the ecology of addiction will be investigated, as well as other factors which are related to the changing incidence of drug addiction in Chicago.

Tables 1 and 2 have been constructed from preliminary information available from this study. These tables provide an approximate picture of what has been happening more recently with respect to the number and type of addict patients from Chicago that have been admitted to the Lexington Hospital since 1935. It shows a large increase of patients during the 1950's. The trends indicate a sharp rise in the number of non-white patients. Table 2 shows trends in narcotics arrests for Chicago from 1942–1968. The data show a general increase in the number of cases during the 1950's and a decline during the mid-1960's. Perhaps more important, there also appears to be another increasing trend during the late 1960's. Addiction in Chicago, as elsewhere in the nation, is becoming a problem of larger scope.

An Evaluation

Any research project, old or new, has both strengths and weaknesses. This is clearly the case with *Opium Addiction in Chicago*. For the most part, the limitations of the research stem from methodological considerations. These are partially due to the obvious point that techniques of the time were less sophisticated than those of today. However, as will be noted below, Dai did not always make the most effective use of those that were in vogue. On the other hand, the strengths of the study lie mainly in its imaginative approach to the research problem and in the substantive findings that it yielded. In spite of its methodological shortcomings, the evidence it presents has added important dimensions to our understanding of addiction.

TABLE 1

ADDICT PATIENTS FROM CHICAGO, ILLINOIS, ADMITTED
TO LEXINGTON HOSPITAL, 1935–1966

YEAR OF ADMISSION	WHITE		NON-WHITE		TOTAL
	Male	Female	Male	Female	
1935	63	*	24	*	87
1936	43	*	26	*	69
1937	29	*	27	*	56
1938	51	*	45	*	96
1939	46	*	56	*	102
1940	37	*	21	*	58
1941	28	4	22	0	54
1942	64	33	39	3	139
1943	48	31	17	2	98
1944	46	15	21	8	90
1945	60	16	13	0	89
1946	42	6	25	0	73
1947	71	28	24	7	130
1948	46	14	64	8	132
1949	79	27	213	25	344
1950	88	40	482	64	674
1951	74	19	256	43	392
1952	92	28	261	65	446
1953	108	33	479	137	757
1954	103	37	398	133	671
1955	105	36	399	131	671
1956	101	51	432	156	740
1957	95	48	494	150	787
1958	102	44	422	140	708
1959	65	31	313	108	517
1960	57	31	282	87	457
1961	70	26	144	61	301
1962	83	25	215	72	395
1963	80	30	230	77	417
1964	63	15	152	46	276
1965	70	17	101	48	236
1966	94	16	158	65	333
Total	2,203	701	5,855	1,636	10,395

*Females were not admitted to the hospital during these years.

TABLE 2

NARCOTICS ARRESTS FOR THE CITY
OF CHICAGO, 1942–1968

YEAR	NUMBER OF ARRESTS*	YEAR	NUMBER OF ARRESTS
1942	376	1956	9,011
1943	378	1957	9,102
1944	370	1958	9,439
1945	400	1959	10,029
1946	692	1960	10,361
1947	711	1961	7,909
1948	736	1962	7,230
1949	1,054	1963	7,369
1950	1,600	1964	6,109
1951	6,000	1965	4,273
1952	7,500	1966	5,279
1953	8,267	1967	5,953
1954	7,639	1968	7,341
1955	7,454		

*The figures for the years 1942–1950 are subject to minor potential errors which could underestimate arrests by as much as one or two per cent.

Deviance research in general continues to suffer from inaccessability of critical data. Investigators since Durkheim have relied heavily on public records of various kinds in the study of suicide, delinquency, crime, and other forms of deviant behavior. The use of information obtained from official sources has frequently been criticized; these criticisms are well known; they center around the issues of validity, reliability, and representativeness; there is little point in rehashing them here.[28] Perhaps the only thing that need be said about the use of such data is that there is little prospect that the situation will improve. Sociological research on sensitive issues will undoubtedly continue to be dependent upon information from official records by virtue of the fact that little else is available in any large-scale sense. The only possible way out of this dilemma is to encourage officials to establish records

[28] See, for example, John C. Ball, "The Reliability and Validity of Interview Data Obtained from 59 Narcotic Drug Addicts," *American Journal of Sociology*, 72, no. 6 (1967): 650-654.

with greater research utility and to develop ways of maximizing validity and reliability of information obtained from such sources, within the limits to which this can be accomplished. This issue is less a criticism of Dai's study, therefore, than a simple noting of the fact that all such studies have inherent limitations along these lines.

A more specific methodological problem arises from Dai's attempt to provide a comparative analysis between areas of high and low addiction rates within the city. Such comparisons should be accomplished by establishing certain criteria of control over those areas that are to be contrasted. For example, it would have been appropriate for Dai to compare areas of high and low rates that had been *matched* on a number of critical variables. Then, he could have tried to sort out factors that were present in high-rate areas but not in low-rate areas. Once located, such key factors could have been studied in all areas of the city with varying addiction rates. Unfortunately, Dai used a procedure that does not permit inferences of this type. His comparison areas not only differed greatly in social characteristics, but they differed sharply with respect to the dependent variable (addiction rates). Such a compounding of factors, of course, places limitations on what comparative analyses can yield.

A different type of methodological problem exists in the section of the monograph which is based upon case studies obtained through the use of prolonged interviews. Dai prefaces this section with extensive cautions to the reader that the cases are neither numerous nor representative enough to provide a basis for conclusive generalizations. In fact, many of the specific case studies are introduced with warnings that the materials do not provide sufficient information for "satisfactory analysis." After posing such cautions repeatedly, Dai then proceeds to make detailed interpretations of each case and to draw rather extensive generalizations from them.

One might overlook this issue, as it is more one of inconsistency than substance. After all, insights concerning possible causal sequences can often be obtained from a detailed study of specific cases. However, the particular hypotheses which Dai induces do not always seem to follow convincingly from the case material he presents. In one instance, for example, Dai concludes that a given woman became addicted because of a combination of factors including post-operative habituation and the influence of friends who were apparently users. In reading the account, however, it was clear that also in the picture were an earlier divorce, an operation resulting in the loss of child-bearing capacity, substantial economic problems, and possible family quarreling over her career in show business. Dai fails to make clear why he chose selectively from the many factors present to construct a possible explanation of this woman's addiction.

The problem of case studies has always been that of evaluating the generalizations obtained from them. At this late date it is scarcely necessary to revive the ancient arguments over the merits of case studies versus the statistical approach. Nevertheless, this issue—which endlessly troubled sociologists in the 1930's—continues to plague the interpretation of the case materials presented by Dai. Perhaps it is worth noting in passing that because of their problems of interpretation, the use of case studies in sociological research has declined regularly over the last half-century. A recent study of research reports in major sociological journals noted that since 1915, the use of case studies in articles has declined from 35 per cent of such publications to less than 18 per cent.[29]

Dai's choice of rather simple statistical methods could be criticized. However, techniques that are common in sociology today had not been widely adopted by sociologists at the time. Multiple and partial regression analyses were being used in other fields, but they had yet to penetrate the social sciences on any widespread basis. The same was true of factor analysis. Psychologists were conversant with early forms of the technique, but its use by sociologists had not yet begun. Applied to Dai's data, these statistical procedures might have yielded more penetrating analyses of both spatial configurations and factors related to addiction. However, such criticism can scarcely be leveled at an individual practitioner when they represent shortcomings of the general state of the art.

In spite of these shortcomings, Dai's monograph remains as a classic that helped give direction to the contemporary study of addiction. To indicate in specific terms what might be considered Dai's more lasting contributions in this monograph, the following can be suggested: (1) He showed how opium addiction spread in the United States as a cul-

---

[29] James L. McCartney: "On Being Scientific: Changing Styles of Presentation of Sociological Research," *American Sociologist*, 5, no. 1 (1970): 31.

tural pattern. It is still spreading, although the facilitating and contributing factors have undoubtedly changed somewhat. More recent research has sought to identify various types of addict populations, each of which have adopted variants of this culture complex. (2) Dai focused attention on the significance of interpersonal variables in the adoption and continued use of drugs by individual addicts. Contemporary research has continued to emphasize the importance of the primary group in understanding the addiction process.[30] (3) Dai also emphasized the role of impersonal (community) variables. He used the ecological approach to show that addiction was concentrated in areas characterized by social disorganization and high rates of deviant behavior. This is still true today. More contemporary studies continue to attempt to unravel relationships among such variables.[31] (4) Dai emphasized the role of psychological considerations in the addiction process. In much more sophisticated ways, we are still attempting to follow this line of investigation. Contemporary students of drug abuse such as Lindesmith continue to emphasize the social-psychological aspects of the problem. (5) Treatment factors were under investigation in Dai's research. Modern approaches to treatment certainly include variables that he studied, although many alternatives are being tried. While Dai emphasized physical separation from other users of drugs, modern programs such as Synanon and other group-treatment centers, attempt to get the addict to adjust to the type of area and type of people within which he must live. (6) Finally, but by no means least significantly, Dai pointed out the inadequacy of the legal approach to controlling addiction. At the time of Dai's writing, major legislation attempting to limit the spread of drugs —the Harrison Act—was less than twenty years old. Dai concluded that it was ineffective as a form of social control and that other means should be sought to combat the increasing use of drugs. We are even more firmly convinced today that these legal approaches have limited value, and are still seeking effective alternatives.

Thus, in spite of its limitations, Bingham Dai's *Opium Addiction in Chicago* remains a lively, insightful, and scientifically important investigation of a major social problem. The present reprinting of the

---

[30] Solomon Kobrin and Harold Finestone, "Drug Addiction Among Young Persons in Chicago," Research Report, 2, no. 10, mimeographed (State of Illinois, Institute for Juvenile Research, 1965).

[31] DeFleur, Ball, and Snarr, *op. cit.*

work will permit it to be brought to the attention of a young and enthusiastic generation of sociologists whose level of concern with the problems of society runs high. One can only hope that, armed with the more sophisticated orientations and techniques of today, plus the leads provided by such pioneers as Bingham Dai, they will be able to make even more significant gains in understanding narcotics addiction.

Washington State University
April, 1970

PREFACE TO THE REPRINT EDITION

This study was completed in 1935. In the thirty-five years that have passed, there have been a number of important changes in the narcotic drug situation. These are expertly documented by Professor Lois B. DeFleur in the Introduction, for which I am deeply grateful. Especially significant are the facts that heroin has become the drug of choice in the recent decades instead of morphine; that narcotic drug addiction has become more a problem of the younger generation than it was in the 1930's; and that while the use of morphine or paregoric among middle-aged whites in the southern states has apparently decreased in the past three decades, the use of heroin by the younger generation in the metropolitan areas all over the country has markedly increased. This is especially so among the members of the minority groups.

Reviewing the situation as a whole, it is exceedingly disheartening to observe that in spite of all the increasingly stringent legal measures adopted by the Federal and local law-enforcement agencies during the past three decades, the problem of narcotic drug addiction in this country has not decreased in magnitude to any appreciable extent; on the contrary, it has in many ways become worse! This fact has led me to believe, as many informed students of the problem do, that a complete reorientation of the public attitude toward narcotic drug addiction is long overdue and that a radical change of policy for its control is urgently needed. More specifically, we should begin seriously to think of the narcotic drug habit as a disease, as we do of alcoholism, and the narcotic drug addict as a patient instead of a criminal, as the Joint Committee on Narcotic Drugs of the American Bar Association and the American Medical Association recommended a decade ago. Furthermore, instead of relying on more stringent punitive measures, our efforts to combat the narcotic drug habit should be directed more toward treatment and prevention.

From this vantage point, this study may be said to have two distinct contributions to make to the further understanding and the eventual solution of the problem of narcotic drug addiction. One is the multi-

disciplinary approach used throughout the study and the other the findings from the case studies that pertain to the formation and the nature
of the narcotic drug habit and to the methods of rehabilitation and prevention.

Before I elaborate on the special value of the multidisciplinary approach to the problem of drug addiction, perhaps a few words may be
of some interest as to how I came to adopt this approach at a time when
it was not generally encouraged in social science circles. From 1929 to
1932, I had the good fortune of studying sociology at the University of
Chicago under Robert E. Park, who was best known as an authority on
urban sociology and race relations, but who unreservedly encouraged
my interest in personality. It was through his recommendation that I
was given the unusual opportunity of studying anthropology at Yale
University under Edward Sapir from 1932 to 1933. This work took the
form of a year-long seminar on culture and personality with representa-
tives from thirteen different cultures as its participants. It was in this
seminar that I came to know Harry Stack Sullivan, who later became
my first analyst. My training analysis was completed in Chicago under
Leon Saul during the two years when I was interviewing drug addicts.
Thus, it was due to a lucky concurrence of my own interests and the
new training facilities just made available that I was enabled to look at
narcotic drug addiction as a problem to be attacked from different
points of view instead of a subject of inquiry for any single discipline,
such as sociology. Nowadays, of course, interdisciplinary courses for
graduate students are available at most of the leading universities,
although to acquire the psychoanalytic approach as a research tool may
still require some special effort.

The special value of the multidisciplinary approach to human behavior lies in its emphasis on the process of interaction between the individual and his socio-cultural environment and in its insistence that the
nature of a given social situation and the individual's perception of it
on the basis of his personality needs, conscious or unconscious, must
be explored at the same time. Only in some such way can we fully
understand the meaning of any given social situation for an individual
and why he responds to it as he does.

When one applies this multidisciplinary approach to the problem of
narcotic drug addiction, one will invariably find, as I did, that most
addicts acquire their habit through association with confirmed drug

users and that it is the individuals with certain unsatisfied personality needs or unresolved emotional problems who are most susceptible to this type of recruitment. The various personality needs and social situations that are conducive to the formation of the drug habit are described in the text. Here I would like to single out one finding that is particularly pertinent to the contemporary scene. It is the fact that over fifty per cent of the cases reported in this study formed their drug habit during their teens and that their one overwhelming desire at that time, as is typical of most adolescents, was to identify with the cynosure of the group they happened to associate with, either at work or at play. Since in most of the places they frequented—the circuses or gambling joints, hotels or restaurants, poolrooms or brothels—the "big shots" were narcotic drug addicts, it was almost as natural for an ambitious youth to aspire to be a narcotic drug user as a sign of prestige and belonging as it was for his less adventurous cousin at home to want to become a missionary when the most glamorous speakers in his church were returned missionaries. While the emulated roles and behaviors in the two instances may differ, the youth's search for identity and his desire to be accepted by, and to belong to, the group are basically the same.

What was said of the drug users reported in this study is even truer of the young addicts of today. The principal difference between the two periods under discussion is that in place of the gambling joint or the red-light district of the 1920's, nowadays the street corner near home, the gang hangout in the neighborhood, and the schoolground have become the main recruiting stations for the future drug users. A little reflection will convince us that these unfortunate youths are drawn to association with drug addicts for prestige or excitement only because their families, their neighborhoods, their schools, and their churches have failed to offer them any recreational or extra-curricular program that is more appealing than taking dope. To condemn these poorly understood and generally neglected youths to life-long criminal careers by the application of the existing narcotic laws is to shift to them the responsibility that really belongs to their elders—their parents, their community leaders, their school teachers, and their religious counselors, who have failed to provide them with enriching and inspiring experiences during their formative years.

In the light of these considerations, it seems the most humane and effective way to combat the spread of the narcotic drug habit among adolescents today is a two-headed program. One part of the program is a stop-gap medical maintenance regimen, such as the use of methadone, for those who have already formed the habit, until they are enabled to seek more radical treatment on a voluntary basis. This would make it possible for them to continue studying or working and to live like decent human beings without resorting to drug peddling or other crimes in order to support their habit. The other part of the program is the improvement of the family atmosphere, the neighborhood organizations, the school environment, and the church facilities of the non-addicted youths so that they will be too engrossed in interesting and satisfying activities to associate with drug users either for prestige or for excitement. This may sound overly idealistic, but it is encouraging to note that both these approaches, on however limited a scale, are being experimented with in New York and some other cities. Particularly noteworthy is the new venture in treatment methods conducted by the Department of Mental Health of Illinois under the direction of Jerome Jaffe, Professor of Psychiatry at the University of Chicago. In this program the special needs of the different types of drug addicts are fully recognized and various treatment methods are being used to meet them. If such experimental efforts could be given sufficient Federal and local support, there is hope that a way may be found to make substantial progress in our war against the narcotic drug habit before another thirty-five years have gone by.

Since the completion of this study in 1935, my career has been that of a psychotherapist, teaching first at Peking Union Medical College in China and later, from 1943 to 1969, in the Department of Psychiatry of Duke University School of Medicine. I have been, therefore, very much out of touch with current narcotic drug research. For helping me catch up with the latest developments in this field through personal communications, I am greatly indebted to the following well-known students of the problem of drug abuse, in addition to Professor DeFleur already mentioned: John A. O'Donnell, Professor of Sociology, University of Kentucky, author of *Narcotic Addicts in Kentucky;* Alfred R. Lindesmith, Professor of Sociology, Indiana University, author of *The Addict and the Law;* Herbert Blumer, Professor of Sociology, University of California at Berkeley, author of "The World of Youthful Drug Use" (a mimeographed statement); and Miss J. J. Fishman, Director of the Narcotic Register Project of the New York City Department of Health.

I am grateful also to the Federal Bureau of Narcotics and Dangerous Drugs for information about existing narcotic laws. However, for the views expressed here I alone am responsible.

With regard to the body of the study itself, I am especially indebted to Mrs. Brantley Henderson, the former Helen Hironimus, Superintendent of the Federal Reformatory for Women at Alderson, West Virginia, for an important portion of the case material. This acknowledgment was regrettably omitted from the first edition, and I am pleased to have the opportunity to record it here.

I should also like to mention my gratitude to Dr. John C. Ball of the Department of Psychiatry, Temple University, whose interest in the work was instrumental in its republication.

This study was first published by the Commercial Press of Shanghai in 1937. Unfortunately, several hundred copies of the book earmarked for shipment to this country were destroyed by Japanese bombs. Hence, this study has not been generally accessible except in its thesis edition available only in a few university libraries. For this reason, I am delighted to have this study included in the Patterson Smith Reprint Series in Criminology, Law Enforcement, and Social Problems, thereby making it available to the general public as well as to serious students of the problem of narcotic drug addiction.

—BINGHAM DAI

Swiss Pine Lake
Spruce Pine, North Carolina
July, 1970

PREFACE TO THE ORIGINAL EDITION

The present study is quite an unexpected but natural outgrowth of the author's deep-rooted interest in the opium problem. As a child he shared his paternal uncle's anti-opium activities, and later had the sad experience of seeing the same uncle end his life as an opium addict. After graduating from college, he was for several years consecutively connected with the Chinese National Anti-Opium Association in Shanghai and the Central Government's Opium Suppression Committee in Nanking, trying first with popular education and later with legislative measures to cope with the opium problem in China. In the course of this experience the conviction dawned on him with increasing momentum that opium addiction is not a problem which mere moral enthusiasm or legal procedure can adequately handle. Ever since then a thirst after a correct understanding of the opium addict and the nature of his habit began to possess him.

It was only natural that after a few years' training in sociology and social psychology the author should turn his newly acquired tools toward his old favorite problem, and the results of this first attempt, made during the years 1933–35, are herein presented. Owing to the complexity of the problem and the rather difficult circumstances under which he worked, this must be considered only as an exploratory study, and his findings cannot be more than tentative. What perhaps may be claimed as original is the application of the sociological and, in a certain sense, the psychiatric approaches to the problem of opium addiction. Instead of looking at the problem purely from the medical, legal, or diplomatic points of view as is generally done, this study considers the opium addict essentially as a member of society and a carrier of culture, and attempts to locate the ætiological factors of opium addiction as well as the effective methods of rehabilitation in the addict's relation with other people and with culture. It is hoped that the results of this study may be of some use to those in whom are entrusted the care of opium addicts and that they may stimulate further studies in this menacing world problem.

The author wishes to express his heart-felt gratitude to all those who have helped to make this study possible. For theoretical orientation he is indebted to all his teachers in sociology and social psychology.

In particular must be mentioned Professors Robert E. Park and Edward Sapir. For untiring efforts in introducing him to the local community and thereby lessening his difficulties as a foreign student, the author is under very great obligation to Professors Ellsworth Faris and E. H. Sutherland, and to Dr. W. L. Treadway of the United States Public Health Service.

Access to the different kinds of data used in this study would not have been possible but for the generosity and friendliness of the following people: Mr. Harry J. Anslinger, United States Commissioner of Narcotics; Mrs. Elizabeth Bass, chief of the Bureau of Narcotics in Chicago; Dr. Frances J. Gerty, superintendent of the Cook County Psychopathic Hospital, and Miss Lera Amlinmeyer, director of its Social Service Department; Lieutenant Cusack and his staff of the Narcotic Division, the Chicago Police Department; Mr. William McGrath, chief of the Federal Probation Office in Chicago; Miss Helen Hazard, superintendent of the Women's Reformatory at Dwight; Dr. J. H. Oughton, superintendent of the Keely Institute; Dr. Harry R. Hoffman, director of the Cook County Behavior Clinic, and Miss Edith Karlin, head of its Social Service Department; Miss Eugenia Brown of the Gospel League; Dr. Ben Reitman; and Mr. Yale Levin. To all these people and others who have kindly volunteered to render data from these sources available for use the author is greatly indebted.

Of the existing literature on the opium problem upon which the author has drawn freely the work of Dr. Charles E. Terry and Dr. Mildred Pellens, entitled *The Opium Problem*, has been most helpful. It is the author's great pleasure to acknowledge his indebtedness to these students of the opium problem both for their writings and for their personal encouragement.

Thanks are due to the Rockefeller Foundation, the Social Science Research Committee of the University of Chicago, and indirectly the Illinois Emergency Relief Commission for financial and staff assistance, without which this study could hardly have been carried to its completion.

Especial gratitude is due to Professor Herbert Blumer for his constant encouragement and friendly assistance in more than one way. He has also kindly read the manuscript and made many valuable criticisms. For errors and discrepancies, however, the author alone is responsible.

The author wishes also to acknowledge his indebtedness to Miss Ida Pruitt of the Peiping Union Medical College for reading the manuscript for publication.

BINGHAM DAI

TABLE OF CONTENTS

LIST OF TABLES

TABLE OF ILLUSTRATIONS

OPIUM ADDICTION IN CHICAGO

CHAPTER I

INTRODUCTION

1. THE MAGNITUDE OF THE OPIUM PROBLEM IN THE UNITED STATES AND IN CHICAGO

THAT the problem of opium addiction[1] has assumed a magnitude of international as well as national importance hardly needs any elaboration. The series of international opium treaties dating from 1912[2] and the existence of such international organs as the League of Nations' Permanent Central Board and the Supervisory Body[3] point to the fact that the problem is not limited to any one nation or race. The seriousness of the problem in this country is indicated by the existence of the federal and state anti-narcotic laws and the regiment of forces for their enforcement. The Federal Bureau of Narcotics with its fifteen branches alone employs about three hundred men and spends nearly two million dollars annually in the enforcement of the Jones-Miller Act and the Harrison Narcotic Act in different parts of the country.[4] And the average

[1] The word "opium" used in this study refers to all opium preparations and derivatives, mainly prepared opium for smoking purposes, morphine, and heroin. "Opium addiction," "chronic opium intoxication," "drug addiction," and the "opium habit" are used interchangeably, all meaning the habitual use of opium for other than strictly medicinal purposes.

[2] The Hague Opium Convention of 1912; the Geneva Convention of 1925; and the Convention for Limiting the Manufacture and Regulating the Distribution of Narcotic Drugs, 1931. See W. W. Willoughby, *Opium as an International Problem* (Baltimore, 1925).

[3] The Permanent Central Board was created by the Geneva Convention of 1925 for gathering statistics on the international trade in narcotic drugs. The Supervisory Body was created by the 1931 Convention for making estimates of the medicinal and scientific requirements of opium for each of the nations concerned.

[4] The Jones-Miller Act, also known as the Narcotic Drugs Import and Export Act, was first passed in 1909 and amended in 1922. The Harrison Narcotic Act, also known as the Federal Internal Revenue Narcotic Laws, was first passed on Dec. 17, 1914, and amended in 1918, 1926, and 1927. All narcotic offenses in this country are violations against these federal revenue laws or state laws of a similar nature; the habitual use of narcotic drugs itself for whatever purpose is not prohibited.

number of the violators of these laws annually committed to the federal institutions only for the past five years exceeds 1,500, constituting, aside from the liquor law violators, practically the largest group of all federal prisoners.[1] Although the exact number of drug users in the country is not known, that there exists in the country an opium problem of a great magnitude is quite evident.

Chicago, being the second largest metropolis in the Union, shares largely in the nation's opium problem. A very conservative estimate of the number of drug users in the city made over ten years ago places it around 5,000.[2] About four years ago, according to a report of the Narcotic Division of the Chicago Police Department, the names of 25,000 drug addicts were found listed in the books when a huge dope ring was exposed.[3] In the past four years or so, the same Narcotic Division alone claims to have handled over 1,000 cases both in the federal and state courts. The Federal Bureau of Narcotics in the city, for a five years' period, 1929–34, apprehended nearly 2,000 cases. For a similar period, the Cook County Psychopathic Hospital alone admitted over 800 patients for the treatment of drug addiction. Data from these sources will be discussed in detail in the following chapters. As a matter of fact, it is not necessary to know the actual number of drug addicts to realize that there are a large number in the city and that the problem is serious.

2. Current Opinions About the Problem and Their Inadequacy

It is not to be inferred from what was cited in the foregoing paragraphs, however, that opium addiction is chiefly a problem of limiting the production of raw opium and the manufacture of narcotic drugs through international agreements. It has often been said in certain quarters that if only the world production of opium could be limited to the amount essential for medicinal and scientific purposes, the problem of drug addiction would automatically resolve itself. Here we will not enter into the problem whether the complete control of opium production, if pos-

---

[1] U. S. Bureau of Prisons, *Federal Offenders*, 1932–33, p. 103.

[2] C. E. Sceleth, "Drug Addiction," *Journal of American Medical Association*, March 1, 1924, p. 679.

[3] W. J. Cusack, "The Narcotic Situation in Chicago," an unpublished report of the Narcotic Division of the Chicago Police Department (1934).

sible, would leave the world in a much better condition, if the underlying causes of opium addiction were not understood; for it is more than probable that so long as these underlying causes exist, the elimination of opium would only mean the ascendancy of some other form of intoxication, the excessive use of alcohol in countries where the opium problem is not serious being a case in point. But the mere fact that after over two decades of international coöperation in this respect certain nations, such as Turkey, Persia, British India, Japan, China, and most of the European countries having colonial possessions in the Far East, still depend on the income from the opium tax to a more or less extent, together with the absence of an international organization capable of enforcing treaty obligations and the remote possibility of there being such an organization in the future, should be sufficient to warn any one who is seriously interested in the problem against looking to international conventions and treaties for its ultimate solution. For the world's output of opium is but an answer to a demand, and the world's demand for narcotic drugs involves problems of human nature that are as yet very little understood.

Nor is drug addiction to be thought of mainly as a penal and correctional problem. The narcotic offenders as a group are notorious for their record of recidivism. The latest report of the Bureau of Prisons states that out of 1,385 narcotic law violators committed to federal institutions during the year 1932–33, 699, or 50.5 per cent, are recidivists.[1] The necessity for a broader conception of the problem cannot be better expressed than in the following words of a federal officer. "It is interesting to observe that repeated prison sentences are imposed more often on drug addicts than on other types of federal prisoners, those with three or more prison sentences occurring twice as often among addicts. This contrast is decidedly greater for the country as a whole, however. This situation of repeated prison sentences challenges the usefulness of handling drug addiction through prison sentence alone."[2] This is equally true of Chicago's drug addicts, as will be seen in a later chapter. The basic assumption behind the present prohibitive measures seems to be that drug addiction is a vice or a crime for which the individual addict must be held responsible. But there seems to be little likelihood that the mere

[1] U. S. Bureau of Prisons, *Federal Offenders*, 1932–33, p. 117.
[2] W. L. Treadway, "Drug Addiction and Measures for Its Prevention in the United States," *The Journal of American Medical Association*, July 30, 1932, p. 372.

increase in the efficiency of law-enforcement or the length of prison sentences will materially mitigate the situation. Perhaps here as elsewhere, as Glueck has well said, "the center of gravity of our problem of crime lies outside the courtroom."[1]

By common consent the treatment of opium addiction has been placed in the hands of the medical profession, and the belief still exists in the minds of many that it is more a medical problem than anything else. Extreme advocates of this view go so far as to say that drug addiction is primarily a physical disease.[2] But here again we are disappointed, for it is the experience of almost every physician who has had anything to do with the treatment of drug addiction at all that while it is comparatively easy to relieve the drug addicts from what are generally called withdrawal symptoms, such a thing as permanent cure is a rare exception, whereas relapse is the general rule. For this reason many hospitals have despaired of their efforts at treating opium addicts, and private physicians shun them. We do not have to go far for the proof of this statement. The Cook County Psychopathic Hospital, for example, has recently discontinued its usual practice of receiving six drug addicts for treatment every week mainly on the ground that the physicians there have not found any satisfactory result from their labors.

The long experience of the Chicago physician known all over the world for his ten-day "cure" is even more illuminating. While he found no difficulty in separating the addict from his drug within ten to fourteen days, he stressed the fact that "no plan of therapy, however logical or successful, can assure freedom from recurrence."[3] It is his conviction that "The desire for the drug after detoxication and subsidence of asthenic symptoms is in the mind only, and is not based on any physical or chemical need."[4] To cope with such a psychological need, therefore, medicine alone is helpless. His conclusion about the matter is: "The solution of the drug evil does not rest on the administration of any specific cure, but rather on the removal, where possible, of the underlying causes for which the drug addiction is merely an expression."[5] To seek such

---

[1] S. and E. T. Glueck, *One Thousand Juvenile Delinquents* (1934), p. viii
[2] E. S. Bishop, *The Narcotic Drug Problem* (1920).
[3] C. E. Sceleth, *A Rational Treatment of the Morphine Habit* (a reprint), p. 11.
[4] *Ibid.*, p. 5.
[5] *Ibid.*, p. 8.

"underlying causes," it seems that we have to go even outside the realm of medicine as it is generally understood.

While there is no desire on our part to belittle the important rôles of international coöperation, domestic governmental control and medical treatment in curbing the spread of opium addiction, we are led by the foregoing considerations to the conclusion that for a more adequate understanding of the problem and for its effective solution a new orientation is required.

3. Some Specific Aspects of the Problem and the State of Existing Knowledge About Them

At the risk of some repetition we are going to present in the following the findings of some carefully conducted studies that were recently made on the problem of drug addiction. These findings will give us a good idea as to the kind of questions asked by students of the problem all over the world and roughly what is already known about each of them, and will at the same time serve to indicate in a more concrete manner the point of departure for the present study. As the works to be cited naturally cover certain grounds that may be quite beyond the province of the present study, only a very general and brief review is here contemplated.

Probably the most comprehensive work on the problem thus far attempted is the report of the Committee on Drug Addictions of New York City that was organized in 1921, consisting of seven authorities in such different fields as pharmacology, physiological chemistry, neuropathology, and others. The report, entitled *The Opium Problem*, appeared in 1928. This monumental work may be said to be a critical review of practically all the available literature on the opium problem, the sources consulted running over six thousand items. This huge amount of material is organized around the following five leading questions: (1) the extent of chronic opium intoxication in this country; (2) its ætiology; (3) its nature and pathology; (4) its treatment; and (5) its solution.[1]

As to the extent of chronic opium intoxication the authors of the report, after having reviewed all the important estimates of the total number of drug addicts in the country, state that they cannot agree to

---

[1] C. E. Terry and M. Pellens, *The Opium Problem* (New York, 1928), p. xii.

the conservative estimate of 110,000, which was made by Kolb and Du Mez of the United States Public Health Service in 1924 on the basis of the annual importations of opiates.[1] The decrease of importations of opium, especially after 1915, according to these authors, was due more to the tightening of prohibitive measures than the actual diminution of the consumption of the drug. The authors' own estimate based on the number of drug addicts registered at the Jacksonville clinic as well as that of the Special Committee of the Department of Treasury, made in 1913 and 1918 respectively, point to 1,000,000 as a more probable figure. These earlier estimates, the authors assert, are better adapted to generalization than most of the surveys made public since the enforcement of the Harrison Narcotic Act.[2]

In the review of the literature on the etiology of chronic opium intoxication, the authors found "a general confusion in the points of view from which the various observers approached the subject." Causes given for opium addiction run the whole gamut from prescription by the physician, self-medication for the relief of pain, and bad associates to psychopathic predisposition. It is the opinion of these authors that "the majority of observers appeared not to differentiate between what might be called predisposing or contributory factors and the immediate object for which the drug was taken." The direct cause is always "the continued taking of the drug over a sufficiently long period to produce upon withdrawal distress of some kind to the patient," whereas the predisposing factors are many. "The determination of the exact rôle played by each of these factors," these authors conclude, "is a matter for the most delicate analysis and one which has received in previous studies practically no consideration, in spite of its very evident importance in the prevention of needless cases of chronic opium intoxication. The more or less limited or selected experiences of the various individual observers point strongly to the need of a broader and more critical type of approach."[3]

As to the nature of chronic opium intoxication, the authors, after passing in review the current notions about the general nature of the problem as well as the scientific literature on the somatic and psychic

[1] L. Kolb and A. G. Du Mez, *The Prevalence and Trend of Drug Addiction in the United States and Factors Influencing It* (Washington, 1924).
[2] Terry and Pellens, *op. cit.*, pp. 1–52, especially 48–9.
[3] *Ibid.*, pp. 94–136, especially 134.

changes due to opium addiction and on such phenomena as tolerance, dependence and withdrawal, observe a similar confusion of opinion. Some maintain that drug addiction is a disease pure and simple; others, a vice or a habit; still others insist that drug addicts are either psychopaths or mental defectives. The authors' conclusions are: "First, that while the evidence of profound somatic and psychic changes is clear, no theory that has sought to explain the exact nature of the phenomena observed in the various stages of chronic opium intoxication either in human beings or in animals has adduced sufficient proof to warrant its unqualified acceptance on the bases usually required for scientific demonstration; second, in view of the preceding, research work along a number of lines is needed to establish unequivocal grounds for a complete understanding of this condition."[1] In other words, whether the addict's dependence on his drug is a physical need based on pathological evidences or rather a psychological one, as Sceleth asserts, with no physical basis, still remains to be determined.

The authors' review of the methods of treating drug addiction employed in many lands and in different periods leads them to state that "for the most part, the treatment of this condition has not emerged from the stage of empiricism." They go on to say: "The various methods described in general indicate that the basis of the majority of them is merely the separation of the patient from the drug. . . . If the separation of the patient from the drug is all that is signified by 'cure,' it is evident that the *modus operandi* and the underlying rationale mean little or nothing and it is readily understood how any treatment with this object in view may result in 'cure.' The word 'cure' should imply the return of the patient, insofar as is possible, to somatic and psychic integrity. In the literature dealing with treatment there is little to indicate that the desirable state of affairs commonly is accomplished."[2]

"Confronted with such a situation," conclude the authors, after having reviewed the measures of international, national and state control now existing, "two courses of action are open to anyone interested in the solution of the problem. The first of these is to continue the search for further information through approved methods of investigation, to corroborate or disprove any one or all of the different theories, or to

---

[1] *Ibid.*, chaps. iv, v, and vi, especially p. 428.
[2] *Ibid.*, pp. 517 ff., especially pp. 627–628.

substitute a new one. Second, pending the determination of knowledge sufficient to permit of the formulation of sound measures for alleviation and control, to view with grave concern the advocacy of any policy which takes into consideration and assumes as its basis exclusively any one of the existing explanations of the nature of this condition."[1]

Thus the one general finding of this important study conducted by the Committee of Drug Addictions seems to be that with respect to such specific problems of opium addiction as its ætiology or causation, its nature and pathology, its treatment and its solution, there is as yet no general agreement, and that this inadequacy of understanding points to the urgent need of an approach at once different and broader than those hitherto employed.

An equally illuminating conclusion is found in one other important study made under the auspices of the Philadelphia Committee for the Clinical Study of Opium Addiction in conjunction with the more extensive investigation just reviewed. This study was conducted strictly along clinical and chemical lines to determine whether objective investigations would reveal any changes that can be measured by physical, chemical or physiologic methods in the addict who is taking daily doses of from $\frac{1}{2}$ to 60 grains of heroin or morphine and that would differentiate him from a normal person, serve to identify the state of opium addiction or would provide indications to guide in his rehabilitation; and at the same time to inquire in a similar fashion into what are generally known as withdrawal symptoms. This study lasted for three years, and altogether 861 patients were investigated. The results may be summarized as follows.

While certain somatic changes were noted, such as a slightly slower average pulse rate, a slightly lower red blood cell count and a higher leucocyte count than those of normal people, together with a slight degree of anæmia and emaciation, which the authors considered more as the result of the addicts' unhygienic surroundings and their impoverished existence than that of the use of drugs itself, they were unable to detect any marked physical deterioration or impairment of physical fitness aside from the addiction *per se* in the series of cases of opium addiction studied during the administration of morphine. "The study shows," conclude the authors, "that morphine addiction is not characterized by physical

[1] *Ibid.*, chaps. x–xiv, especially p. 926.

deterioration or impairment of physical fitness aside from the addiction *per se*. There is no evidence of change in the circulatory, hepatic, renal or endocrine functions. When it is considered that these subjects had been addicted for at least five years, some of them for as long as twenty years, these negative observations are highly significant."[1]

The abrupt withdrawal of morphine too, according to these authors, was accompanied by only slight changes in the physiologic mechanisms studied, changes which afforded no adequate explanation of the withdrawal symptoms.

Having thus failed to discover any definite physical and physiological basis of opium addiction, the authors rightly pointed out: "It indicates, however, the necessity for a study of the addict from some new standpoint in order to reveal the factors which induce and maintain the state of addiction and which on abrupt withdrawal of the drug elicit the withdrawal symptoms."[2]

It is the task of the present study to develop such a new standpoint and to apply it to the investigation of those problems raised but not answered by previous studies. The reader must not be surprised, therefore, if from now on he should find his attention drawn almost exclusively to a field quite beyond the boundaries of international relations, law and medicine, for we are going to look at the opium addict from a quite different perspective.

4. THE SOCIOLOGICAL POINT OF VIEW

It seems to us that the study and treatment of opium addiction hitherto attempted has been centered too much around the phenomenon as an isolated event and around the addict as a separate individual. Thus, opium addiction has been thought of either as a disease or a vice and studied as such with little or no consideration of the relation between this behavior of the addict and his personality as a whole. The cure of drug addiction is generally supposed to lie in a single therapeutic procedure or a magical chemical substitute yet to be discovered. If the addict is taken into account at all, he is usually looked upon by the law-enforcement officers, physicians and the general public as an individual with a diseased body, or a weak will-power, or a defective mentality, or

---

[1] A. B. Light and others, *Opium Addiction* (Chicago, 1929-30), pp. 115-16.
[2] *Ibid.*, p. 116.

still a psychopathic personality, as though the whole problem of drug addiction were, as one physician put it, "entirely a matter of the individual,"[1] little or no attention having been paid to the relation between the drug addict and his social and cultural *milieu*. Such a point of view is so contrary to the fact of human behavior that it has quite naturally led those students who adopted it away from the real issues of the problem, and explains to a large extent the very meager results of many previous studies.

The sociological point of view has as its basis the organic conception of the relation between the individual and society. "A separate individual," according to this conception, "is an abstraction unknown to experience."[2] For the individual is always born into a group and brought up in a culture. Roughly speaking, we may say that there are two principal sets of influences that shape and mold not only the exterior mannerism but the innermost being of an individual, that give him desires and habits, in fact, character and personality,[3] and that remain with him as long as he lives. For the purpose of this study, one may be conveniently called the "social," and the other the "cultural."[4] The former refers to the affectional and prestige relations between the individual and other members of his group, and the latter to the conditioning of the individual's behavior by the folkways and mores of his group, or culture, the word, "culture" here, according to the usage of the ethnologist, being taken to mean the totality of cultural patterns as abstracted from behavior.[5] Such social and cultural influences or conditions, both in their objective and subjective aspects, constitute the human environment or situation to which human behavior is a response. In this sense, it may be said that every human individual, be he a holy man or an opium addict, is invariably a social as well as a cultural being; in fact, if the opium addict were not so, it would be impossible to understand why opium addiction should constitute such a problem as it does. And the individual's behavior, be it a virtue or a vice, therefore, must be considered as a response to the social and cul-

---

[1] C. E. Sceleth, *A Rational Treatment of the Morphine Habit* (a reprint), p. 11.
[2] C. H. Cooley, *Human Nature and the Social Order*, pp. 1–2.
[3] R. E. Park, "Personality and Cultural Conflict," *Publication of the Sociological Society of America*, XXV (1931), pp. 96–7.
[4] A similar distinction is found in Kimball Young, *Social Psychology*, pp. 4–7. In actual behavior, however, such a distinction is very difficult to maintain.
[5] Edward Sapir, An unpublished lecture on "The Impact of Culture upon Personality" (Yale University, 1933).

tural situation as he defines it. It is probably in some such sense that Park emphasizes, "the actions of the individual can be understood and explained only by considering them in the social and cultural context in which they occurred."[1]

To put the same point of view in a more concise manner, we may say that we propose to study the opium addict not as a separate individual, but as a person, that is, an individual who has status or a rôle in his group and an individual whose behavior may be considered as a response to the rôle as he conceives of it.[2]

It follows from what is said that the human personality is not a mere conglomeration of isolated traits or habits; it is always an organization, a unity, except perhaps in the case of the mentally deranged; and the center of gravity that organizes and unifies the personality is the individual's conception of his rôle or task among his fellow beings.[3] If this view of the human personality is tenable, it is evident that no habits or traits of a person, including opium addiction, can be understood or explained except by considering them in the light of his personality as a whole. And to study a habit in the light of the total personality organization of a person, from what was said in the preceding paragraphs, always means a study of the social and cultural *milieu* to which the person's social rôle or task is oriented, and in which the habit under investigation is formed and maintained. It is undoubtedly in some such sense that Dewey stresses the importance of studying and remedying social conditions in understanding and correcting a bad habit.[4]

To sum up, the sociological point of view as it is applied to the study of opium addiction is to look at the habit in the light of the total personality of the addict, and to study the addict with reference to his social and cultural situations. It may also be said to be a configurational and situational approach.[5]

[1] R. E. Park, "Sociology," *Research in the Social Sciences*, ed. Wilson Gee (1929), p. 44.

[2] R. E. Park and E. W. Burgess, *Introduction to the Science of Sociology* (Chicago, 1924), p. 55.

[3] *Ibid.*, p. 70. This view is shared by Individual Psychology as well as Psychoanalysis. For the latter's view of personality expressed in similar terms, see Paul Schilder, "Personality in the Light of Psychoanalysis," *The Biology of the Individual*, ed. J. R. Hunt and others (1934), pp. 269 ff.

[4] J. Dewey, *Human Nature and Conduct* (New York, 1922), p. 29.

[5] W. I. and D. S. Thomas, *The Child in America* (New York, 1928), p. 506.

5. PROBLEMS AND METHODS OF STUDY

The problems of opium addiction from the sociological point of view and the methods we employ in this study, in the order in which the materials of this report will be presented in the following chapters, may be briefly stated as follows.

First of all, we will consider opium addiction as a cultural pattern and deal with it as such apart from actual behavior. The questions we are going to ask are: how does opium addiction originate and spread, especially in this country and in Chicago, and what forms does it now assume, —in other words, what is the natural history of opium addiction, and what is the relation of this particular cultural pattern to the general cultural complex as a whole? To be sure, we must also give due consideration to the well-known pharmacological properties and physiological effects of opium, but these properties and effects of the drug alone do not make its addiction a prevailing pattern; the less are they sufficient to render it a grave social problem. It is our hypothesis that there are definite sequences of events that lead to the spread of opium addiction among a certain group of people and to the formation of the opium habit in a certain individual, just as there are in the diffusion of any other cultural pattern. An account of such sequences of events, however sketchy it may be in the present report, is deemed necessary to bring to light the fact that opium addiction is not a vice inherent in any individual or race as the uninformed public is disposed to think. The point of view and the method of procedure to be followed here is something like that of the cultural anthropologist in dealing with any cultural pattern.

Assuming as we do that all cultural patterns are transmitted to individuals by the group, a sister-problem to the preceding one is to ask who constitute the group through which the pattern of opium addiction is transmitted and what their characteristics are. They are, of course, the opium addicts. In order to have some idea of their general characteristics, we have collected data on such facts as age, sex, nationality, education, occupation, etc., from the following agencies or institutions for the past five or more years: the Cook County Psychopathic Hospital, the Federal Bureau of Narcotics, the Narcotic Division of the Chicago Police Department, the Women's Reformatory at Dwight, the Municipal Psychiatric Clinic, and the private Keeley Institute at Dwight. Such characteristics of opium addicts will be compared with those of the general population of the city whenever possible.

Perhaps the most pressing problem of this study, one that follows directly the preceding two, is: how is the pattern of opium addiction taken over by the individual or how is the pattern transmitted by the group of confirmed addicts to the addict-to-be? It is self-evident that the process in every case presupposes a social situation. In order to understand the process, therefore, the logical thing to do is to explore all the possible social situations in which different drug addicts got started in their habit, in which their habit was firmly established and in which "cures" and relapses took place. To do this two principal methods are employed in this study: the one may be called the ecological approach and the other the prolonged interview method. The latter is supplemented whenever possible by autobiographical accounts written by addicts themselves.

The ecological approach aims at locating opium addicts in the ecological organization of the city. In other words, it is to find out where addicts live and where their haunts or "hang-outs" are. Such a knowledge of the spatial distribution of drug addicts in the city is considered as an essential, though preliminary, step in exploring what may be called the addicts' social and cultural environment, in the light of which only can we expect to understand drug addiction.[1] For this purpose we shall use the addicts' residences and the places of their offense. The relative incidence of opium addiction in the different areas of the city will be shown in some detail on the map.

The prolonged interview method aims at exploring the social and cultural situations as the addict defines them, the situations that have conditioned his life in the past and that are confronting him at present. Such a knowledge of the addict's own social and cultural world is essential, for it is to this world of his own and not to the observer's world that the addict reacts as he does. The prolonged interview method is used instead of the ordinary interview method, not only because of the well-known reluctance of a drug addict to tell anything about himself to a stranger in the first one or two interviews, but because of the physical necessity of having more than one interview to explore not only the

[1] R. E. Park, "The City: Suggestions for the Investigation of Human Behavior in the Urban Environment," *The City*, ed. R. E. Park, E. W. Burgess, and R. D. McKenzie (Chicago, 1925), pp. 1 ff.

experiences that are directly connected with the formation and maintenance of the drug habit, but the total personality of the addict as well.

Perhaps the most distinguished feature of the prolonged interview method is the facility it affords to observe the reaction of the addict to the interviewer, which reaction, if correctly interpreted, may be taken to be indicative of the total personality organization of the addict. In other words, the addict's attitude towards the interviewer may be taken as a fairly accurate index of his attitude towards all other people in actual life-situations. It may be pointed out here that this is the basic assumption of the technique of psychoanalysis. Although we have not been able to use the psychoanalytic technique to any noticeable extent in this study, possible use of this basic assumption for the purpose of sociological research is sufficiently indicated in some of our case studies.

What is implied in the foregoing discussion of the prolonged interview method is that we cannot expect to understand and explain drug addiction unless we consider it in the light of the total personality of the drug addict. For a knowledge of social situations alone as it is generally understood in current sociological study is not sufficient to account for the fact that under similar social situations only certain individuals form the drug habit while others do not. Thus we are faced with a no less important problem than the preceding ones of discovering what it is in a person that may predispose him to the lure of narcotics. It seems to us that this is not only a problem of discovering the previous attitudes to a particular object or situation, but one of exploring the general emotional trends or reaction patterns in an individual which in a more or less compulsive manner predispose him to this or that line of reaction to practically all social and cultural situations. Thus, an individual with an intense feeling of inferiority will probably react to the world around him in a combative manner all the time, and a person with a father-hatred, let us say, may encounter endless difficulties in dealing with men. It is probably on the basis of such emotional inadequacies that narcotics come in conveniently as a buffer between the person and difficult life-situations. The task before us, therefore, is to find out what these personality trends or emotional reaction patterns are in opium addicts that may be pointed out as the predisposing factors in the formation and the continuance of their habit. It seems to the writer that this can be best done by the technique of psychoanalysis, but our experience shows that a careful use of the prolonged interview method may yield some promising results.

In the last analysis, we shall find that opium addiction is essentially a problem of the one and the many, a problem of the relation between the individual and society, between personality and culture. Our hypothesis is that most of the life-problems of a drug addict, that find a temporary solution in the use of narcotics, arise from his association with his fellow beings and from the necessity to conform to the demands of culture. We must try with particular care, therefore, to inquire into the nature of those group associations and culture demands that prove themselves such a tax on the mental energy of drug addicts, and to discover just where the difficulties lie.

In brief, in a sociological study of opium addiction we consider the following as our major problems: (1) the natural history of opium addiction as a cultural pattern; (2) the characteristics of opium addicts as a group; (3) the social situations in which the pattern of opium addiction is taken over by the individual addict, and in which "cures" and relapses occur; (4) the more or less persistent trends in an addict's personality that may be said to have predisposed him to the habitual use of narcotic drugs; and (5) the relation between an opium addict and his group and its culture. It is only after we have achieved some understanding of these major issues that we can state with some degree of assurance what the nature of opium addiction really is and where the solution of the problem seems to lie.

CHAPTER II

A CONSIDERATION OF CERTAIN PHARMACOLOGICAL, HISTORICAL, AND CULTURAL ASPECTS OF OPIUM ADDICTION

SO widespread is the popular conception of opium addiction as a vice of the weak-minded individual or the evil of an unprogressive race that little does the general public realize that back of the practice there is a long history and that there are just as definite sequences of events leading to its genesis and diffusion as there are in the case of any other cultural trait. In order to correct this current prejudice and to sharpen our knowledge of the factors that contribute to the spread of opium addiction among any group of people, we are going in this chapter to invite the reader to look at opium addiction not as a law-enforcement officer or a reformer, but as a cultural anthropologist, who is interested in locating the source of a personal habit outside the individual, that is, in culture, and in following, in this case, the natural history of opium addiction as a cultural pattern. As a prerequisite for this adventure, we shall equip ourselves first with the rudiments of the physical and pharmacological properties of the drug or drugs we have inclusively called opium, and with some general knowledge of their physiological as well as psychological effects on man. We shall then be briefly concerned with the history of opium as a therapeutic agent, and finally with the factors and conditions that marked the transition from the use of opium as a therapeutic agent to its use as a source of euphoria or pleasure. In the end we shall find that this brief historical excursion will give us a useful point of view from which to approach the problem in our immediate environs.

1. OPIUM AS A DEPRESSANT OF THE CENTRAL NERVOUS SYSTEM

The word "opium," as has been indicated in the foregoing chapter, is used in this study to refer to all opium preparations and derivatives, particularly prepared opium for smoking purposes, morphine and heroin. Here a more detailed description of these drugs is in order.

Opium is the juice from the unripe seed capsule of the opium poppy (*Papaver somniferum*). It is usually obtained by incising the unripe capsule with a knife and scraping the coagulated juice into a vessel. In this state it is generally known as raw opium. From this naturally dried juice, the prepared opium for smoking purposes is obtained by the processes of dissolving, boiling, roasting, and fermentation. It must be borne in mind that raw opium is a complicated chemical mixture, containing in itself, besides fats, acids, and many other substances, about twenty-five bases, generally known as alkaloids, of which morphine, $C_{17}H_{19}O_3N$, is present in greatest abundance (about 10 per cent), and codeine, $C_{18}H_{21}O_3N$, called in chemistry, methylmorphine, forms from 0.1 to 3 per cent. The last principal drug, heroin, $C_{17}H_{17}NO_3(COCH_3)_2$, also known as diacetylmorphine, is an artificial alkaloid, produced by heating morphine with acetic anhydride. These then are the principal drugs with which we shall be concerned, except that occasionally we may come across cocaine, $C_{17}H_{21}O_4N$, which is an alkaloid from the leaves of a plant generally known as coca, but which, since it is not habit-forming in the sense opium is, will not be emphasized in our discussion.[1]

There are two principles of pharmacology that are particularly important for our inquiry. One is that the action of drugs on the tissues of an organism is always selective in character, that is, particular drugs affect only particular organs of the body. Drugs are generally divided into those of local action, which affect only the site of their application and which operate before they are absorbed into the blood stream, and those of general action, which show their effects after they are absorbed into the blood stream. Even the latter kind of drugs are found to be selective in their action. Gunn gives the example of using the extract of pituitary gland for the purpose of stimulating the uterus in labor. It is clear that if it had an equal effect on the muscle of the bronchi, an undesirable attack of asthma would follow, and the therapeutic use of the drug for the purpose mentioned would be lost. In fact, it is this selective action that makes the therapeutic use of any drug possible.[2]

---

[1] John A. Killian, "Narcotic Drugs," *The Menace of Narcotic Drugs*, ed. E. G. Payne (New York, 1931). For more detailed descriptions of the chemical properties of opium, see U. S. Public Health Service, *Chemistry of the Opium Alkaloids* (Washington, 1932).

[2] J. A. Gunn, *An Introduction to Pharmacology and Therapeutics* (London, 1929), pp. 4–6.

The other important principle is that the effects of drugs on the organism are always quantitative, and never qualitative. That is to say, when a cell is affected by a poison, the extent of its activity is changed but not the kind. "No drug can, for example, cause a nerve-cell to contract rhythmically, or a cardiac cell to exhibit reflex action, or a salivary gland to secrete bile. All a drug can do is to increase or decrease the excitability of a nerve-cell, make the heart go slower or faster, or make a salivary gland eliminate more or less of its normal secretion. In other words, *drugs can only change activity of organs quantitatively, not qualitatively.* . . ."[1] On the basis of this fact, the pharmacological action of a drug is generally described as stimulation or depression, and drugs, accordingly, are classified as stimulants or depressants. The stimulants are those drugs which increase the activity of any organ or function, and the depressants those which lessen the activity. And because of the selective character of their action, drugs are further classified into stimulants or depressants of this or that organ or system. In fact, the same drug may be found to be a stimulant to one organ and a depressant to the other at the same time. It must also be noted that whether a drug acts as a stimulant or as a depressant depends to a large extent on the dose taken.

According to these basic principles and for reasons to be further explained, the drugs that concern us most in this study, that is, opium and its derivatives, are known in pharmacology as depressants of the central nervous system, or more popularly known as narcotics.

2. The Pharmacological Effects of Opium and Their Socio-psychological Implications

The pharmacological effect of opium on man may be described either as therapeutic or euphoric.

The therapeutic effect of opium is so well known that it does not require more than a passing mention in this discussion. The superiority of opium over other drugs lies chiefly in its special analgesic action, that is, the relieving of pain, for morphine, the active principle of opium, so depresses or decreases the activity of the central nervous system that the sensation of pain is not duly registered in the sensory centers of the cortex, and the person using the drug is thereby rendered insensitive to pain

[1] *Ibid.,* p. 7.

of whatever kind, as long as the effect of the drug lasts. It is this special quality of opium that makes it a master anæsthetic of all medicine and renders it an indispensable part of modern therapeutics. And through depressing the sensory and motor areas in the brain, it must be noted, the narcotic effect extends to the functions of the whole body, particularly respiration, which explains the collapse of a person after a fatal dose of morphine, the safe medicinal dose of the drug being from $\frac{1}{8}$ to $\frac{1}{4}$ grain; the peristaltic movement of the stomach, which explains the universal phenomenon of constipation among drug addicts; and the secretion of glands, which explains in part the loss of sexual·passion on the part of almost all confirmed drug addicts. The only cortical area that is stimulated instead of being depressed is the oculomotor center, and that accounts for the contraction of the addict's pupils, giving them the familiar "pin-point" appearance. One other exception must be made for the sweat glands, which are stimulated to greater activity through asphyxia following the depression of the respiratory center, and this increased perspiration gives the person a feeling of warmth throughout the body.[1]

There is one point in connection with the depressing function of opium which must be emphasized in this discussion, and that is the order in which the hierarchical structure of the brain is affected by drugs like opium. This is important, because it has immense psychological as well as sociological implications. With respect to this specific point the writer cannot do better than quote one who is not only an authority in dynamic psychology but has done research in the effects of drugs:

> The nervous system is built up in layers of which the oldest are the lowest and are of relatively simple functions; the spinal cord (and its upper end which forms part of the brain) is the first or lowest layer, comprising the oldest and simplest structures and functions. The second layer is the mid-brain, comprising the cerebellum and the masses of tissue loosely designated as the basal ganglia, and making up all of the brain between the cerebral hemispheres and the spinal layer. The cerebral hemispheres, which in the human brain greatly preponderate in size over all the rest of the nervous system, comprise two principal layers; the third layer which is directly connected with the first and second layers, and a fourth which is connected with the two lower layers only indirectly, namely, through the medium of the third or sensori-motor layer . . . . .

[1] A. R. Cushny, *Pharmacology and Therapeutics* (10th ed., 1934), pp. 270–77.

All the evidence regarding the function of these anatomical layers converges to show that each higher layer modifies and controls the functioning of the lower layers, without superceding those functions. By the administration of narcotic or anæsthetic drugs, such as chloroform and ether and alcohol, the functions of these layers seem to be abolished in the order from above downwards. Under increasing dosage of such drugs, a man shows first some impairment of the highest functions of mind and brain, loss of critical self-consciousness and impairment of judgment and reasoning; the fourth layer is progressively put out of action, until he lies at the level of one of the higher animals—utilizing only the three lower layers; he lives, for the time, a life of sense-perception and uncontrolled affective responses. At a further stage, his sensorimotor functions are impaired; though he can still be stirred to outbursts of crude and violent affective response, during which he must be admitted to be conscious in a low indiscriminating fashion (comparable to the responses of a lower vertebrate animal to sense-impressions). And, at a third stage, he lies unconscious, his life processes sustained and regulated by only the first or lowest layer of the nervous system. If the dose of the drug is pushed beyond this point, the functions of the first layer are gravely impaired, and the man dies, generally from arrest of the rhythmic working of heart or lung.

Observations of the effects of brain injuries, both accidental and surgically induced, bear out these indications of the hierarchical relations of the four brain-layers.[1]

What is important to note here is that the part of the brain that is most easily affected by a dose of opium is the seat of what McDougall calls the highest functions, that is, the power of critical self-consciousness and the faculty of judgment and reasoning; and that, by decreasing these important functions of the brain and mind, the person may be rendered insensitive not only to pain of a purely physical nature, but to pain of all kinds, such as emotional conflicts, failures and disappointments, and the sense of guilt or shame—in other words, pains and afflictions that are characteristic of man as a member of society and as the carrier of a culture. Psychologically speaking, it may be stated that one of the major sources of mental conflicts, namely, undue inhibitions or repressions, are thus taken off by opium for the time being, and the individual's secret desires are given a chance to express themselves either in the form of overt behavior or fantasy. The well-known use of opium as an aid

[1] Wm. McDougall, *The Energies of Men* (1933), pp. 319–21.

in enhancing the pleasure from the sex act is a case in point.   Sociologically speaking, it means the relegating of social obligations and cultural demands to the background and the individual for a moment at least is allowed to live entirely for himself.   In other words, the person under the influence of opium is enjoying a moral holiday.   Now if we consider the almost unlimited extent to which a man can be made to suffer by the stresses and strains of life and by the expectations and demands society makes on him, it is not difficult to understand that such a moment of Nirvana as described above is not just a moment of forgetfulness; instead, by contrast to the former state, it may be considered as a moment of positive pleasure, and the person thus affected is usually overwhelmed by a sense of well-being.   From this point of view, the euphoric effect of opium may be characterized as one of false psychological stimulation.[1]   Herein then lies the secret not only of the magical power of opium for the relief of physical pain, but its infinite charm for man as a social and cultural being.

We have yet to consider another aspect of the euphoric effect of opium. For the sense of elation or the feeling of well-being following a dose of morphine to the initiated does not seem to be entirely negative in the sense of a psychological relief from the strains of life as stated in the preceding paragraph; along with this, according to a number of authors, there seems to be a phase of true physiological as well as psychological stimulation, which precedes that of depression, thus constituting together what may be called a cycle of stimulation and depression.   This cycle as seen in the results of psychological experiments has been graphically represented as follows:[2]

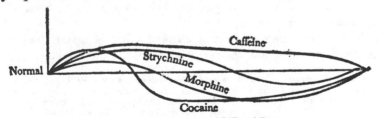

Fig. 1.   Temporal Action of Different Drugs

Here the mental effect of morphine is represented along with those of caffeine, strychnine, and cocaine, and "the action of morphine,"

[1] J. A. Gunn, *op. cit.*, p. 107.
[2] A. G. Bills, *General Experimental Psychology* (1934), p. 485.

according to the same author, "rises very gradually to a maximum of stimulation, followed by a descent below normal where it remains for a long time." In fact, this phenomenon, according to some authors, agrees with the "general law of biology that diminution of the functions of any organ of the body is preceded by an increase of functional energy, the expression of the primary excitation."[1] Others who may not extend this general principle to all narcotics also maintain that the reason why opium alone is a drug of addiction is that it produces "a preliminary stage of pleasurable excitement," while hypnotics, such as bromide or any drug of the veronal group, do not.[2] What is back of this excitement still remains a moot question in pharmacology. Probably it is nothing more than a false stimulation on the physiologic level, such as the increase of perspiration and its accompanying feeling of warmth throughout the body due to asphyxia, leading ultimately to depression; but at the moment it is felt by the organism as true stimulation. Whatever the ultimate explanation of the phenomenon may be, it seems that the experiential existence of such a cycle or curve of excitement-relaxation following a dose of morphine as represented above may be safely taken as the best interpretation of present facts.

It may be pointed out here that there seems to be a great deal of similarity between this form of artificially induced pleasurable sensation and natural orgasm following the excitement of the sex organ, and it seems understandable how this form of self-indulgence might be continuously resorted to by certain individuals, though perhaps unpremeditatedly in the beginning, either as a substitute for normal coitus or as a release from a nervous tension. Though mainly speculative, this is pointed out here as a possible physiologic, or shall we say erotic, basis of the strong hold of opium over man.[3]

In the beginning opium is taken either for its therapeutic or its euphoric effect, but in the end the result is practically the same, and here we

---

[1] L. Lewin, *Phantastica: Narcotics and Stimulating Drugs* (1931), pp. 28–9. See also Cushny, *op. cit.*, p. 19, in which the authors express agreement to this general principle in the great majority of cases; Wm. McDougall, *The Effect of Alcohol and Some Other Drugs during Normal and Fatigued Conditions* (1920), pp. 14–5; M. H. Severs, "Acute and Chronic Narcotic Drug Poisoning" (Unpublished Ph.D. thesis, University of Chicago, 1928), pp. 23–4.

[2] Sir Wm. Willcox, "Medico-legal Aspects of Alcohol and Drug Addiction," *British Journal of Inebriety*, XXXI (1934), p. 139; R. D. Gillespie, "Insomnia and Drug Addiction," *British Journal of Inebriety*, XXVIII (1930), p. 9.

[3] Sandor Rado, "The Psychic Effects of Intoxication," *Psycho-analytic Review*, XVIII (1931), pp. 69 ff.

come to the most peculiar and the most discussed aspect of the problem of opium addiction. For the continued use of opium for a certain length of time, which may vary from a week to several months, almost invariably results in making the individual an opium addict, except in cases where the individual is not cognizant of the nature of the drug he has been taking or has not learned to identify the physical discomfort experienced by him upon withdrawal with the effect of the drug. An opium addict may be defined as a person who, not requiring the continued use of opium for the relief of the symptoms of organic disease (for which it might be originally taken), has acquired as a result of repeated administration a strong dependence on the drug and an overpowering desire for its continuance, and in whom withdrawal of the drug leads to definite symptoms of mental or physical distress or disorder, such as yawning, restlessness, vomiting, diarrhea, perspiration, and extreme weakness.[1] In other words, the repeated use of the drug has created a craving, and the craving has to be continually satisfied. The use of the drug was once a voluntary act; it now has become strongly appetitive, which makes it a compulsory habit.

But what is it in opium that is capable of inducing such a strong dependence in the individual using the drug, and what is the nature of the craving or the withdrawal symptoms that compel one to continue its use? These are some of the most disputed questions in pharmacology, and it would be unwise, therefore, for us to go far afield and to attempt more than a very cursory mention of what seem to be the most plausible explanations on pharmacological grounds alone. The concensus of opinion of students in the field seems to be that there are no morphological changes in the cellular tissues in the phenomenon of the withdrawal symptoms,[2] but that the continued use of opium for a certain length of time has the effect of establishing in the organism an artificial functional equilibrium. It is described by Lewin in these words, "The life of the cell has adapted itself to or was dominated by the drug, and if it is lacking a craving appears."[3] Others call it an "altered metabolism"[4] or simply

---

[1] The definition is adapted from *The Departmental Committee Report of 1926*, by British Ministry of Health, quoted in Wm. Willcox, "The Prevention and Arrest of Drug Addiction," *British Journal of Inebriety*, XXIV (1926).

[2] *Supra*, pp. 13–4.

[3] Lewin, *op. cit.*, p. 21.

[4] Willcox, *British Journal of Inebriety*, XXXI, p. 132.

maintain that "the body becomes educated to the new relationship."[1] From this point of view, the withdrawal symptoms, such as restlessness, irritability, insomnia, etc., as mentioned above, may be roughly considered as the attempts of the organism to achieve chemical equilibration on the one hand and adjustment to the environment on the other when the narcotics are taken away from it, and the craving for a further dose as a desire to be freed from this agonizing process of readjustment and to remain in what has been called the "altered metabolism." But the effect of a new dose alleviates the condition only for a short while by restoring the lost artificial equilibrium and giving the organism a false sense of well-being at the same time; eventually as the effect of the drug wears off the feared physiologic process is due to reappear, for the relief of which again another dose is required. Furthermore, as the central nervous system can readily acquire tolerance to the action of depressants, it is not sufficient that the administration of the drug should be continued; it must be given in increasing dosages.[2]

Some such functional basis due to the pharmacological action of the drug alone, therefore, should be kept in mind when we discuss withdrawal symptoms. But from what was said about the euphoric effect of opium in the preceding paragraphs, it should be self-evident that the phenomenon before us is a very complicated one. For almost every pharmacological action is psychological in its effect. What affects the brain affects the personality as well. Consequently, it is difficult to say whether the addict's craving for opium is due to a physiologic urge to recover the lost artificial functional equilibrium or more a psychological desire to reënter the state of Nirvana as we have called it. We are inclined to adopt the latter view, and evidences in support of it will be advanced when we come in a later chapter to discuss what the opium habit means to the individual. It is fitting to point out here that recent experimental evidences also seem to point quite definitely to the conclusion that the basis of withdrawal symptoms is emotional rather than pharmacological. The following passage from the work of Light and his colleagues is especially illuminating:

In favor of an emotional basis as a cause for the withdrawal symptoms, we wish to cite our negative observations. Despite

[1] B. Legewie, *Delirium bei Morphinismus*, u.s.w., quoted in Terry and Pellens, *op. cit.*, p. 400.
[2] J. A. Gunn, "Cellular Immunity," etc., quoted in Terry and Pellens, *op. cit.*, p. 397.

the fact that the addicts claim to be so weak as to be scarcely able to move, their response to the staircase climbing test was carried out with the same efficiency as when drugs were administered, with the exception of the respiratory response; following the read-ministration of the drug, the response was, if anything, poorer. Such differences as exist in basal blood pressure, heart rate and respiratory rate are too small to indicate any significant change. Addicts will admit that when they are unable to obtain drugs and when withdrawal symptoms with extreme weakness have become severe, the assurance of an available supply at a considerable distance will cause them to travel this distance with remarkable speed and efficiency.[1]

It is reasonable to suppose, therefore, that the reasons that cause the withdrawal symptoms are probably the same as those which cause the addict to seek after and enjoy the euphoric or the therapeutic effect of opium and to continue to use the drug, till the pharmacological factor, i.e., whatever modification there is in the cell due to the chemical effect of the drug, comes in and adds to the links of an unbreakable chain, so to speak, that has long been in the process of formation. We refer, of course, to the possible inadequacies in the personality of the addict and the vicissitudes of his existence that have made life difficult for him. From this point of view, therefore, the really important thing to inquire into is not so much the effects of the drug as the individual's need for them. And to inquire into a man's need for narcotics, we have indicated already, little can be gained from studying him as an individual, for almost all of his troubles and difficulties for which opium is resorted to as a relief, with the possible exception of organic diseases, come from his association with his fellow-beings. Thus a brief excursion into the pharmacological effects of opium only makes it clearer that the real locus of our problem lies neither in the drug or the addict as an individual but in the relation between the addict and his society.

3. THE NATURAL HISTORY OF THE EUPHORIC USE OF OPIUM

Thus far we have made some working acquaintance with the pharmacological action of opium and with its therapeutic as well as euphoric effects. Since the therapeutic use of opium is limited to medical practice and does not lead to so many cases of addiction as to constitute a major social problem, our attention in this study will be centered mainly on the

[1] A. B. Light and others, *op. cit.*, p. 64.

use of the drug for its euphoric effect. It is not to be taken for granted, as is done by many, that the capacity of opium of producing euphoric effects by itself is sufficient to account for its prevalent use. As a matter of fact, the majority of opium addicts had only the slightest idea of what the effect of the drug was when they first came in contact with it. It may almost be said that most of them begin to use opium for very much the same reason as we begin to smoke tobacco, and few of us smoke tobacco because we know what effect it will produce. It seems, therefore, the spread of opium addiction is very much like the spread of a cultural practice. This observation is contrary to the very popular notion that indulgence in the use of opium springs directly, so to speak, from the evil nature of a degenerated individual or an unprogressive race. Quite on the contrary, we believe that there are certain constellations of conditions or sequences of events that so unavoidably lead to the genesis and the spread of opium addiction among a group of people as to constitute what may be called a natural history. A knowledge of this history will not only prevent us from blaming the drug addict for conditions for which he is not responsible, but will also give us a rational basis for curbing its further spread and for future prevention. However, the history of opium is still very fragmentary, and an account of the conditions we have in mind that occasioned the development of the euphoric use of the drug is yet to be written. So the best we can do here is to give only a bare outline, leaving the details to be filled in by our future historian.

According to the best authorities, the properties of opium were known as early as some seven thousand years before the Christian era among the Sumerians, a non-Semitic people who descended from the uplands of Central Asia into Southern Mesopotamia. The first mention of the drug is found on the Assyrian Medical Tablets.[1] The method of collecting opium juice described on these tablets is practically the same as used at the present day in the opium-producing countries from the "cradle of opium," i.e., Mesopotamia, to the neighboring countries both to the West and the East. From the Assyrians or Babylonians the knowledge of opium was passed on to the Persians and the Egyptians, then to the Greeks and the Romans, and finally to the heirs of most classical heritage, the Arabs. And through these Mohammedan con-

---

[1] Terry and Pellens, *op. cit.*, pp. 53–4.

querors and traders the seeds of opium were carried to the Far East, to Persia, India, and China. Thus a complete history of opium would involve a history of the cultures of all these peoples and their contacts with each other. Here we are mainly interested in the transition, so to speak, from the early therapeutic use of opium to its later more popular euphoric use, from the use of the drug exclusively for the cure of physical ailment to its use for pleasure. Without going into minor details, the following milestones may be pointed out as worth our special attention.

First of all, it seems the use of opium in the early days was closely associated with the religious cult of a people and assumed something of a sacred character. The knowledge and use of the drug was the exclusive privilege of a certain class: the magicians, warriors or priests; it was unknown to the common people. From this point of view, the later development of the euphoric use of opium by the masses may be considered as the secularization of a sacred plant. Thus the magical and superstitious character of the Egyptian *Ebers Papyri*, dated about 1550 B. C., in which opium was mentioned, is well known. Among the early Greeks, who acquired the knowledge of the drug from the Egyptians, the cup of Helen, mentioned by Homer both in *Iliad* and the *Odyssey*, was the special privilege of the warriors. "Only the initiated, the 'heroes,' made use of it."[1] Among the early Romans, the poppy was held sacred to Ceres. Lewin has an interesting observation on this point:

> It is interesting to note that the poppy-head belonged to the mysteries of Ceres, for she took papaver "to forget the pain," *ad oblivionem doloris*. This is why a small earthen statue of Ceres-Isis with a torch holds poppy-heads in her hand. Everywhere in antique art we meet with the poppy as a mythological symbol of sleep, and even a personification of the dispenser of sleep, the god who gives sleep. . . . he is presented as a bearded man leaning over the sleeper and pouring on his eyelids the poppy-juice contained in a vessel of horn which he holds in his hand.

> On the coffin of the sleeping Ariadne, the bearded God of Sleep is holding poppy-heads and an opium-horn in his hand. At a later date the God of Sleep, Somnus, is depicted as a young genie carrying poppies and an opium-horn, or with a poppy-stalk in his hand.[2]

---

[1] Lewin, *op. cit.*, pp. 32–5. This author maintains that the nepenthes mentioned in the *Odyssey* is the juice of opium.
[2] *Ibid.*, pp. 36–7.

That a powerful drug, whose properties were then only vaguely understood, should in those times be endowed with a supernatural character
is only natural and is, in fact, a very common phenomenon. Furthermore, these observations seem to suggest that the use of opium at this
stage, though enjoyed by the individual, was often linked up with some
social function; the use of the drug for the pleasure of the individual was
either unknown or not emphasized. An example near at hand is the
use of Peyote by the American Indians, which among some tribes has
even developed into a religion all of its own, and serves as some form of
integrating influence in the face of White domination.[1]

Historical evidences seem to show that it was in the great ancient
cities like Athens and Rome that the process of secularization of the
drug spoken of in the preceding paragraph first took place. Here the
knowledge of its beneficial properties gradually ceased to be the exclusive
privilege of the minority, and its use for both therapeutic and
euphoric purposes spread. Among the well-known physicians of the
classical days, who used opium extensively in their practice, may be
mentioned Pliny, Celsus, and Galen. The last named "spoke enthusiasti-
cally of the virtues of opium confections, and the drug was soon so
popular in Rome that it fell into the hands of shop-keepers and itinerant
quacks."[2] The euphoric use of the drug also began to be noticeable.
The following observation is illuminating.

The seductive power of opium, which incites an incessant renewal
of its use, as millions of experiences and human nature itself prove,
found its victims in Rome and in Greece, who desired a state of mental detachment from the life of the world. The short descriptions
which are given to us by the naturalists Theophrastus (third century
B. C.), Pliny, and Dioscorides (first century A. D.) show that the
toxic effects of the drug were already well known, effects which
were judged so important that Diagoras of Melos and Erasistratus,
in the fifth and third centuries before Christ, recommended the
complete avoidance of its use. But the employment of "poppies
soaked with the sleep of Lethe," has never been abandoned. Not
only the dragon which dwelt in and protected the garden of the

[1] V. Petrullo, *The Diabolic Root* (Philadelphia: University of Pennsylvania Press,
1934), p. 3.
[2] D. I. Macht, "The History of Opium and Some of Its Preparations and Alkaloids,"
Journal of American Medical Association, February 6, 1915, quoted in Terry and
Pellens, *op. cit.*, p. 56.

Hesperides, lying in the far-off country of the Moors . . . . succumbed
to its action . . . . but also innumerable human beings.[1]

In the Middle Ages in Europe, the therapeutic use of opium became
very prevalent. The famous physician Paracelsus (1490–1540), according to one author, "owed much of his success to the bold way in
which he administered opium to his patients. He is said to have carried
opium in the pommel of his saddle and called it the 'stone of immor-
tality.'"[2] The four well-known compounds of opium, called mithridatum,
theriaca, philenium, and diascordium were widely used by the physician
of this period for a great variety of ailments.[3] Cases of addiction due to
this prevalent form of medication and other reasons must have increased.
On the basis of the publications of the sixteenth to the eighteenth century, one author says of the addicts, "Some of these are reported to have
continued the consumption of opium in increasing doses for a number of
years, one woman, for example, taking in forty years sixty-three pounds
of 'fluid opium,' i.e., tincture of opium. Another consumed four grams
a day for nineteen years, twenty-seven kilos in all. A third, led to use
it as an anodyne by an accident, is said to have introduced one hundred
kilos of the drug into his system in the course of thirty-four years."[4]

For the transmission of the knowledge and the use of opium to the Orient,
we must take into account the influence of Mohammedanism, which
rose in the seventh century and spread speedily eastward in the following
one. The Arabs were well fitted for the job, for they were not only
great conquerors, but traders, and, besides, great opium-consumers
themselves.[5] Coincident with the arrival of the Moslems in India in
about the eighth century appear the first notices of opium in Sanskrit
medical works.[6] During practically the same period, known as the
Tang Dynasty in the history of China (618–907 A.D.), the drug was first
mentioned in the Chinese medical literature. But the process of obtaining opium from the poppy was not known there till the end of the
fifteenth century. The Arabic origin of this knowledge is indicated by

[1] Lewin, op. cit., p. 36. The Latin sentences in the text are omitted here.
[2] Macht, op. cit., quoted in Terry and Pellens, op. cit., p. 57.
[3] Payne, op. cit., pp. 12–3.
[4] Lewin, op. cit., p. 39.
[5] Payne, op. cit., p. 8. It is suggested that the prevalence of opium addiction
among the Moslems is due to their prohibition against the use of wine.
[6] D. E. Owen, British Opium Policy in China and India (New Haven: Yale
University Press, 1934), p. 1.

the Chinese word for opium, *A-fu-yung* or *ya-pien*, which is the Arabic *afyun*, derived from the Greek name *opion*.[1] And "for almost nine centuries following the introduction," says a well-known author, "the Chinese used opium exclusively for dysentery, and its use for purposes of euphoria was unknown to them."[2] For it was not until the second half of the eighteenth century that opium addiction in our sense of the word developed to any noticeable extent in China.

The subsequent development of the euphoric use of opium in China is especially interesting from our point of view, for in it we shall see something of the constellation of conditions we spoke of in a preceding paragraph that characterizes the diffusion of most cultural patterns. In this particular instance, strangely enough, we have to take into account the most diverse influences. First in order we may mention the missionary spirit of Christianity and the individualistic monetary motive of early European explorers and traders. For it is a well-known fact that the Portuguese navigators first sought the Orient "for Christians and spices."[3] The Dutch and the British adventurers who came after the Portuguese differed from them only in being more successful in attaining both of these objectives. The other important influence came from the culture of the American Indians in the form of tobacco. This is not the place to go into the social and economic conditions in Europe of the fifteenth and the sixteenth centuries that led to the great voyages of discovery or the growth of individualism, as Thorndike calls it, that inspired the early explorers and their sponsors.[4] But something of the complexity of the sequence of events that led to the euphoric use of opium in China may be glimpsed from the following story of opium-smoking.

An interesting problem is presented by the interrelation of opium and tobacco smoking. A new investigation of this subject which I made on the basis of Chinese sources has led me to the conclusion that opium smoking sprang up as a sequel of tobacco-smoking not earlier than the beginning of the eighteenth century. Before tobacco became known in Asia, opium was taken internally, either in the

---

[1] J. Edkins, *The Poppy in China*, quoted in H. B. Morse, *The Trade and Administration of the Chinese Empire* (1908), pp. 323–26.
[2] J. Marks, "The Opium Habit," *Social Science*, ed. Leroy Allen (1929), pp. 429 ff.
[3] Owen, *op. cit.*, p. 2.
[4] L. Thorndike, *A Short History of Civilization* (1926), p. 387.

form of pills, or was drunk as a liquid. The Hollanders, who ex-
ported large quantities of opium from India to Java, were the first
who prepared a mixture of opium with tobacco by diluting opium
in water, and who offered this compound for smoking to the natives
of Java. This fact is stated in perfect agreement by E. Kaempfer,
a physician in the service of the Dutch East India Company, who
visited Batavia in 1689, and by contemporaneous Chinese documents.
A Chinese author, who wrote a history of the island of Formosa,
which was under Dutch Rule from 1624 to 1655, even intimates
that the inhabitants of Batavia, who were originally excellent fight-
ers and had never lost a battle, were enervated and conquered by
the Hollanders by means of opium prepared by the latter for smoking
purposes. Be this as it may, the custom was soon imitated by the
Chinese on Formosa, and smoking-opium was smuggled into that
country from Batavia despite prohibitory regulations of the Chinese
authorities. Opium was then boiled in copper kettles, and the
mass was invariably blended with tobacco; the price for this product
was several times greater than that for tobacco alone. It was a
much later development to smoke opium in its pure state. The
opium pipe, as it still exists, was invented by Chinese in Formosa
in the first part of the eighteenth century . . . . . This is not the place
to go into the details of opium-smoking; it is mentioned here merely
in order to show that the opium-pipe is based on the tobacco-pipe
and that opium-smoking has grown out of tobacco-smoking.[1]

It is interesting to note that it is along the coastal cities, which were
the first to come in contact with Western cultures, that opium-smoking
first grew. From Formosa the habit spread to its nearest city, Amoy
in Fukien and to Canton in Kwangtung. In fact, when the first anti-
opium edict was issued in 1729, opium-smoking was a local affair, confined to the said coastal cities,[2] and it was not until the beginning of the
nineteenth century, when the opium trade was greatly augmented by
the British East India Company, that the habit spread further inland.
Hence the drastic measures taken by the Chinese Imperial Government
that led to the Opium War of 1839. The importance of taking into
account the monetary motive of early European merchants is here clearly
seen; for while the Chinese authorities, ignorant of the then world situation, considered opium traffic entirely as a moral issue, to the British it
was predominantly an economic one. The truth is succinctly expressed

[1] B. Laufer, *Tobacco and Its Use in Asia* (Chicago: Field Museum of Natural
History, 1924), pp. 23–4.
[2] Owen, *op. cit.*, p. 16.

by an English author who says that the Opium War "was due to the seizure by the Chinese of some two million pounds worth of contraband opium, and to the desire of the British Government to protect the large revenue derived from opium by the East India Company and the profit made from the illicit trade in opium by British merchants."[1]

To follow the further development of the euphoric use of opium in China, one would be tempted to inquire into such important facts as how China once almost entirely suppressed the use of opium for euphoria by the end of 1917; how in the following years, owing to internal political, social, and economic conditions, the drug habit returned until it became what is often called a "national vice"; and how the smuggling in of manufactured narcotic drugs, such as morphine which was isolated in 1803 by a German chemist, named Serturner, and heroin which was first synthetically produced in 1898, complicated the whole problem and has made futile even the most drastic measures of suppression;—but space does not permit this highly interesting undertaking here.[2]   Suffice it to conclude that even with the Chinese, who are generally thought of by the uninformed as an inborn opium-smoking race, we have found that the growth of the euphoric use of opium is connected with definite and traceable sequences of events that have more to do with the conditions of the most diverse cultures than with the native characteristics of the people.   We shall find this point helpful in the study of any group of people who happen to be "dope users" in a modern city or anywhere else, for, as we shall see presently, there are also traceable sequences of events that lead to the spread of the habit among them, that cannot be explained by the innate characteristics of individual addicts.   For no individual is born a morphine addict, just as no race is born an opium-smoking people.   Opium addiction as a cultural pattern can be explained only in terms of culture.[3]

Considering the fact that opium-smoking developed in the Far East in the beginning of the nineteenth century as a result of increasing contact with the West and the further fact that during practically the

[1] L. A. Lyall, *China* (1934), p. 163.
[2] Readers interested in the details of the story may consult among other works the following: W. T. Dunn, *The Opium Traffic in the International Aspect;* The International Anti-Opium Association, *The War Against Opium* (1922); W. T. Wu, *The Chinese Opium Problem;* Bingham Dai (ed.), *Opium: A World Problem*, Vols I–II 'Shanghai: The Chinese National Anti-opium Association, 1927–29).
[3] R. H. Lowie, *Culture and Ethnology*, p. 66.

same period the euphoric use of opium became increasingly popular in Europe as indicated by the writings and examples of such notables as De Quincey, Coleridge, Francis Thompson, and others, and in this country as well, as we shall see presently, one is tempted to characterize opium addiction as a "vice" or "disease" of the nineteenth century. Again we must leave it to our future historian to relate this phenomenon with other phenomena of the same period in order to discover the cultural conditions or the habits of mind that contributed toward the rapid growth of this highly individualistic form of self-indulgence. The following observation of a historian of medicine is quite suggestive, and is here introduced to furnish food for our deliberation:

> It is also apparent that in every epoch certain diseases are in the foreground and that they are characteristic of this epoch and fit into its whole structure. It seems as though the powers that ordain the style for and that stamp their impress upon a certain epoch affect even disease.
> The Middle Ages, for instance, were dominated by diseases of the common people—such as the plague, leprosy, and the epidemic neuroses—which appeared in the 6th and the 14th centuries, thus outlining that period in history. In the Renaissance it was syphilis, a distinctly individualistic disease, to which no one is subject but which is acquired through a volitional act.
> In the discordant Baroque era the foreground is occupied by diseases which might be called deficiency diseases like camp-fever, scurvy and ergotism on one hand and on the other by diseases which might be called luxury diseases like gout, dropsy and hypochondriasis. Tuberculosis of the lungs, chlorosis and similar disease are pathological expressions of the romantic period, while the 19th century, with its tremendously increased industrialization, the development of great cities and the accelerated life tempo, brought about industrial diseases, general nervousness and neuroses of many different kinds.[1]

What seem to be the most general factors closely associated with the increase of opium addiction in the nineteenth century are the psychology of exploitation, which is a product of industrialization and which is at the back of the clandestine trade in opium all over the world, and the possible increase of mental conflicts as suggested by Sigerist, which follows the breaking down of the earlier forms of social control and

- H. E. Sigerist, *Man and Medicine* (1932), p. 180.

which may explain the increasing need for narcotics on the part of many individuals.

4. THE SPREAD OF OPIUM ADDICTION IN THE UNITED STATES AND IN CHICAGO

As has been suggested in a preceding paragraph, in America as well as in the world at large it was in the beginning of the nineteenth century that the euphoric use of opium became increasingly popular. Medical authorities like Handy and Seaman, writing in as late as 1791 and 1792, did not mention the danger of chronic opium intoxication.[1] Probably before the nineteenth century there were not enough drug addicts in this country to attract the attention of the medical profession. But by 1832 the euphoric use of opium seemed to have grown to a sufficiently alarming extent to call forth the following warning:

> Opium should never be exhibited simply to rouse the spirits, to awaken the fancy or to give a temporary exertion to brilliant wit, this practice is most deleterious . . . . .
> Fearful of names, rather than of consequences, opium is continually resorted to by many of both sexes, but particularly by females, and these of the higher circles, as a substitute for the stimulus ordinarily afforded by gin or brandy . . . . . But there is another class who resort to opium in some one or other of its forms, either from indolence, or carelessness, or both; I mean mothers, nurses, and those to whom are trusted the charge of infants. The youthful, inconsiderate mother and the idle nurse, too frequently resort to opium to hush the infant's cries, which might have been done by the ordinary and only best means of nursing.
>
> . . . .
>
> But the injudicious use of opium is not confined alone to mothers and nurses, many practitioners of medicine are also culpable.[2]

In tracing the subsequent development of the euphoric use of opium in this country, one must take into account the following factors. Here

[1] Hast Handy, *On Opium*. (Thesis, Philadelphia, 1791); Valentine Seaman, *An Inaugural Dissertation on Opium* (Philadelphia, 1792). Both works are mentioned in Terry and Pellens, *op. cit.*, pp. 59–60.

[2] W. G. Smith, *On Opium Embracing Its History, Chemical Analysis and Use and Abuse as a Medicine* (New York, 1832). Mentioned in Terry and Pellens, *op. cit.*, pp. 60–1.

we have drawn freely from an article by Charles E. Terry on this very topic.[1]

Terry considers as an important influence certain writings of this period. Among the earliest and by far the most important of these was Thomas De Quincey's "Confessions of an English Opium-Eater." It is doubtful if any single work has had a more far-reaching influence in stimulating its readers to undertake hazardous experiments with opium than has De Quincey's masterpiece, the forerunner of a host of other less brilliant but equally morbid productions.

The next important factor in the spread of addiction was the discovery of the hypodermic syringe by Rynd of Dublin in 1845 and Wood of Edinburgh in 1853. By the employment of this instrument and the injection of morphine and other derivatives of opium under the skin, it was thought that the so-called opium appetite would not be stimulated, as it had been heretofore by oral administration. That this was not realized is evidenced by the fact that the hypodermic use of morphine as a drug of addiction has become in this country as well as in Europe the most common method of administration.

Wars are mentioned as the next important factor in the increase of drug addiction in which opium was used to a large extent for its analgesic effects. In particular may be mentioned the Civil War and the last World War. So marked was the effect of the former that opium addiction came to be known in this country after 1865 as the "army disease." The World War also gave rise to many victims not only in this country but in Europe as well, where the marked increase is a matter of frequent comment in medical writings.

The extolling of opium by medical writers and the susceptibility of the public to therapeutic suggestions culminated in the nineteenth century in the development of a host of patent remedies containing opium or its derivatives. The peak of the patent-medicine industry in the United States was reached just prior to the passage of the Pure Food and Drugs Act in 1906. The decline of the industry began at this time and was further affected in 1914 with the passage of the Harrison Narcotic Act.

The discovery of heroin in 1898, as mentioned in a preceding paragraph, was a further impetus given to the use of opium. It was first claimed

[1] C. E. Terry, "The Development and Causes of Opium Addiction as a Social Problem," *Journal of Educational Sociology*, February, 1931.

that heroin was free from habit-forming properties and was useful in
the treatment of opium addiction.   Medical literature for the next ten
or twelve years continued to advocate the use of heroin and it was not
until about 1910 that the picture began to change and the profession
began to realize that heroin was as dangerous as morphine or other opium
derivatives in addiction-forming properties.   But its greater potency,
the ease with which it could be sniffed, and the rapidity of its absorption
through the mucous membrane of the nose all led to early popularity of
this drug as a drug of addiction.   Although at the present time the
importation and manufacture of this drug are prohibited in this country,
it continues to be the most handled drug, because its amorphous form
permits easily of adulteration and makes it thereby more profitable in
the illicit traffic.   Recently it has supplanted morphine to a considerable
degree as a drug of addiction in every part of the country except on the
Pacific coast.[1]

The influence of illicit traffic mentioned above in the spread of drug
addiction in this country cannot be measured.   It defies all prohibitive
efforts, and through the operation of the retail peddlers supplies the needs
of most drug addicts.   The rôle of illicit traffic in creating new drug
users, though not well defined, should also be kept in view.

All these factors no doubt have contributed toward the increase of
opium addiction in the last century.   But there is one other factor which
probably has more to do with the spread of the euphoric use of the drug
than any other factor thus far mentioned, and this is the underworld
environment.   For while the ignorance and carelessness of physicians
in prescribing opium might have been responsible for a large number
of addicts in the early days when the habit-forming properties of the drug
were not well known, toward the end of the last century this factor
became increasingly less important, not only because the medical profession became better informed, but the knowledge of the euphoric
effects of the drug had gradually become a common property of the
so-called underworld.   In fact, with respect to heroin, it has been stated
that the underworld knew of its habit-forming character long before the
average physician did.[2]   Kolb and Du Mez in 1924 reported an observation made by Simon, stating that less than 2 per cent of approximately

---

[1] U. S. Bureau of Narcotics, *Traffic in Opium and Other Narcotic Drugs*, 1932, p. 11.
[2] Terry and Pellens, *op. cit.*, p. 84.

10,000 addicts arrested or committed to hospitals in New York City during the previous three years owed their addiction to physicians. "The latter figures," added the authors, "are supported by our own findings. Examinations made by one of us during the past two years have shown that less than 5 per cent of the cases of recent addictions are caused by physicians."[1] Treadway, writing in 1930, pointed to a similar observation, saying, "It has been estimated that 80 per cent of the present-day addiction occurs in the land of 'Hobohemia,' or the underworld . . . ."[2]   And it has been found that it was in the underworld of San Francisco that opium-smoking first spread since the year 1868.[3] On the basis of these evidences, it may be stated, at least of the last generation in this country, that it is in proportion to the extent to which opium addiction becomes a habit of the underworld that it constitutes a major social problem.

The trend of addiction for the country at large is something for which we do not have accurate statistics. According to Kolb and Du Mez, the peak was reached in 1900, their estimate of the total number of addicts for the country then being 264,000. After 1900, the number of addicts is said to have steadily decreased.[4] This observation was based on the amount of opium and opium alkaloids imported and available for consumption, and smuggled opium was not considered important enough to affect the direction of the trend. But the experience of the law-enforcement forces during subsequent years does not confirm this assumption. While official reports state that possibly there has not been any increase in addiction during recent years, the existence of a large contraband trade in opium is frankly acknowledged.[5] For this reason, larger estimates of the total number of addicts, as given in the preceding chapter, seem more probable, and the trend herein depicted is doubtful.

Something of an upward trend since 1900, however, seems to be indicated by the increasing number of commitments to federal institutions for the violation of the narcotic drug laws since 1915, in which year the

1 Kolb and Du Mez, op. cit., p. 23.
2 W. L. Treadway, "Some Epidemiological Features of Drug Addiction," British Journal of Inebriety, October, 1930, p. 50.
3 Terry and Pellens, op. cit., p. 73.
4 Kolb and Du Mez, op. cit., pp. 14 ff.
5 U. S. Bureau of Narcotics, Traffic in Opium and Other Narcotic Drugs, 1930, p. 13.

Harrison Narcotic Act went into effect.[1] With only 63 for 1915, the number of commitments to federal institutions alone increased to 287 in 1920, and jumped up to 1,880 in 1925. The peak was reached in 1929, with a total of 1,889 commitments, after which year there has been a noticeable decrease. With 1929 commitments as the base, the percentages of decrease for the past few years are found to be 13.1 for the year 1929–30, 22 for the year 1930–31, 18.9 for the year 1931–32, and 26.7 for the year 1932–33. Both the increase and the decrease of these commitments may be due to more than one factor. Among others may be mentioned efficiency in enforcing the narcotic drug laws and the amount of appropriations for the enforcement, which, as a matter of fact, has decreased from $1,712,998 for the year 1930–31 to $1,400,000 for 1933–34.[2] So the exact relation between this trend of prison commitments and the actual trend of drug addiction is difficult to ascertain.

Besides this temporal trend of drug addiction, the reader may be interested in knowing something about the spatial distribution of opium addicts in the whole country. Again this is a subject for which we cannot expect to have accurate data. But the following map prepared by the Narcotic Division of the United States Public Health Service on the basis of estimated average annual drug addiction among violators of the Harrison Narcotic Act for the years, 1922–1928, is suggestive.

According to Map 1 the states of relatively heavy addiction in terms of absolute numbers seem to be along the coasts, especially Massachusetts, New York, New Jersey, Maryland and Virginia on the Atlantic coast, and Washington and California on the Pacific. The other states of heavy addiction in the sense as stated above are found in the Mid-West and the Near-East, along the Mississippi and the Ohio rivers. They are Illinois, Missouri, Michigan, Ohio, and Pennsylvania. The southern states like Tennessee, Oklahoma, Texas, Louisiana, Georgia, and Florida are not far behind. It is interesting to note that the states in the West, except those already mentioned, are relatively free of drug addiction. The same is

---

[1] U. S. Bureau of Prisons, *Federal Offenders*, 1932–33, pp. 103, 137. It is to be noted that not all of these violators of drug laws are drug addicts, the percentage of addicts among them having been estimated to be about 40. The actual percentage may be higher. Thus, of the total of 2,158 unregistered violators of the Harrison Narcotic Law apprehended between July 1 and October 31, 1929, 1,593, or 74 per cent, were addicts, and of the 249 registered offenders, 67, or 27 per cent, were addicts. See W. L. Treadway, *Further Observations on the Epidemiology of Narcotic Drug Addiction* (1930), p. 1.

[2] U. S. Bureau of Narcotics, *Traffic in Opium*, 1930, p. 12; *Ibid*, 1933, p. 12.

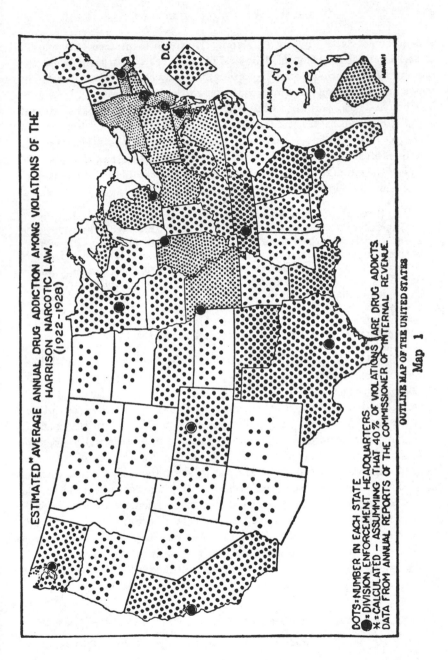

ESTIMATED* AVERAGE ANNUAL DRUG ADDICTION AMONG VIOLATIONS OF THE
HARRISON NARCOTIC LAW.
(1922-1928)

DOTS= NUMBER IN EACH STATE
●= DIVISION ENFORCEMENT HEADQUARTERS
*= CALCULATED – ASSUMING THAT 40% OF VIOLATIONS ARE DRUG ADDICTS
DATA FROM ANNUAL REPORTS OF THE COMMISSIONER OF INTERNAL REVENUE.

OUTLINE MAP OF THE UNITED STATES

Map 1

true of some states in New England. How representative this map is of the actual distribution of drug addiction in the country and what the factors are that bring about the different extent of addiction in different states are interesting questions that are worth closer study.

What has been said about the conditions or factors that have brought about the spread of drug addiction in the county is more or less true of Chicago. The careless therapeutic use of opium in the early days, for example, must have resulted in making a large number of addicts. In the city, the extent of addiction became quite noticeable by 1880, as may be seen in the following report by Earle:

> The three divisions of the city were visited, and localities inhabited by the different classes and nationalities were thoroughly canvassed. I was greatly surprised to find that druggists on the West Side were patronized to a greater extent (excepting a few on Clark Street) than in any other part of the city. Foreign druggists (German and Scandinavian) seem to exhibit more conscientious scruples in regard to the trade than our own nationality. I learned from some of these gentlemen that in Denmark, and, if I mistake not, in Norway and Sweden, the trade is absolutely forbidden. Fifty druggists have 235 customers, or an average of nearly five to each store.[1]

By 1895 the number of opium addicts must have greatly multiplied. Cobbe, a local opium addict, mentioned a number of people in his autobiography using an enormous quantity of opium. Thus one swallowed 7,680 drops of laudanum every day, which, according to the author, is equal to 110 grains of morphine. A resident of Northern Illinois took 250 grains of morphine daily, and a gentleman in Southern Illinois used 80 grains every day hypodermically. He added, "Hundreds of instances might be given from personal knowledge of individuals (whose diurnal addiction ranged from the equivalent of 20 grains of morphine to 190 grains of that salt), attesting the increasing tendencies of the habit."[2] What the author reported about the quantity of drug used by other addicts may not be accurate, but his numerous associations with drug users serve to indicate the prevalence of the habit at that time.

The extent to which opium addiction reached during the following decade or two may be seen in the following observation by Chicago's

---

[1] C. W. Earle, "The Opium Habit," *Chicago Medical Review*, 1880. Quoted in Terry and Pellens, *op. cit.*, p. 16.
[2] W. R. Cobbe, *Doctor Judas: A Portrayal of the Opium Habit* (Chicago, 1895).

best-known authority on the subject. After complaining about the spasmodic and fruitless attempts that had been made by the community in checking the growth of addiction, Sceleth said in 1921, "Chicago is the home of thousands of these poor miserable wretches, whose lives are but despairing struggles for the poison that lulls them to the false rest and solace of insanity. Year after year I have watched their constantly increasing numbers until I have begun to wonder whether the American of the future is to be a drug-nurtured, dope-fed being. Years ago this habit was seldom met with outside the dive or gilded brothel; but to-day, in hundreds of homes of all classes, the recruiting of victims of the drug curse goes steadily on."[1]

Let us stop here and ask what the most important factors are that brought about this apparent increase of drug addiction in the city. In the report cited above, Sceleth mentioned patent medicine as an important one. But, above all, he emphasized a factor which we have found to be mainly responsible for the spread of opium addiction in the country at large, and that is what we have called the underworld. He says in another place, "Fifteen or twenty years ago, most addicts acquired the habit through physical disease or discomfort. Today the number of new addictions through physicians' prescriptions is small. The great majority of cases now result from association with addicts, following their advice in taking a 'shot' or a 'sniff' for 'what ails you' and searching for new sensations. These are the pleasure users."[2] The foregoing observation is further collaborated by one who has unusually long and intimate contact not only with the opium addicts of Chicago but with the underworld in general as well. He convincingly points out in the following statement that the underworld has been and still is the most common road to drug addiction.[3]

In Chicago in 1885 I had my first experience with dope. At 16th and Clark St., Chicago, I lived across the street from a house of prostitution. The Madame was an old rheumatic, fat woman who seldom left a big chair. She always sat in the window. She called me in one day and gave me a morphine bottle and fifty cents and told me to go to the drug store and get it filled. I was just a

---

[1] The House of Correction of the City of Chicago, *A Retrospect Covering a Half Century of Endeavor* 1871–1921, pp. 55–56.
[2] Sceleth, *Journal of the American Medical Association*, March 1, 1924, pp. 679 ff.
[3] Ben L. Reitman, "The Underworld the Most Common Road to Drug Addiction," an unpublished statement prepared for this study.

child but the druggist took the bottle and the money, and filled the bottle with morphine and I brought it back to the Madame. For a well-filled half a century I have been studying the drug traffic, drug addiction and narcotics in its many phases and ramifications.

I believe I am conservative in estimating that I have known personally ten thousand drug addicts and at least one thousand were my personal friends and patients.

The larger portion of drug addicts were met while I was a physician at the Chicago House of Correction, the Cook County Jail, Chicago, Ill. and while I was a prison-physician at the Warrensville jail in Cleveland, Ohio.

I also contacted hundreds of prisoner-addicts while I was a prisoner in about fifty jails throughout America. Most of the dope fiend prisoners I met in the jails of New York, San Francisco and Pueblo, Col.

For over thirty years I have been a practicing physician and a large percent of my patients were underworld types: prostitutes, pimps, and criminals, and many of them were drug addicts.

I have also met several hundred legitimate, apparently decent, honest people who were drug addicts. I know at least one hundred doctors who are addicted to the use of morphine or cocaine.

Out of my experience and observation I am certain that the majority of all drug addicts have their genesis in the Underworld. The beginning of nine-tenths of all users of opium in its various forms, and cocaine, is in an environment that we could correctly label as criminal, anti-social and "illegitimate." The Underworld contains more accessible narcotics than the respectable world. For the past ten years it has been difficult for a drug addict to legitimately, legally obtain drugs. The largest source of narcotics is in the Underworld. And most drug addicts have to have an Underworld connection to obtain them.

Thus we have followed, however briefly, the trail of the poppy, so to speak, from the time when it was held as a sacred plant to the time when it came to be considered as an evil weed, and we have discovered some of the social and cultural conditions that marked this process of secularization and that popularized not only the therapeutic but the euphoric effects of the drug. From the earliest time to the present day, we have found that it is in the city environment that the euphoric use of opium finds its most fertile soil, but that its rapid spread throughout the world did not begin until the beginning of the nineteenth century. We further discovered that among all the conditions that have been responsible for the wide spread of the opium habit, the underworld environment is the most important, particularly since the beginning of the present century. This is especially true of the city which is our immediate object of study.

The next logical question to ask is what this underworld environment is and how in such an environment the pattern of opium addiction is passed on to the individual. We shall try to answer this and other related questions in the following chapters.

CHAPTER III

CHARACTERISTICS OF OPIUM ADDICTS IN CHICAGO

HAVING explored to some extent the natural history of opium addiction, we shall attempt in this chapter to answer the question who the opium addicts are and in what way, if any, they differ from other people. The chief sources of our data are the Federal Bureau of Narcotics in Chicago, the Narcotic Division of the Chicago Police Department, and the Cook County Psychopathic Hospital. Data from the first two sources are based on the records of arrests made by these agencies for the violation of the Harrison Narcotic Act or the narcotic laws of the state of Illinois for the years, 1929–34, and the years, 1931–33, respectively.[1] Those from the hospital are based on the records of admissions for the treatment of drug addiction for the years, 1928–33. In order to avoid overlapping as far as possible under the circumstances, an attempt has been made to compare the records of these different agencies and those of different years in the same agency, and, as a result, we have discarded the records of 426 recidivists from the Bureau of Narcotics, and those of 358 offenders from the City Narcotic Division, as they were later transferred to the Bureau of Narcotics. A number of records from the hospital were also laid aside because of repetition. Altogether we have secured data on 2,518 drug addicts and 327 drug peddlers, who were declared to be non-addicts, and these data cover approximately a period of six years, from 1928 to 1934.

Besides, we have on hand similar information about 118 female addicts who have served time in the Women's Reformatory at Dwight, and 259 patients admitted to the Keeley Institute for the cure of drug addiction. Data from these sources are treated separately, because most of the cases in the former institution were already included in the records of the City Narcotic Division, and because more than half of the patients

---

[1] It was not possible to take data from these different agencies for a uniform period of time as originally intended, because a uniform system of record amenable to scientific analysis was not used by the Bureau of Narcotics in the city until July, 1929, and the Narcotic Division of Chicago Police Department did not begin its work until 1931.

in the latter institution were not residents of Chicago. But they will be presented whenever they show variation from, or serve to supplement what is lacking in, our main body of data as described above.

The reliability of all these data is a question that is very difficult to ascertain. Most of them were originally obtained from addicts by law-enforcement officers or hospital authorities who were not primarily concerned with scientific research. Furthermore, drug addicts as a whole, as it is well known, are liable to make statements that are expedient rather than true. Such considerations, therefore, must be borne in mind when one comes to interpret the data to be presented in the following.

Our data have another limitation in that we do not have comparable data about the characteristics of the general population, although comparison between opium addicts in Chicago and Chicago's general population is possible in some respects. The absence of reliable comparable data regarding the non-addict population, however, does not invalidate all research into the general make-up of drug addicts. As in the case of similar studies,[1] a descriptive account of the characteristics of drug addicts in Chicago is believed to be of value in the practical task of understanding drug addiction and of determining upon rational and effective measures of meeting the problems they present to the community. Bearing all these points in mind, let us now examine the characteristics of opium addicts in Chicago as revealed by our data.

1. SOME GENERAL CHARACTERISTICS

Age. Of 2,439 drug addicts of whom the age at their arrest or admission to the Psychopathic Hospital was known, 12 (.5%) were between 15 and 19; 177 (7.3%) between 20 and 24; 423 (17.3%) between 25 and 29; 535 (21.9%) between 30 and 34; 450 (18.4%) between 35 and 39; 369 (15.1%) between 40 and 44; 209 (8.6%) between 45 and 49; 142 (5.9%) between 50 and 54; 68 (2.8%) between 55 and 59; and 54 (2.2%) were 60 or over. The small percentage of cases under 20 seems to show that in Chicago drug addiction is mainly a problem of the adult population, the most common age group among these addicts being between 30 and 34.

A slight variation from this general age distribution is noticed among the female patients admitted to the Psychopathic Hospital taken by

---

[1] Glueck, *op. cit.*, pp. 63–5.

themselves. Out of 287 cases, 3 (1.0%) were between 15 and 19; 29 (10.1%) between 20 and 24; 74 (25.8%) between 25 and 29; 65 (22.6%) between 30 and 34; 44 (15.3%) between 35 and 39; 39 (13.6%) between 40 and 44; and the remaining 33 (11.5%) were 45 or over. There seemed to be a larger percentage of young female addicts between 20 and 29 among the hospital patients than among the offenders of the narcotic laws.

Sex. In 2,518 cases in which this information was available, 1,789 (73.0%) were males, and 672 (27.0%) females, the proportion of male to female addicts being approximately 3 to 1. Among the drug-peddlers, who were declared as non-addicts, 273 (85.3%) were male; and 47 (14.7%) female, the proportion of male to female non-addict peddlers being approximately 6 to 1.

Color. In 2,431 cases in which this factor was known, 1,876 (77.1%) were classified as white; 420 (17.3%) black; 133 (5.5%) yellow; and 2 (.1%) red. Table I compares this distribution of color with that of the general population of Chicago.

TABLE I

THE RACE RATIO AMONG DRUG ADDICTS AND THE GENERAL
POPULATION OF CHICAGO

(*Percentages*)

Color	Drug Addicts	General Population of Chicago, 1930[a]
White	77.1	92.3
Negro	17.3	6.9
Other races	5.6	.8
TOTAL	100.0	100.0

(a) E. W. Burgess and Charles Newcomb (ed.), *Census Data of the City of Chicago*, 1930, p. xv.

It will be noted that while the majority of Chicago's drug addicts were white, the Negro addicts have more than twice the incidence of Negroes in the general population, and addicts of other races about seven times the incidence of other races in the general population, most of the latter being Chinese.

Nationality. In 2,299 cases in which this fact was recorded, 2,005 (87.2%) were classified as American; 89 (3.9%) Chinese; 69 (3.0%) Mexican; 28 (1.2%) Italian; 25 (1.1%) Jewish; 15 (.7%) Irish; 12 (.6%) German; and 53 (2.3%) all other nationalities, such as the Polish, the Spanish, the French, the Russian, etc. That so many nationalities are involved clearly suggests that the explanation of drug addiction is not to be found in the nationality or racial factor alone, as has been popularly supposed.[1]

2. NATAL CIRCUMSTANCES AND FAMILY BACKGROUND

Nativity. Of 1,520 drug addicts of whom this fact was reported, 1,419 (93.4%) were native-born; and 101 (6.6%) foreign-born. It is interesting to note that among the native-born group, 22.9 per cent were born in the city of Chicago, 16.3 per cent in other places of the state of Illinois, and 59.8 per cent in other states of the Union. These figures suggest that opium addiction in Chicago is mainly a problem of the native-born, but that relatively a smaller percentage of them are natives of Chicago; most of them came from other localities or states and lived here as strangers. The significance of this fact can be shown only in the study of individual cases.

Nature of community. The nature of the early environment of this group of drug addicts may be seen to a certain extent in the kind of community from which they came. Out of 1,441 cases in which this information was available, 1,190 (82.6%) were reported to have come from urban communities; 74 (5.1%) suburban; and 177 (12.3%) rural.[2] These figures seem to suggest that the majority of drug addicts are products of the urban environment.

Nativity of parents. Out of 1,113 cases in which parentage was known, in 708 (63.6%) both parents were born in the United States; in 283 (25.4%) both parents were born in foreign countries; and in 122 (11.0%) parentage was mixed, including a few cases in which the birthplace of one of the parents was unknown. The percentage of foreign-born parents

---

[1] The reader may be interested in the following discussion of the fallacy of explaining alcoholism or drug addiction in terms of the racial factor. W. M. Feldman, "Racial Aspects of Alcoholism," *British Journal of Inebriety*, XXI (1923).

[2] As specified by the instructions in the federal records, "urban" and "suburban" refer to communities having a population of 2,500 or more. All other places are considered as rural.

is slightly larger in the case of the female addicts in the Women's Reformatory at Dwight. Out of 109 cases, 77 (70.7%) had native-born parents; and 32 (29.3%) foreign-born parents, including one case in which the birthplace of the father was unknown. In at least one-fourth of our cases, therefore, we have to consider the possible influence of the natural conflict of the cultural and ethical standards and attitudes between the American-born younger generation and the foreign-born elder, as has been emphasized by criminologists.[1]

Physical and mental condition of parents. From the point of view of both the heredity and the environment of drug addicts, it is of interest to inquire into the physical and mental condition of their parents. The following information about the family medical history of drug patients in the Keeley Institute, however meager, is suggestive. Among the fathers of 117 cases, in which this information was available, 25 (21.4%) were reported to have had no physical or mental trouble; the remaining 92 (78.6%) had ailments of one kind or the other. Of these 92 fathers, 49 (53.3%) used liquor; 7 (7.6%) had heart trouble; 6 (6.5%) either died of or had cancer; 5 (5.4%) had apoplexy; 4 (4.3%) were reported to have been paralyzed; and the remaining 21 (22.8%) together had a great variety of ailments, such as hemorrhage, diabetes, kidney trouble, tuberculosis, asthma, and others. Of the 84 mothers, about whom this information was available, 32 (38.1%) had no serious physical or mental difficulties. Of the 52 mothers who had ailments, 11 (21.1%) died of cancer; 6 (11.5%) had kidney trouble; 5 (9.6%) tuberculosis, 5 (9.6%) heart trouble; 5 (9.6%) were said to have been nervous; 4 (7.7%) paralyzed; 3 (5.8%) epileptic; and the remaining 13 (25.0%) had most of the ailments enumerated above in connection with the fathers. Three major physical or mental handicaps, therefore, are most common among the parents of this group of addicts: namely, the use of liquor, cancer, and heart trouble. While it is difficult to draw any inference on the basis of such insufficient data, some of the ways in which these habits or diseases on the part of the parents affect the early life of addicts may be seen in our case studies.

Rank in the family. It has been quite generally recognized by psychiatrists that the status of a child in the family has a determining effect upon his later development into an adult personality. Information of

---

[1] E. H. Sutherland, *Criminology* (1924), p. 101.

this nature is lacking in our main body of data. But what we found among the inmates of the Women's Reformatory is suggestive. Of 97 cases in which relationship with siblings was reported, 25 (25.8%) were the youngest in the family; 19 (19.6) the oldest; 16 (16.5%) the only child; 16 (16.5%) the second child; and the remaining 21 (21.6%) occupied other intermediate positions. It is difficult, however, to determine how far these figures may be representative of other drug addicts under study.

Age of leaving home. One other fairly accurate index of the family background of drug addicts is the age at which they left home. Information on this point is also lacking in our main body of data. The following figures we obtained from the Women's Reformatory are quite illuminating. Of 115 female addicts about whom this information was available, 4 only never left home. The remaining 111 left home at the following ages: 1 (.9%) before 13; 10 (9.0%) between 13 and 14; 38 (34.2%) between 15 and 16; 25 (22.5%) between 17 and 18; 15 (13.5%) between 19 and 20; and 22 (19.8%) after 20. It was not definitely stated whether these addicts ran away from home or left home for some good reason, but that about half of this group left home by the age of 16 is sociologically significant. In the first place, running away from or leaving home at such an early age has been found to be in many cases a reaction to an unfavorable home environment.[1] In the second place, eagerness to run away from an unpleasant home often places the girl at the mercy of a still more unfavorable environment outside the home, leading in many cases to serious personal disorganization. This will be shown in some of our case studies.

3. RELIGION AND EDUCATION

Religion. Of 801 cases in which this fact was known, 395 (49.3%) were reported to have been Protestant; 361 (45.1%) Catholic; 39 (4.9%) Jewish; 1 (.1%) had some other form of religion; and 5 (.6%) none. The percentage of Catholics is relatively higher with the group of female addicts in the Women's Reformatory. Of 118 cases, 60 (50.8%) were Catholic; 48 (40.7%) Protestant; 4 (3.4%) Christian Scientists; 2 (1.7%) Jewish; and 4 (3.4%) none. These figures show that almost all of these drug addicts have received one form of religious training or the other, although at the time this information was solicited many of them might

---

[1] C. P. Armstrong, *660 Runaway Boys* (1932), p. 192.

not profess the religion with which they had been brought up. One interesting question arises in examining these figures as to whether the early religious training of these addicts had been beneficial or detrimental to their later development, or whether their religious background had anything to do with their drug habit. The statistical data on hand, however, give us no clue to this question, but something about the relation between their religious background and their life-organization as a whole will be said when we come to the study of individual cases.

Education. Drug addicts are generally thought of either as mental defectives or people who have little or no education. It is interesting, therefore, to find out how much education our group of addicts have had and how they compare with the general population of Chicago in this particular respect. Of 1,253 cases in which this factor was known, 186 (11.7%) either had no education or reached the grades from first to fourth in the elementary school; 674 (54.6%) reached the grades from fifth to eighth; 317 (25.2%) had high school education, complete or incomplete; and 66 (5.3%) had education beyond the high school. Table II compares the education of these addicts with that of the general population of Chicago.

TABLE II

THE EDUCATION OF DRUG ADDICTS AND OF THE GENERAL POPULATION
OF CHICAGO 18 YEARS OLD AND OVER

(*Percentages*)

Grades or Years Reached	Drug Addicts	General Population, 1934 a
None and 1–4	14.9	11.6
5–8	54.6	49.5
9–12	25.2	30.1
13 and over	5.3	8.8
TOTAL	100.0	100.0

(a) Charles Newcomb and Richard Lang (ed.), *Census Data of the City of Chicago* (1934), Table VI.

According to Table II, the percentage of addicts receiving secondary and higher education appears relatively lower compared with the general population, while that of addicts receiving elementary education is higher. It seems that the education of drug addicts is not particularly deficient compared with that of the general population.

Among our group of drug addicts, it is interesting to note that the female group seem to be relatively better educated than the male group. Table III is based on the records of 940 male and 297 female addicts.

TABLE III

THE EDUCATION OF MALE AND FEMALE ADDICTS

(*Percentages*)

Grades or Years Reached	Male	Female
None and 1–4............................	16.7	8.8
5–8	55.2	53.5
9–12.......................................	23.5	30.3
13 and over.............................	4.6	7.4
TOTAL.............................	100.0	100.0

Age of leaving school. The importance of the school as an early environment of addicts is next only to that of the home. The age at which they left school may serve to indicate to a certain extent the degree to which they were adjusted to the school environment. Of 1,094 cases of whom this fact was known, 10 (.9%) left school at the age of 8 or less; 9 (.8%) at 9; 22 (2.0%) at 10; 14 (1.3%) at 11; 59 (5.4%) at 12; 82 (7.5%) at 13; 231 (21.1%) at 14; 185 (16.9%) at 15; 176 (16.1%) at 16; and 306 (28.0%) at 17 and over. In other words, more than half of these addicts left school by the age of 15, and about three-fourths of them did so by 16. What did they do after leaving school at such an early age? And what kind of environment took the place of the school? On these points we have no statistical data. But a partial answer to these questions may be found in the kinds of occupation they engaged in after quitting school, to be presented in the following.

4. OCCUPATION, EMPLOYMENT, AND ECONOMIC STATUS

Occupation. In 2,022 cases in which information about their occupation was available, 390 or about one-fifth were reported to have had no occupation or such non-gainful occupations as "housewife" or "student." Among the 1,632 cases who had had occupation of some kind, 520 (31.9%) were reported as having been engaged in manufacturing industries; 492 (30.1%) in domestic and personal service; 383 (23.5%) in business or clerical work, or what was classified in the census as trade industries; 90 (5.5%) in transportation and communication; 61 (3.7%) in recreation and amusement; 38 (2.3%) in other professional or semi-professional activities; 17 (1.0%) in agriculture or mining; 7 (.4%) in public service; and 24 (1.5%) in illegal or criminal professions. Table IV compares the occupations of drug addicts in a rough way with those of the general population of Chicago.

TABLE IV

THE OCCUPATION OF DRUG ADDICTS AND OF THE GENERAL POPULATION
OF CHICAGO 10 YEARS OLD AND OVER, 1930[a]

(*Percentages*)

Occupation Groups	Drug Addicts	General Population
Manufacturing industries	31.9	43.8
Domestic and personal service	30.1	12.0
Business or trade industries	23.5	23.1
Transportation and communication	5.5	11.6
Recreation and amusement	3.7	1.2
Other professional or semi-professional	2.3	5.9
Agriculture and mining	1.0	.3
Public service	.4	2.0
Illegal professions	1.5	.....
TOTAL	99.9	99.9

(a) Burgess and Newcomb, *op. cit.*, p. xv.

It will be noted that whereas with the general population domestic and personal service ranks third with respect to the number of people engaged in it, it is second with our group of addicts. The latter also exceed the general population in the occupation group, called recreation and amusement. The percentage of addicts who were definitely known as having pursued illegal professions also deserves notice.

When the number of addicts as well as that of the general population engaged in those various occupations enumerated above was counted according to sex, the following result was obtained. The percentages for the addicts in Table V are based on the occupational records of 1,297 male and 207 female addicts, the data for the general population being the same as those in Table IV.

TABLE V

THE OCCUPATION OF DRUG ADDICTS AND OF THE GENERAL POPULATION OF CHICAGO 10 YEARS OLD AND OVER, CLASSIFIED BY SEX

(*Percentages*)

Occupation Groups	Drug Addicts		General Population	
	Male	Female	Male	Female
Manufacturing industries	34.9	4.8	48.1	31.6
Trade industries............	25.9	14.5	23.2	22.8
Domestic and personal service......................	24.8	59.9	7.4	25.1
Transportation and communication	6.3	2.4	13.2	6.9
Recreation and amusement........................	3.9	4.3	1.1	1.4
Other professional or semi-professional.........	1.5	8.7	4.0	11.4
Agriculture and mining...	1.2	.....	.4	.....
Public service.................	.5	.....	2.5	.7
Illegal professions	.9	5.3	.....	.....
TOTAL......................	99.9	99.9	99.9	99.9

According to Table V, the male addicts greatly exceed the male general population in domestic and personal service, and also to a noticeable extent in recreation and amusement. The same is true also of the female addicts compared with the female general population. Without going into the possible reasons for these addicts being engaged more than the general population in these two occupational groups, it is interesting to note that such occupations as a waiter or waitress, or a show-man or show-girl tend to keep those engaged in them constantly "on the go," and thus subject them to that kind of environment and life with a high degree of mobility which presumably is somewhat conducive to different forms of disorganization.

That the preceding figures on occupation may not be representative of all addicts is shown by the data we secured from the Keeley Institute.[1] Here the addict-patients apparently belonged to a relatively higher economic status. Out of 210 cases in which information about their occupations was available, 100 (47.6%) were engaged in professional activities; 54 (25.7%) in business or trade industries; 16 (7.6%) in manufacturing industries; 16 (7.6%) in agriculture or mining; only 13 (6.2%) in domestic and personal service; 6 (2.9%) in transportation and communication; 3 (1.4%) in recreation and amusement; and 2 (1.0%) in public service. It is interesting to note that among the 100 addicts who were professional, 59, or about 60 per cent, were physicians. It is needless to say that the knowledge of the properties of opium and the accessibility to it in the case of physicians are factors that we must consider in accounting for their addiction to drugs.

Employment. Of 1,049 cases in which information about employment was available, 186 (17.7%) were reported as having had regular employment; and 863 (82.3%) irregular. The causes of the irregularity of employment were not known. It might be due to the incapacity on the part of addicts to hold any job for any considerable length of time. It might be due also to the general economic situation. But that the majority of these addicts did not have regular jobs is a fact of considerable importance.

Of 92 female addicts in the Women's Reformatory information about whose employment at the time of arrest was available, 78 (84.8%) were reported as not working; and 14 (15.2%) as working.

Economic status. Of 1,135 cases in which information about their economic status was available, 161 (14.2%) were reported as being dependent; 892 (78.6%) as marginal; and 82 (7.2%) as comfortable.[2]

The irregularity of employment and the low economic status of most of these addicts raises the question as to how they managed to subsist and, further, to keep their expensive habit. A

---

[1] It is also to be noted that in the group of addicts dealt with in the preceding paragraphs, we did not include 346 doctors and druggists, who had been licensed to deal in drugs and had violated the narcotic laws, for we were not permitted by the Bureau of Narcotics to use data on this group of "registered" offenders.

[2] Per instructions in the federal records, from which alone our data on addicts' economic status were drawn, "dependent" means lacking in the necessities of life or receiving aid from other people, and "marginal" refers to the intermediate position between self-supporting and dependency.

partial answer to this question is to be found in their criminal records to be presented in a later section.

5. MARITAL STATUS AND FAMILIAL TIES

Marital status.   Of 1,401 male addicts whose marital status was known, 745 (53.2%) were reported as single; 532 (38.0%) as married; 59 (4.2%) as widowed; 26 (1.8%) as separated; 38 (2.7%) as divorced; and 1 (.1%) as a common law husband.   Of 533 female addicts whose marital status was known, 118 (22.1%) were reported as single; 281 (52.7%) as married; 74 (13.9%) as widowed; 24 (4.5%) as separated; 35 (6.6%) as divorced; and 1 (.2%) as a common law wife.   Table VI compares the marital status of male and female addicts.

TABLE VI

THE MARITAL STATUS OF MALE AND FEMALE ADDICTS

(Percentages)

Marital Status	Male	Female
Single	53.2	22.1
Married	38.0	52.7
Widowed	4.2	13.9
Separated	1.8	4.5
Divorced	2.7	6.6
Common law	.1	.2
TOTAL	100.0	100.0

Thus relatively speaking, considerably more of the male addicts were single than the female addicts, while the percentages of female addicts being widowed, separated or divorced are all larger than those for male addicts.[1]   The proportion of broken homes due to separation or divorce in our group of addicts as a whole, however, does not seem to be any greater than that in the general population.   According to the figures presented above, out of 1,071 addicts married, 123 were separated or

---

[1] It is interesting to note that practically the same phenomenon was found among the prison population at large.   See E. R. Groves and W. F. Ogburn, *American Marriage and Family Relationships* (1928), pp. 141-5.

divorced, the proportion of homes thus broken to marriages being slightly more than 1 in 8, which was also true of the general population of Chicago for 1930.[1] As to what these different marital conditions mean to the individual addict, some understanding can be achieved only by the study of individual cases.

Age at marriage. The age at marriage of our main group of addicts is unknown. But the data we secured from the Women's Reformatory are suggestive. Out of 100 female addicts whose age at marriage was known, 12 were married between 10 and 14; 48 between 15 and 19; 26 between 20 and 24; and the remaining 14 at 25 or over. Thus 60 per cent of this group of female addicts were married before 20. This tendency toward early marriage is probably true of most of the female addicts, and the reasons for it deserve close notice. Through some of our interviews with drug addicts, one reason was found to be rather common, and that is the girl's dissatisfaction with her home. Needless to say, hasty marriages of this sort often result in broken homes and unhappiness. More of this will be said in a later chapter.

Number of children. From the data on marital status it was found that about 62 per cent or two-thirds of the male addicts and about 48 per cent or one-third of the female addicts were either single or devoid of family obligations to a greater or less extent by being widowed, separated or divorced. It is interesting to know how many of the once married had children, who might serve as a form of familial tie. Out of 600 cases in which this information was available, 120 (20.0%) had one; 83 (13.8%) more than one; and 397 (66.2%) none. In other words, about two-thirds of this group had no children. It seems that in the case of our group of drug addicts the family as an integrating influence played a rather insignificant rôle.

6. PHYSICAL AND MENTAL CONDITION

Physical condition. In the records of the Bureau of Narcotics notice was taken of the ailments or deformities of the addicts arrested, if any. Of 1,065 cases in which this information was available, 5 (.5%) were either blind or deaf to a greater or less degree; 68 (6.4%) crippled in some fashion, having broken bones, etc.; 121 (11.3%) had ailments of a more or less serious nature, such as heart trouble, kidney disturbance, syphilis,

---

[1] W. F. Ogburn, "The Family and Its Functions," *Recent Social Trends in the United States* (one volume edition, 1933), p. 690.

lung disease, and others; and 871 (81.8%) were reported to have no physical ailment or deformity. At least four-fifths of our main group of addicts, therefore, were apparently in good or fairly normal physical condition at the time of their arrest. While these figures do not represent the result of accurate medical examination, they do serve to show that at least in the experience of most of these addicts the factor of organic disease, considered either as a cause or an effect of drug addiction, was apparently not very important.

The exclusively female group of addicts in the Women's Reformatory presented a somewhat different picture. Out of 118 cases, 44 (37.0%) were inflicted by venereal diseases; 15 (13.0%) by other ailments of a more or less serious nature; and 59 (50.0%) by none, except such feminine troubles as abortion, miscarriage, and "underweight." The large percentage of addicts in this group having venereal disease was probably due to the fact that many of them had to resort to prostitution in order to maintain their opium habit. At least 4 out of 72 cases in which information about their occupation was available, or 5.5 per cent, gave prostitution as their profession.

Statistical information about the physical condition of addicts admitted to the Psychopathic Hospital was not available. But something of the condition probably most of them were in when they were attempting to quit the habit may be glimpsed from the data we secured from the Keeley Institute. As most of the 259 addicts at the time of their admission complained of more than one ailment, these ailments or troubles are listed in the following not according to the absolute number of persons, but according to the relative frequency with which they were mentioned. Nervousness was mentioned by 161 addicts; despondency by 134; insomnia by 114; heart trouble by 89; cough by 70; gonorrhea by 64; constipation by 55; biliousness or malaise by 41; rheumatism by 32; hemorrhoids by 30; and pneumonia by 30, not to mention many others that were mentioned by less than 30 addicts. It is interesting to note again that most of the troubles frequently mentioned were not organic diseases; they were either transitory emotional reactions accompanying the attempt to quit the drug habit or merely functional disturbances due to the depressing effect of opium.

Mental condition: intelligence. Data on general intelligence as shown by the results of psychological tests are lacking in regard to our main group of addicts. But what we know about the inmates in the Women's

Reformatory may be of interest. Of 114 female addicts to whom psychological tests were given, 58 (50.9%) had I. Q. above 90, and may be considered as normal or supernormal; 28 (24.6%) between 80 and 89 and may be considered as dull normal; 19 (16.7%) between 70 and 79 to be considered as borderline; and 9 (7.8%) below 70, being definitely mental defectives.[1] Owing to the smallness of this sample and the lack of comparable data about the general population, it is difficult to draw any inference from these figures. But a study of women delinquents made by the Bureau of Social Hygiene some years ago seemed to show that the intelligence of those who were drug users was relatively superior to that of those who were not.[2] Some definitely assert that drug addiction is uncommon among mental defectives.[3]

Mental condition: personality and personality anomalies. Personality, as viewed by the psychiatrist, may be said to be "the integrated activity of all the reaction-tendencies of the daily life of the individual."[4] And personality abnormalities, besides mental deficiency and epilepsy, are generally classified under the following categories: psychoses organic or functional, which are marked by definite disorder in the mental processes; neuroses, which do not involve serious mental impairment, but which are marked by the failure to make the necessary emotional adjustments in life; and such reaction types without psychosis as alcoholism, drug addiction, and psychopathic personality.[5] By "psychopathic personality" is generally meant the kind of maladjustment that arises "on a basis of inherent anomalies of judgment, temperament, character, ethical sense, or sexual make-up."[6] From this point of view then let us consider the personality and personality abnormalities of drug addicts.

It is regrettable that data on this important aspect of the problem of drug addiction were not available, except those we secured from the Women's Reformatory. Out of 95 cases in which psychiatric diagnosis was known, 88 (92.6%) were found to have a psychopathic personality,

---

[1] Lewis M. Terman, *The Measurement of Intelligence*, pp. 65–104.

[2] Bureau of Social Hygiene, *A Study of Women Delinquents*, p. 486.

[3] E. W. Norwood, "Mental Defectiveness and Alcoholism and Drug Addiction," *British Journal of Inebriety*, XXIX (1932), p. 163.

[4] D. K. Henderson and R. D. Gillespie, *A Text Book of Psychiatry* (London, 1932), p. 99.

[5] *Ibid*, pp. 17–19.

[6] Aaron J. Rosanoff, *Manual of Psychiatry* (6th ed.), p. 689. Quoted in Glueck. *op. cit.*, pp. 325–26.

described as inadequate, egocentric, morally inadequate, or emotionally unstable; 6 (6.3%) had psychoses, partly manic-depressive and partly associated with menopause; and 1 (1.0%) was marked, "questionable traumatic mental enfeeblement," i.e., mental deficiency due to injuries done to the central nervous system.   In the records of the Psychopathic Hospital, the psychiatric diagnosis of drug patients, with a few exceptions, was invariably "Drug addiction without psychosis." The same was true of the records in the Municipal Psychiatric Institute, from which data on 60 drug addicts were secured.

These figures, however unsatisfactory, serve to show that in the judgment of psychiatrists, most of the addicts under investigation were not mentally so ill that they might be considered as psychotic or insane. But they were considered markedly inadequate either in their emotional adjustments to life situations or in value-judgments or in both.   One author definitely classifies drug addiction as a form of neurosis.   In that sense, all drug addicts have what he calls the neurotic type of personality which has failed to maintain its equilibrium.[1] A mere classification of drug addicts and their habit, however, must be thought of only as a preliminary step toward the real understanding of drug addiction.   As to what constitutes a neurotic personality, in what ways these addicts had failed to make their adjustments in life, and what psychologic functions drugs served in their case, in our opinion light can come only from a study of the individual addict in relation to his social and cultural *milieu*.   And this will be undertaken in a later chapter.

Habits other than the use of opium.   Postponing our consideration of the drug habit to a later section, let us now examine some other habits which these addicts might have indulged in and which may serve to indicate their mental condition to a certain extent.   We shall take up first the use of alcohol.   Out of 1,129 federal cases in which this information was available, 969 (85.8%) were reported as total abstainers; 153 (13.5%) as moderate users; and 7 (.6%) as excessive users.   Practically the same proportion of drinkers to non-drinkers holds for the group of addicts in the Women's Reformatory.   Of 113 cases in which this fact was known, 91 (80.5%) were total abstainers; and 22 (19.5%) used liquor to a greater or less extent.

These figures seem to suggest that the majority of these drug addicts did not use liquor at all.   Perhaps an exception should be made in the

[1] Karl A. Menninger, *The Human Mind* (New York, 1930), pp. 116, 120.

case of those addicts who had been "cured" and who were fighting against
a relapse.   In such cases, we have found that liquor was often resorted
to as a temporary, though unsatisfactory, substitute for opium.   When
we consider the fact that both opium and alcohol are depressants of the
central nervous system and that their pharmacological effects seem
practically the same,[1] it becomes an interesting problem why some people
take to opium, while others to liquor.   The explanation probably does
not lie in the properties of the said drugs alone, nor yet in the personality
make-up of the individual considered by itself.   We expect to throw
some light on this problem in a later discussion of the social situations
related to drug addiction.

A much more popular habit among drug addicts is the use of tobacco.
Of 116 cases in the Women's Reformatory in which this information was
available, 101 (87.1%) smoked cigarettes regularly; and 15 (12.9%) did
not.   Of 223 cases in the Keeley Institute in which this fact was known,
153 (68.5%) used tobacco; and 70 (31.5%) did not.   Among the 153
addicts who used tobacco, 139 inhaled it.   We have been told that nico-
tine, the principal element of tobacco, is as much a depressant of the
central nervous system as a stimulant,[2] and has thereby effects similar
to those of opium and alcohol.   But the use of tobacco is so common
among the general population that it is difficult to use it as an indication
of the mental condition supposedly peculiar to drug addicts.

7.   The Drug Habit

Drugs used.   We shall now consider the habit of these addicts which
concerns us most, and begin with the kinds of drug they used.   Of 1,887
cases in which this fact was known, 940 (49.8%) used morphine; 236
(12.5%) heroin; 221 (11.7%) morphine and heroin; 175 (9.3%) morphine,
heroin, and cocaine; 133 (7.0%) prepared opium; 49 (2.6%) prepared
opium and opium alkaloids, i.e., morphine and heroin; 48 (2.5%)
marahuana;[3] 41 (2.2%) cocaine; 14 (.7%) morphine and opium compounds; and 30 (1.6%) other drugs, such as veronal and luminal.   Morphine, therefore, was by far the most popular drug with Chicago's ad-

---

[1] Cushny, *op. cit.* (9th ed.), pp. 186–87.   Also H. Emerson (ed.), *Alcohol and Man*
(1932), pp. 268–69.

[2] Cushny, *op. cit.* (9th ed.), p. 332.   Also Walter L. Mendenhall, *Tobacco* (1930),
p. 37.

[3] The sale and possession of marahuana is restricted only by the laws of Illinois.
See *Illinois Revised Statutes* (1933), c. 91, §§134–156.

dicts. During the past couple of years, however, heroin seemed to have been used more than morphine. One reason given to us by addicts we knew is the exacting price of morphine compared with that of heroin. Thus on the basis of samples bought by the federal agents, it was found that in 1933 illicit morphine in Chicago cost $90–110 per ounce, while an equal amount of heroin was sold for only $38–40.[1] Another reason is the amorphous form in which heroin comes. This makes adulteration easy and renders heroin a more profitable drug for the peddlers. Possibly it was also due to the fact that very small supplies of morphine were available in Europe for the illicit traffic.[2] But morphine seems to have been the favorite drug not only of the addicts in Chicago but those of the country at large. This is shown by the fact that out of 2,320 drug addicts in the federal penal and correctional institutions as of June 30, 1930, 1,493, or 64.4 per cent, used morphine; 236, or 10.2 per cent, heroin; and the rest, these drugs in combination or other drugs.[3] The pharmacological and psychological reasons for this preference for morphine against heroin, if any, remain to be investigated.

How administered. We shall next examine the ways in which drugs were used by these addicts. Out of 1,587 cases in which this information was available, 1,361 (85.8%) used them hypodermically, that is, by injection under the skin; 128 (8.1%) in the form of smoking; 30 (1.9%) intravenously, that is, injection through the veins; 26 (1.6%) by sniffing; 22 (1.4%) by mouth; 13 (.8%) both hypodermically and by smoking; and 7 (.4%) by other combinations of these methods. These figures show that the hypodermic method was the most popular with these addicts. Opium-smoking probably was limited mainly to the Chinese group, and was indulged in by relatively few American addicts. The intravenous method seemed to be limited to even a smaller number of addicts. As to how these methods were chosen and transmitted and what they might possibly mean to the individual addict, something will be said in a later connection.

Daily dosage. How much drug these addicts used each day is our next question. Of 1,352 cases in which this fact was known, 19 (1.4%) took less than a grain every day; 38 (2.8%) between one and less than 2 grains; 54 (4.0%) between 2 and less than 3 grains; 208 (15.4%) between

---

[1] U. S. Bureau of Narcotics, *Traffic in Opium*, 1933, p. 51.
[2] U. S. Bureau of Narcotics, *Traffic in Opium*, 1932, p. 11.
[3] U. S. Bureau of Prisons, *Federal Penal and Correctional Institutions*, 1930, p. 80.

3 and less than 5 grains; 463 (34.2%) between 5 and 9 grains; 340 (25.1%) between 10 and 14 grains; 115 (8.5%) between 15 and 19 grains; 5£ (4.1%) between 20 and 24 grains; 15 (1.1%) between 25 and 29 grains; and 45 (3.3%) 30 grains or more. According to these figures, over two-fifths of this group of addicts used less than 5 grains a day; nearly two-fifths used 5 to 9 grains; and about one-fifth used 10 grains or more.

It is interesting to inquire whether sex makes any difference in the amount of drug used. Table VII compares the daily dosage of male and that of female addicts, data used being the same as described above.

TABLE VII

THE DAILY DOSAGE OF MALE AND FEMALE ADDICTS[a]

(*Percentages*)

Daily Dosage	Male	Female
Less than half gr.	.3	1.1
Half gr. but less than 1 gr.	.8	1.1
1 gr. but less than 2 gr.	2.5	3.6
2 gr. but less than 3 gr.	3.6	5.0
3 gr. but less than 5 gr.	15.4	15.3
5–9 gr.	33.6	35.8
10–14 gr.	26.1	22.5
15–19 gr.	8.4	8.9
20–24 gr.	4.0	4.4
25–29 gr.	1.2	.8
30 gr. and over	4.0	1.4
TOTAL.............................	99.9	99.9

(a) The percentages for male addicts are based on 992 cases, and those for the female on 360 cases.

According to Table VII, it seems that, relatively speaking, male addicts were more apt to use large doses than female addicts. From the pharmacological point of view, this variation is understandable. For the effect of a drug generally depends upon its concentration in the blood, and consequently upon the volume of the blood. Thus the size and weight of a person become important factors in determining the effective dosage of a drug.[1] It is probable that for the same amount of satisfaction, a male addict has to take a relatively larger dose than a female

[1] J. A. Gunn, *An Introduction to Pharmacology and Therapeutics* (1929), pp. 8–11

one.   Other factors that might have contributed to this variation in dosage between the sexes or among addicts of the same sex remain to be discovered.   It may be pointed out here that even with the same individual, we have found that the daily dosage may vary with the supply of drug at hand and, most important of all, with the emotional state he or she may be in.   Fear, for example, almost invariably causes an addict to increase his dose.[1]   Some such situations will be entered into at some length when we come to the discussion of individual cases.

Reasons for addiction.   We come now to one of the most interesting problems of drug addiction, and that is, why and how these addicts first began to use drugs and finally formed what we call the drug habit.   Of 1,068 cases in which information relevant to this problem was available, 657 (61.4%) gave as their reason for addiction the influence of other addicts; 291 (27.2%) self-medication to relieve physical pain or discomfort; 39 (3.7%) previous use of drug in medical treatment; 33 (3.1%) to relieve emotional distress; 31 (2.9%) curiosity; 10 (.9%) to overcome drunkenness; 3 (.3%) suicide; and 4 (.4%) other reasons not specified. These figures indicate that so far as our group of addicts are concerned, the most important ætiological factor of their addiction was the influence of other addicts, and that the use of drug in medical treatment was relatively unimportant.

TABLE VIII

REASONS FOR ADDICTION GIVEN BY MALE AND FEMALE ADDICTS

(Percentages)

Reasons for Addiction	Male	Female
The influence of other addicts	65.6	50.5
Self-medication to relieve physical pain or discomfort	24.8	33.6
Previous use in medical treatment	2.8	5.9
To relieve emotional distress	2.6	4.5
Curiosity	2.6	3.8
To overcome drunkenness	1.2	.4
Suicide	.....	1.0
Other reasons	.4	.3
TOTAL	100.0	100.0

[1] Light, and others, *op. cit.*, p. 33.

We shall next find out whether these ætiological reasons vary with the sexes. Table VIII compares the reasons given by male, and those by female, addicts, the percentages to be presented being based on 777 male and 289 female addicts.

Table VIII seems to suggest that, relatively speaking, in our group of addicts more women resorted to opium as a relief from either physical pain or emotional difficulty than men, while more men started the habit through direct association with addicts than women. It is interesting to note that suicide as an ætiological reason was not mentioned at all by the male group. The reasons for this slight variation deserve closer study.

Needless to say, all those ætiological reasons given by both male and female addicts are altogether too general and vague to enlighten us as to the specific ways in which they were initiated into the use of drugs by other addicts, or the various life-situations that had caused them emotional distress. Such specific sequences of event that led to the formation of the drug habit can be understood only by studying the individual addict in relation to social situations.

Age at which addiction was established. Of 1,592 cases in which this fact was known, 19 (1.2%) were reported as having formed their drug habit under 15; 194 (12.2%) between 15 and 19; 494 (31.0%) between 20 and 24; 438 (27.5%) between 25 and 29; 224 (14.1%) between 30 and 34; 117 (7.3%) between 35 and 39; 53 (3.3%) between 40 and 44; 34 (2.1%) between 45 and 49; 12 (.8%) between 50 and 54; 4 (.3%) between 55 and 59; and 3 (.2%) at 60 or over. The most common age group during which addiction was established seemed to be between 20 and 24. Stated in a slightly different fashion, we may say that 13.4 per cent of these addicts formed their habit under 20; 58.5 per cent between 20 and 29; and 28.1 per cent at 30 or over.

It is also of interest to see whether the age of addiction differs with the sexes. Table IX compares the age of addiction of male addicts and that of female ones, the percentages listed in the following being based on 1,172 cases of male, and 419 cases of female, addicts.

According to Table IX, it seems that more of the female than the male addicts formed their drug habit before they were twenty-five years old; but from the age of twenty-five on the incidence of addiction was relatively more common among the male, than among the female, addicts.

TABLE IX

THE AGE OF ADDICTION OF MALE AND FEMALE ADDICTS

(*Percentages*)

Age of Addiction	Male	Female
Under 15 years	1.0	1.9
15–19	11.2	14.8
20–24	29.7	34.6
25–29	27.9	26.5
30–34	14.6	12.7
35–39	8.1	5.3
40–44	4.0	1.7
45–49	2.4	1.4
50–54	.7	.9
55–59	.3	.....
60 or over	.1	.2
TOTAL	100.0	100.0

Duration of habit. Of 1,591 cases in which this fact was recorded, 119 (7.5%) had had their habit for less than a year; 258 (16.2%) for 1 to 2 years; 167 (10.5%) for 3 to 4 years; 313 (19.7%) for 5 to 9 years; 263 (16.5%) for 10 to 14 years; 176 (11.1%) for 15 to 19 years; 138 (8.7%) for 20 to 24 years; 79 (5.0%) for 25 to 29 years; and 78 (4.8%) for 30 or more years. In other words, 34.2 per cent of this group of addicts had used drugs for less than five years; 36.2 per cent for from five to fourteen years; and 29.6 per cent for fifteen or more years.

Remembering that our data cover a period of approximately six years, i.e., 1928–1934,[1] we are enabled by the preceding figures to make the following observations. First, the fact that over one-third of these addicts had a habit that is less than five years old indicates that opium addiction in Chicago has not been on such a decline in recent years as some people suppose. Then, another third or more of these addicts had used drugs for from five to fourteen years. These over two-thirds of our cases must have formed their habit after 1914, the year in which the Harrison Narcotic Act was passed, and their addiction in spite of the law raises the important problem as to how far prohibitive measures could be relied upon as a means of preventing people from using narcotic

[1] The total number of addicts for each of these years for whom we have data is as follows: 10 for 1928; 291 for 1929; 433 for 1930; 408 for 1931; 663 for 1932; 536 for 1933; 103 for 1934; and 74 not reported as to years, the total being 2,518.

drugs. Nor did the narcotic laws seem to have much correctional effect on the remaining third of our cases, most of whom formed their habit before 1914, and must have come under the purview of the law more than once. All these considerations point to the urgent need for further study of the opium problem in the community and for more effective measures both for the purpose of rehabilitating those who are addicts already and for preventing future cases of addiction.

Number of previous treatments. Of 992 federal cases in which this information was available, 778 (78.4%) were reported to have had no previous medical treatment, confinement in prisons being not included; 162 (16.4%) had one; and 52 (5.2%) more than one. Of 183 hospital cases in which this fact was known, 35 (19.1%) had no previous medical treatment; 73 (39.8%) had one; 75 (41.0%) more than one. If these figures were reliable, it seems the tendency among the hospital cases was to seek medical treatment as often as they could, while that of the majority of our federal cases was more to go on with their habit until they were arrested or imprisoned and compelled to quit it. Such a difference in attitude towards one's drug habit between the federal offenders and the hospital patients undoubtedly implies many other factors, which can be isolated and understood only by studying individual cases of both groups.

8. DRUG ADDICTION AND CRIME

One of the most disputed questions in regard to drug addiction is its relation to crime. The general public, aroused by sensational news and spectacular police activities, is apt to identify what they call the "dope fiend" with a hideous criminal, and to brand all drug addicts as such. The addicts we came to know, on the other hand, strongly resented this popular stigmatization, and considered it as sheer prejudice, that comes from ignorance. Without joining either side of the dispute, let us examine the data we have at hand on the previous criminal records of these addicts, all of which were taken from the records of the Bureau of Narcotics in Chicago. We shall first deal with the number of previous criminal records, and then with the types of crime that had been committed.

Number of previous criminal records. Of 1,098 federal cases in which this information was available, 221 (20.1%) had one previous criminal record; 120 (10.9%) 2; 84 (7.6%) 3; 80 (7.3%) 4; 49 (4.5%) 5; 43 (3.9%) 6; 31 (2.8%) 7; 14 (1.3%) 8; 20 (1.8%) 9; 75 (6.8%) 10 or more; and 361 (32.9%) none.[1] In other words, about one-third of this group of addicts had had no previous record before their present arrest. Had it not been for the narcotic laws, these addicts probably would not have had anything to do with criminalism. The remaining two-thirds may be considered as recidivists for all offenses.

Perhaps a better index of the possible relation between drug addiction and criminalism is the number of addicts of this group who had had no criminal record before they formed the drug habit, but who began to engage in criminal activities after addiction. Out of 1,047 cases in which both the year of addiction and the number of previous criminal records were known, it is found that 846 (80.8%) had had no criminal records before addiction; only 201 (19.2%) had had criminal records of some kind. In one-fifth of our cases, therefore, drug seemed to have little to do with their criminal career prior to addiction, but in the remaining four-fifths it seems that participation in crime becomes marked after addiction.

But since most of these criminal records, as we shall see presently, are records of the violation of the Harrison Narcotic Act or crimes related to it, we must suspend our judgment as to whether or not after addiction to narcotic drugs these addicts turned to be criminals as they are usually understood, until we have occasion to examine the types of crime they committed.

Types of crime committed. The types of crime committed by addicts may also be divided into those before and those after addiction. We shall first take up the former. In the records of 201 of our cases as mentioned in the foregoing paragraph, we found the following types of offense for which they had been arrested or imprisoned, the number following each type being the frequency with which it appeared in the records: offenses against property, not involving violence, such as larceny, 91; disorderly conduct and vagrancy, 61; offenses against property, involving violence, such as robbery, 49; violation of narcotic laws, 40; sex offenses, not involving violence, 9; offenses against the person, such

---

[1] It must be noted that what appeared originally as criminal records included also arrests for investigation. These figures, therefore, should not be taken to represent absolute convictions. They represent rather the addicts' conflicts with the law. Detailed types of crime committed after addiction will be discussed in a later section.

as assault and battery, 8; sex offenses involving violence, such as rape, 2; violation of liquor laws, 2; violation of parole or probation, 1; and all other offenses, including arrests for investigation, 77. Bearing in mind the order of frequency of these pre-addiction offenses, let us now compare them with those committed by addicts after their addiction to drugs. The latter are listed in Table X according to their order of importance, together with the frequency with which each type of crime had been committed. All the percentages in the following table are based on previous criminal records, the present narcotic offense being excluded.

TABLE X

TYPES OF CRIME COMMITTED BY DRUG ADDICTS AFTER ADDICTION AND THE
FREQUENCY WITH WHICH EACH TYPE HAD BEEN COMMITTED[a]

(*Percentages*)

Types of Crime	Number of Previous Criminal Records							Total
	None	1	2	3	4	5	6 and over	
Violation of narcotic laws	51.2	46.9	20.5	15.3	10.6	3.7	3.0	99.9
Offenses vs. property, not involving violence	80.4	8.9	2.8	3.0	1.6	.8	2.5	100.0
Disorderly conduct and vagrancy	85.2	8.6	3.2	1.9	.4	.4	.3	100.0
Offense vs. property, involving violence	94.9	3.7	.6	.5	.1	.....	.2	100.0
Violation of parole or probation	98.7	.9	.3	.....	.....	.....	.....	99.9
Violation of liquor laws	98.7	.9	.4	.....	.....	.....	.....	100.0
Offenses vs. the person	99.1	.8	.....	.....	.....	.1	.....	100.0
Sex offenses, not involving violence	98.8	.7	.2	.....	.4	.....	.2	100.0
Sex offenses, involving violence	100.0	.....	.....	.....	.....	.....	.....	100.0

(a) Except for the violation of narcotic laws information about which was available in 1,047 cases, the percentages for all other types of crime are based on a total number of 1,046 addicts.

One noticeable difference between the types of crime committed by addicts before addiction and those after addiction seems to be that whereas before addiction the most common crime committed by them was larceny or similar offenses against property, after addiction it was

the violation of narcotic laws.   And it is important to note in this connection that, just as in the case of federal narcotic offenders in general,[1]
nearly 50 per cent of these addicts are recidivists.   This finding again
leads us to question the efficacy of purely prohibitive measures in coping
with the opium problem in the city.

The next common types of crime committed by addicts after addiction,
according to Table X, are offenses against property, disorderly conduct,
and vagrancy.   This is rather to be expected, when we take into account
the low economic status of most of these addicts and the necessity of
their maintaining an expensive habit.   In this connection, it is interesting to note that comparatively few of them resorted to violence in their
criminal activities.   The small percentage of addicts committing such
crimes as robbery, assault and battery, homicide and others that involve
the use of force seems to discredit the view shared by many that the use
of drugs has the effect of causing an individual to be a heartless
criminal.[2]   On the contrary, our figures suggest that most of the crimes
committed by addicts were of a peaceful nature, that involve more the
use of wit than that of force.[3]

It is also interesting to note that very few of these addicts had violated
any of the liquor laws or committed sex offenses with or without violence.
This is quite understandable, when we recall the fact that most of them
were total abstainers so far as liquor is concerned, and the further fact
that the pharmacological effect of opium is always depressing in the end,
especially with regard to the functioning of sex organs.

These findings point to the conclusion that most of these addicts became criminals mainly because of conflict with narcotic laws, and that
there is little indication in the data at hand that the use of opium has
any casual relationship to anti-social activities other than those which
are closely related to the maintenance of the drug habit.

Time between addiction and first known criminal record.   Inasmuch as
most of the crimes committed by addicts were related to the maintenance of their drug habit, and in that sense may be said to have been

---

[1] *Supra*, p. 3.

[2] For an example of writings sharing the popular notion stated above, see May
D. Baily, "Drug Peddling, Addiction and Criminals," *Journal of Criminal Law and
Criminology*, May–June, 1932.

[3] For similar findings about addicts in an eastern penitentiary, see J. F. Fishman
and V. T. Perlman, "The Real Narcotic Addict," *American Mercury*, January, 1932,
pp. 100 ff.

caused by it, we are naturally led to inquire into the time between the formation of their drug habit and the beginning of what may be conveniently called their criminal career. Of 498 cases in which there was no criminal record before addiction and in which both the year of addiction and the year of first known criminal record were available, 61 (12.2%) began to have conflict with the law in the same year in which addiction was established. The following cases began to have criminal records after the year of addiction: 36 (7.2%) 1 year after addiction; 33 (6.6%) 2 years; 44 (8.8%) 3 years; 25 (5.0%) 4 years; 114 (22.9%) 5 to 9 years; 185 (37.2%) 10 or more years. Thus over 60 per cent of this group of addicts began to engage in criminal activities five or more years after they had been addicted to drugs. This seems to suggest that most of them probably would not have been what we call criminals had it not been for their drug habit, and that probably anti-social acts were not resorted to until they were unable to support their habit by legitimate means.

9. SUMMARY

The significant points indicated by our statistical data thus far are as follows:

(1) Drug addiction in Chicago is mainly a problem of the adult population, as shown by the fact that less than one per cent of our group of addicts were under twenty. The most common age group is between 30 and 34.

(2) Drug addiction in Chicago is not confined to any one color, race or nationality, although the incidence of addiction may vary with different racial or nationality groups. Thus, about fourth-fifths of our group of addicts were white, nearly one-fifth Negroes, and the rest include more than one race. Hence the necessity of seeking an explanation of drug addiction in other than racial or nationality factors.

(3) With the exception of a little over 6 per cent, all of our group of addicts were native-born, although only one-fifth of them were natives of the city of Chicago. Most of them were born and brought up in other urban communities and came to stay in Chicago for various lengths of time.

(4) A fourth of these addicts had foreign-born parents, a factor having to do with the possible clash of cultures between native-born children and foreign-born parents and the relationship of this, in turn, to personal

disorganization and to drug addiction. Other interesting points about the family background of these addicts are their rank in the family and the age of their leaving home. A limited amount of data shows that the youngest, the oldest, the only child and the second child were the most common positions they occupied in the family, and that most of them left home before 16.

(5) Practically all of those addicts about whose religious background we have information had had some form of religious training during their childhood, mostly Christian. By what we know about the rôle religion plays in the lives of a certain number of addicts, we are led to point out the possible conflict between the addicts' early religious training and their later adjustments in life as a factor that is worth our close notice in accounting for their predisposition to the use of narcotics.

(6) Our data on the native intelligence and the education of drug addicts do not seem to support the popular notion that addicts are either mental defectives or people lacking badly in education. On the contrary, psychological tests on a limited number of cases showed that over half of them might be considered as normal or supernormal with respect to intelligence. Where comparable data on education about the general population of Chicago were available, it was found that addicts compared quite favorably with the general population. The latter leads slightly in the percentage of people receiving secondary or higher education. Of addicts there were only a little over 2 per cent who might be considered as illiterate.

(7) In regard to occupation, addicts led the general population of Chicago appreciably in two occupational groups: namely, domestic and personal service, and recreation and amusement. In these two groups of occupation over one-third of addicts had been engaged. Their employment, however, was irregular; less than a fifth had had what may be called regular employment. Their economic status, consequently, was low; nine-tenths of them were reported as either lacking in the necessities of life or incapable of self-support by legitimate means.

(8) Most of these addicts did not seem to have much of what may be called familial ties. Our data on their marital status show that about two-thirds of the male cases and about one-third of the female ones were either single or devoid of family obligations to a greater or less extent by being widowed, separated or divorced. And of those who had had families, over two-thirds had no children.

(9) The chronic use of drugs did not seem to have much deteriorating effect on the body. Four-fifths of our federal cases were reported as having no physical ailment or deformity at the time of their arrest. This is significant when we consider the fact that about two-thirds of our group of addicts had used drugs for from five to thirty or more years.

(10) A psychiatric examination of the mental condition of a limited number of addicts revealed that while they were not psychotic, they were decidedly inadequate in their emotional adjustments. Such addicts were said to have a psychopathic personality. But it remains to be found out what these emotional inadequacies consist of and how they are related to drug addiction.

(11) As to the drug habit, the following points are interesting. About half of the addicts under investigation used morphine; a tenth, heroin; less than a tenth, prepared opium; and the rest used these and other drugs in various combinations. The most popular method of using these drugs was hypodermic injection, true of four-fifths of our cases. And the most common dosage used varied from 5 to 9 grains a day. Perhaps the most significant finding in this connection is the fact that about two-thirds of these addicts gave as their reason for addiction bad associates or the influence of other addicts.

(12) The criminal records of federal cases show that four-fifths of them had had no known conflict with the law prior to their addiction, and that after addiction the most common types of crimes committed by them were violation of narcotic laws, offenses against property, disorderly conduct and vagrancy,—crimes either directly or indirectly caused by their drug habit and by the existence of narcotic laws.

The above delineation of the traits and activities of drug addicts in Chicago is by no means complete. Thus, we have not yet touched on such other characteristics of drug addicts as a group as their attitude toward each other and toward non-users, their codes of conduct, their special lingo, and their traditions concerning the technique of using drugs and many other matters. But instead of going beyond our space here and dwelling on each of the characteristics just mentioned in a vague and general manner, we propose to reserve a discussion of them for a later chapter, where we shall let the addicts speak for themselves and where such characteristics as have not been dealt with will be revealed in concrete life situations.

CHAPTER IV

THE DISTRIBUTION OF OPIUM ADDICTS IN CHICAGO

IN the preceding chapter we were chiefly concerned with the question who the drug addicts are and in what way, if any, they differ from the general population. From now on we propose to go further and take up the more difficult but interesting problem how these addicts acquired their drug habit and why it was so difficult for them to give up the habit once it was formed. It is pertinent to recall at this juncture that about two-thirds of these addicts ascribed their addiction to the influence of other addicts. Needless to say, this process of acquiring the drug habit cannot take place in a social vacuum; it presupposes a *milieu* that may be considered as especially conducive to drug addiction. In order to fully understand drug addiction, therefore, a thoroughgoing exploration of this social and cultural *milieu* of drug addicts is of the greatest importance.

As a preliminary step and an indispensable aid to the said exploration, we shall attempt in this chapter to map and to describe briefly the spatial distribution of opium addiction areas as well as the centers of drug peddling in Chicago. This is what was in an earlier chapter called the ecological approach, and is similar to that used in studies of delinquency by Clifford R. Shaw,[1] of suicide by Ruth S. Cavan,[2] of vice by Walter C. Reckless,[3] and of insanity by Robert E. L. Faris.[4] Our aim is to discover some more information about the relation of the ecological structure of a city to its cultural and social environment, and that of the latter, in turn, to drug addiction.

1. AREAS OF OPIUM ADDICTION IN CHICAGO

We shall first present our data on the distribution of opium addicts in the ecological configuration of Chicago. For the purpose of research, the 935 census tracts of the city have been grouped into 75 com-

---

[1] C. R. Shaw, *Delinquency Areas* (Chicago, 1930).
[2] Ruth S. Cavan, *Suicide* (Chicago, 1928).
[3] W. C. Reckless, *Vice in Chicago* (Chicago, 1933).
[4] R. E. L. Faris, "An Ecological Study of Insanity in the City" (Unpublished Ph.D. thesis, University of Chicago, 1931).

munities, and this grouping was used in most of the previous studies mentioned above. But the great disparity between the sizes, and thereby the population, of these 75 communities has made necessary a regrouping of the said census tracts into 120 sub-communities. It is on the base map of the latter kind, prepared by the Social Science Research Committee, that our data are to be spotted. The procedure we followed in calculating the opium addiction rates for the 120 sub-communities is something as follows.

Out of the total number of addicts dealt with in the preceding chapter, the addresses of 2,619 cases, in which information about sex was available, were selected and sorted according to the location of the 120 sub-communities. The total number of addicts thus found in each sub-community for a period of six years, i.e., 1928–1934, was divided by 6 times the average population 20 years and over of that sub-community for 1930 and 1934, the adult population alone being used, because only half of one per cent of these addicts were below twenty years of age. The result was then expressed in terms of 100,000 population 20 years and over for each of the 120 sub-communities, for the years 1928 to 1934. These rates are classified into intervals of 50, and are represented by a scheme of cross-hatching on Map 2. The exact rates for each of the 120 sub-communities together with the population figures may be found in Appendix I.[1]

It will be seen on examination of Map 2, that areas with high rates of opium addiction are either included in or adjacent to the central business district (sub-community 74); that those with low or no rates of addiction are near the outskirts of the city, and that the decrease in addiction rates seems to be uniformly proportional to the distance from the Loop. Such differences in the rate of addiction are not likely due to chance. The task before us, therefore, is to find out whether there are some differences in the ecological features and population characteristics of these areas that may account in a certain measure for the difference in addiction rates.

As a basis for comparison, let us first have some acquaintance with the areas in which no cases of opium addiction were reported. While the absence of record does not necessarily mean the actual absence of drug addicts, it is believed that what we can find out about the areas

---

[1] For advice on the method of calculating opium addiction rates as detailed above the author is indebted to Prof. William F. Ogburn.

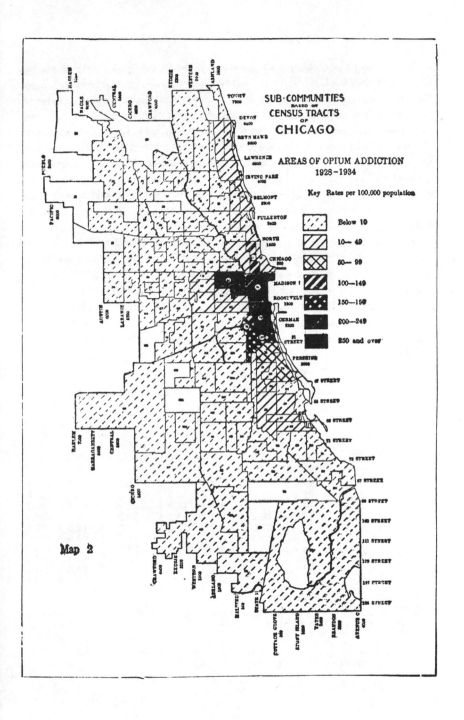

Map 2

with no rate of addiction may greatly aid us in understanding the areas with high rates of addiction. Altogether there are thirteen sub-communities that were apparently free of drug addiction. Space, however, does not allow us to go into the characteristics of each of these sub-communities. In the following, therefore, only one area, i.e., sub-community 25, is selected for a sample study, and the information about those factors listed is based on the 1934 census data of Chicago.[1] The census tracts instead of the sub-communities are referred to, not only because such data are not yet available in terms of sub-communities, but a knowledge about the census tracts included in an area serves to give us a more detailed picture of the area as a whole.

Sub-community 25 is composed of 10 census tracts and has a total population of 26,702 according to the 1934 census, and an average population of 17,808, 20 years and over—average of 1930 and 1934 figures. Its eastern boundary begins on Kedzie Ave., at 3200 west of State St. and its southern limit on Lawrence Ave., at 4800 north of Madison, the center of the area being approximately 8 miles from the center of the metropolis. Some of the known characteristics of this area are as follows:

TABLE XI

CHARACTERISTICS OF AN AREA WITH NO RATE OF OPIUM ADDICTION:
SUB-COMMUNITY 25
(Percentages)

Census Tracts	Median Rental[a]	Homes Owned	Vacant Units	Population[b]	Residence under 1 Yr.	People Married	Sex Ratio[c]
152	42.8	75.8	2.0	1.1	10.1	65.6	108.8
153	42.4	59.9	2.1	4.5	16.0	65.9	102.6
154	74.5	72.6	1.7	18.9	12.8	66.5	97.8
155	74.5	73.4	0.7	38.4	10.3	73.8	96.9
156	44.9	57.0	4.9	-11.2	18.2	70.5	97.8
157	44.9	38.4	4.1	3.1	23.2	63.9	93.6
158	44.9	38.4	4.1	-9.3	23.2	76.7	113.8
159	49.8	23.3	3.4	10.1	26.6	59.2	73.2
160	48.7	59.6	4.1	-2.2	16.1	64.6	101.8
161	39.9	43.8	5.3	-5.8	21.0	65.5	99.7

(a) Rental is in dollars per month.
(b) Figures without sign mean percentages of increase from 1930 to 1934; those with minus sign mean decrease during the same period.
(c) Number of males per 100 females.

[1] The census data used here were taken from the file of the Social Science Research Committee of the University of Chicago.

It will be noticed from the above table that the median rentals of homes in all the census tracts except three are above 44 dollars. According to the classification used in the 1934 census, such rentals indicate the highest economic class; rentals of the other three tracts are also considered as high. This index alone is sufficient to give us some idea as to the high economic status of people living in sub-community 25. The fact is further shown by the relatively large percentage of homes owned.

The low percentage of vacant dwelling units may be taken as an indication of the fact that the area under investigation was a growing community, and that it was not so invaded by industry as to become unfit for residential purpose. This is further indicated by the considerable increase of population from 1930 to 1934 for the area as a whole.

A relatively low degree of mobility is seen in the small percentage of families having lived for less than a year at the address where their census was taken.[1] In all but 1 of the 10 census tracts, the number of families whose length of residence is 5 or more years exceeds 40 per cent. This fact seems to indicate a relatively high degree of stable communal life.

The large percentage of married people is another indication of the relatively stable and probably also well-adjusted life of the people living in this area. This is further suggested by the absence of great disparity between the number of males and that of females.

In the preceding table, data on education and some other factors have not been included. But it was found that in all but 2 of the tracts two-thirds of the population 18 years and over had received high school education.

Thus we are given a picture of a growing community with few dwelling units unoccupied. Most of the occupants had high school education. They mostly lived in families, and either owned homes or paid high rentals, and relatively few of the families had a length of residence of less than a year. While not all of these characteristics can be said to be true of the other 12 areas in which no cases of opium addiction were known, a careful examination fails to reveal any great dissimilarity between them in respect to such major factors as the ownership of homes, the number of vacant dwelling units, residence under 1 year, the number of people married, and the sex ratio. In a general way, therefore, sub-

---

[1] For the definition of "family," see Newcomb and Lang. *op. cit.*, p. 160. It is to be noted that single persons living alone were counted as families.

community 25 may be taken as fairly representative of the areas with no known cases of addiction.

Having had some notion about the areas with no addiction rate, let us now examine the areas with relatively high rates of addiction. In Table XII are listed, according to the order of magnitude, those areas with addiction rates above 16, which is the average rate for the city as a whole.

TABLE XII

OPIUM ADDICTION RATES FOR THE CITY OF CHICAGO, BY SUB-COMMUNITIES
HAVING OVER 16 ADDICTS PER 100,000 POPULATION,
20 YEARS AND OLDER (1928–34)

Sub-Com-munities	Average Population of 1930 and 1934, 20 Years and Over			Annual Average Number of Addicts, 1928–1934			Rate per 100,000 Population		
	Total	Male	Female	Total	Male	Female	Total	Male	Female
61	20,284	16,029	4,255	60.8	53.0	7.8	299.9	330.6	184.0
75	7,508	3,518	3,990	21.0	15.0	6.0	279.7	426.4	150.4
74	5,435	4,412	1,023	12.8	10.8	2.0	236.1	245.6	195.4
76	10,080	6,172	3,908	17.8	17.6	.2	176.9	286.2	4.3
77	13,052	6,894	6,158	22.5	14.5	8.0	172.4	210.3	129.9
21	29,034	17,520	11,514	40.1	25.6	14.5	138.3	146.5	125.9
79	18,371	8,890	9,481	13.8	7.3	6.5	75.3	82.5	68.6
78	25,081	12,693	12,388	15.3	10.7	4.6	61.1	84.0	37.7
62	20,090	10,833	9,257	9.8	6.0	3.8	48.9	55.4	41.4
7	33,050	16,361	16,689	14.0	9.0	5.0	42.4	55.0	29.9
81	26,844	13,240	13,604	10.6	8.3	2.3	39.7	62.9	17.2
18	20,689	10,235	10,454	8.0	5.2	2.8	38.7	50.5	27.1
82	19,514	9,490	10,024	6.3	3.5	2.8	32.4	36.9	28.3
13	24,436	12,616	12,020	7.1	3.1	4.0	29.3	25.5	33.3
20	16,789	9,197	7,592	5.0	2.8	2.2	29.8	30.8	28.5
83	15,158	7,146	8,012	3.8	3.0	.8	25.3	42.0	10.4
6	24,855	11,374	13,481	5.5	3.5	2.0	22.1	30.8	14.8
14	19,657	8,237	11,420	4.3	2.7	1.6	22.0	32.4	14.6
22	16,344	6,276	8,068	3.0	1.8	1.2	20.9	29.2	14.5
87	20,427	10,013	10,414	4.0	2.5	1.5	19.6	25.0	4.4
85	36,775	17,848	18,927	7.0	5.0	2.0	19.0	28.0	10.6
88	21,278	10,277	11,001	3.8	2.5	1.3	18.0	24.3	12.1

Sub-community 61. Sub-community 61 is the area that has the highest rate of addiction. It has an average population of 20,284,—average of 1930 and 1934 populations, 20 years and older—and an annual average of 60 addicts in our record, the rate per 100,000 people being approximately 300.   This area is adjacent to the central business district, surrounded by West Kinzie on the North, the Chicago River on the East, West Van Buren on the South, and Ashland Avenue on the West.   It includes the notorious West Madison Street, generally known as Chicago's Hobohemia, the land of the homeless and the jobless, the center of employment bureaus, pawnshops, and flophouses.[1]   This area may also be conveniently referred to as the Near West Side, on account of its proximity to the Loop.   To have a little more precise notion about the ecological character of the area, let us study the characteristics of the nine census tracts included in it with reference to some of what may be considered as significant factors.   It is to be noted that the census data used here and in the following pages apply mainly to the conditions in 1934; inference on the basis of these data about conditions in other years, therefore, must be made with reservation.

TABLE XIII

CHARACTERISTICS OF SUB-COMMUNITY 61

(Percentages)

Census Tracts	Median Rental[a]	Homes Owned	Vacant Units	Popula-tion[b]	Residence under 1 Yr.	People Married	Sex Ratio
415..................	18.2	6.6	24.0	−27.1	31.4	41.7	203.8
416..................	14.9	2.4	25.1	21.4	31.6	21.8	652.7
417..................	14.9	2.4	25.1	127.9	31.6	14.0	20100.0
418..................	19.8	9.8	21.8	−19.7	41.0	40.6	141.0
419..................	14.9	3.0	28.2	7.7	31.1	21.8	609.3
420..................	14.9	3.0	28.2	1.7	31.1	11.1	2133.6
422..................	15.1	16.9	15.2	−17.8	19.7	43.8	145.2
423..................	14.7	2.3	32.5	−29.7	24.0	29.6	324.6
424..................	11.9	11.8	7.9	−60.9	15.4	29.6	107.7

(a) In dollars per month.
(b) Percentage of increase or decrease from 1930 to 1934.

On examining Table XIII, one cannot help being impressed by the great contrast between sub-community 61 and sub-community 25, which we used as a sample of those areas with no addiction rate.   Whereas the lowest median rental per month in sub-community 25 was $39.9,

[1] Cavan, op. cit., p. 91.

the highest in sub-community 61 was $19.8. According to the scale used in the 1934 census, rentals in sub-community 61 may all be classified under the lowest economic class.[1] The low economic status of this area is further indicated by the very small percentages of homes owned.

Another great contrast between sub-community 61 and sub-community 25 is seen in the population trends of these areas. Sub-community 25 was characterized by something of a steady increase in population, whereas in sub-community 61 there was a marked increase in one tract and a great decrease in the other, signs of a highly irregular and artificial demographical process. From this one would naturally expect most of the occupants of this area to be transitory migrants. This is clearly indicated by the relatively large percentage of residence under 1 year. This area, therefore, may be said to be one with a very high degree of mobility.

Sub-community 61 also seems to be an area marked by a high degree of physical deterioration. This is shown by the low rentals mentioned above, and further indicated by the fact that in practically all of the nine census tracts included in this community a fourth of the dwelling units were not occupied.

A still greater contrast between sub-community 61 and our non-addiction area is found in the sex ratio and the percentage of people married. In tracts 417 and 420 of the former, for example, males exceeded females by the thousand. Most of the occupants of this area seemed to lead a lonely and isolated life, as shown by the fact that, in 3 of the 9 tracts, only two-fifths of the population were married, while for the rest of the area the percentage of the married is even much lower.

People living in this area were also less well educated than those of our non-addiction area referred to above, as shown by the fact that in none of the nine tracts was there more than a third of the population 18 years and over who had received high school education, the percentage of those receiving higher education being still lower.

Compared with sub-community 25, therefore, sub-community 61 may be characterized as an area of cheap lodging houses and very low rentals, occupied mainly by a highly mobile population, with single males predominating in number. The physical feature of the area was one of marked deterioration.

---

[1] Newcomb and Lang, *op. cit.*, Map 2, pp. 672–73.

Sub-community 75. Sub-community 75 is the area that has next to the highest addiction rate. The average adult population of this area for 1930 and 1934 is 7,508, and the annual average number of addicts of whom we had record is 21, the rate per 100,000 being 279. This area may be called the Near South Side in relation to the central business district. It is surrounded by Roosevelt Rd. on the North, Lake Michigan on the East, 26th St. on the South, and the South branch Chicago River, W. Cermak and W. 18th St. on the West. It includes the well-known S. State St. and 22nd St. Some of the characteristics of this area as shown by the 1934 census are presented in Table XIV.

TABLE XIV

CHARACTERISTICS OF SUB-COMMUNITY 75

(Percentages)

Census Tracts	Median Rental[a]	Homes Owned	Vacant Units	Population[b]	Per Cent Negroes	Residence under 1 Yr.	People Married	Sex Ratio
517	40.1	6.5	43.5	−36.3	4.6	24.9	37.7	139.7
518	.....	.....	.....	−100.0	.....	.....	.....	.....
519	26.7	8.1	36.3	−33.1	2.7	24.1	44.2	97.4
520	20.0	1.5	23.5	−11.4	19.4	26.3	48.6	134.5
521	20.1	0.4	20.4	26.1	86.7	32.6	62.2	96.4
522	12.3	1.4	40.4	−5.3	80.1	21.9	49.0	120.1

(a) In dollars per month.
(b) Per cent of increase or decrease from 1930 to 1934.

It is interesting to note that the ecological features of sub-community 75 are similar to those of sub-community 61 in more than one respect. The differences seem mainly a matter of degree. Thus, the median rental of this area is also low compared with that of our non-addiction area referred to above, although it is somewhat higher than that of sub-community 61. Other features in favor of this area are the relatively more normal distribution of males and females in its population and the higher percentage of people married. But the decrease of population in this area is very marked, and the percentage of dwelling units unoccupied is also higher. In most essentials, therefore, what was said of sub-community 61 seems applicable to sub-community 75.

There is one other distinctive feature of this area that has not been mentioned, and that is, in tracts 521 and 522 over a fourth of the population were Negroes. The preponderance of Negroes in these tracts might have had something to do with the relatively high addiction rate of this area, as indicated by the fact that of a total of 126 addicts in this area of whom we had record, 45 came from these two tracts. It may be noted in this connection that these tracts, beginning from somewhere near 18th St. and leading southward between S. Clark St. and S. State St., mark the beginning of Chicago's Black Belt, which extends some six miles south to 71st St.

Sub-community 74. Sub-community 74 is the central business district, occupied mostly by business and commercial buildings. The average adult population of this area for 1930 and 1934 is 5,435, and the annual average of addicts of whom we had record is approximately 13, the rate per 100,000 population being 236. It is delimited by the Chicago River on the North, Lake Michigan on the East, Roosevelt Rd. on the South, and the South branch Chicago River on the West. It includes a part of W. Madison St. that leads to sub-community 61, and a part of S. State St. that leads to sub-community 75. Both of these streets and others in the area, such as W. Van Buren and W. Harrison are the havens of unattached men, noted for their cheap hotels, small restaurants, and low class amusements. The characteristics of this area as shown by the 1934 census data are listed in Table XV.

TABLE XV

CHARACTERISTICS OF SUB-COMMUNITY 74

(*Percentages*)

Census Tracts	Median Rental[a]	Homes Owned	Vacant Units	Population[b]	Per Cent Negroes	Residence under 1 Yr.	People Married	Sex Ratio
511	14.7	1.4	26.0	−51.7	.....	24.1	26.6	619.6
512	14.7	1.4	26.0	−33.3	.....	24.1	26.6	300.0
513	14.7	.....	26.0	−9.9	.....	.....	22.4	284.7
514	14.7	1.4	26.0	−57.5	16.8	24.1	17.4	743.3
515	14.7	1.4	26.0	−46.2	.....	24.1	26.3	244.4
516	14.7	1.4	26.0	−59.2	2.5	24.1	21.3	279.1

(a) In dollars per month.
(b) Percentage of increase or decrease from 1930 to 1934.

It will be seen from Table XV that the median rental for the dwelling places of this area is even lower than that of sub-community 61, which has the highest rate of addiction. Such low rentals and the fact that less than 1.4 per cent of the dwelling units in all of the tracts included in this area were owned seem to suggest that a great majority of the occupants must have lived in cheap lodging houses or hotels. Our figures further show that about one-third of these dwelling units were unoccupied. This phenomenon was accompanied by a uniform decrease of population in all of the six tracts. These facts, together with the marked preponderance of males over females and the very low percentage of people married, seem to confirm our general impression that this area is the land of the homeless men, a part of Chicago's Hobohemia.

Sub-community 76. Sub-community 76 is situated southwest of sub-community 75. It has an average adult population of 10,080 for 1930 and 1934, and a yearly average of approximately 18 addicts in our records, and the rate per 100,000 is nearly 177. The main boundaries of this area are West 18th Street on the North, South Clark Street, Federal Avenue, and Wentworth Avenue on the East, West Pershing Street on the South, and Stewart Avenue, South Canal Street, and the South branch Chicago River on the West. It includes Chicago's Chinatown, situated on 22nd and Wentworth, noted for its opium-smoking "hangouts." Some of the ecological features of this area may be glimpsed from the following table.

TABLE XVI

CHARACTERISTICS OF SUB-COMMUNITY 76

(Percentages)

Census Tracts	Median Rental[a]	Homes Owned	Vacant Units	Population[b]	Residence under 1 Year	Education 9–12 Years	People Married	Sex Ratio
523..........	14.3	5.9	1.2	−28.9	12.4	14.4	74.7	514.4
524..........	14.3	21.0	14.4	7.2	16.7	9.1	43.5	172.7
525..........	14.2	19.8	22.0	−9.5	20.2	10.0	58.3	94.2
526..........	14.2	35.1	16.4	−3.7	19.7	10.9	55.0	115.0
527..........	17.0	26.7	17.4	−0.9	17.9	12.7	55.2	105.3
528..........	17.0	27.7	16.0	−6.9	19.5	10.9	53.1	101.5
529..........	17.0	27.7	16.0	24.8	19.5	17.4	63.5	108.0
530......,...	20.3	31.3	13.5	−25.3	16.5	9.9	54.3	132.6
531..........	20.3	31.3	13.5	−15.4	16.5	11.6	62.3	103.3
532..........	20.3	34.1	8.1	3.8	19.4	11.8	58.8	102.3
533..........	20.3	34.1	28.9	−14.5	16.3	18.3	58.0	119.1
534..........	18.6	34.3	15.3	−5.2	20.9	15.0	57.9	105.8

(a) In dollars per month.
(b) Percentage of increase or decrease from 1930 to 1934.

According to Table XVI, sub-community 76 is also characterized by very low rentals, and by a considerable proportion of vacant dwelling units. These facts together with the marked decrease of population from 1930 to 1934 seem to suggest a high degree of physical deterioration in the community. It is also interesting to note that the percentage of people in this area receiving high school education is unusually low, and that in all of the census tracts included in this area except two the percentage of people receiving education under 5 years is below 40. This would lead us to infer that a large number of the occupants of this area were either uneducated or very poorly educated.

In regard to the percentage of married people, sex ratio, and the length of residence, however, sub-community 76 does not compare very unfavorably with our sample of non-addiction areas, i.e., sub-community 25. It would seem that a large majority of the population in this area led a comparably more stable life than those in the areas with higher addiction rates described in the preceding pages. But it is important to note that in two of the tracts included in this area there were a considerable number of Chinese immigrants—79.4% in tract 523 and 9.8% in tract 524[1]—and that most of the married men among this group left their families in their home country. It is to be further noted that out of a total of 107 addicts in this area of whom we had record, 97 came from these two tracts. Recalling the fact that nearly 4 per cent of our group of addicts were Chinese, we shall not be far wrong in saying that the presence of a large number of Chinese immigrants in the area was in no small measure responsible for its relatively high rate of addiction.

Sub-community 77. Sub-community 77 is situated directly south of sub-community 75, with 26th Street as its northern boundary and Lake Michigan as its eastern limit. East 31st Street and West 35th Street from its southern border, and Wentworth Avenue separates it from sub-community 76 on the West. This area has an average adult population of 13,052 for 1930 and 1934 and an annual average of nearly 23 addicts in our record. The rate per 100,000 is 172. Some of the ecological features of this area are listed in Table XVII.

On examining Table XVII, it will be noticed that in many respects this area is similar to sub-community 76, especially with reference to rentals, vacant dwelling units, the decrease of population, the percentage

---

[1] Newcomb and Lang, *op. cit.*, Table 4 and Supplement, pp. 399, 668.

TABLE XVII

CHARACTERISTICS OF SUB-COMMUNITY 77

(Percentages)

Census Tracts	Median Rental[a]	Homes Owned	Vacant Units	Popula-tion[b]	Per Cent Negroes	Residence under 1 Year	People Married	Sex Ratio
535...........	13.8	29.4	11.2	−27.0	71.4	17.4	61.2	99.6
536...........	16.1	6.1	11.3	−25.8	78.4	26.8	50.2	128.8
537...........	16.1	6.1	11.3	−3.1	81.9	26.8	59.7	115.1
539...........	14.3	9.0	14.4	−10.4	92.1	34.5	53.4	124.5
540...........	16.2	4.4	11.1	−31.4	94.0	34.5	49.2	24.7
541...........	16.2	4.4	11.1	−10.2	97.0	34.5	60.6	93.3
543...........	22.2	6.9	26.8	3.5	63.8	36.7	40.3	210.3
544...........	22.2	4.5	22.7	2.8	87.4	39.4	51.1	108.1
548...........	20.3	11.3	17.2	−31.2	72.2	39.8	59.5	100.3
549...........	18.1	7.6	18.1	−0.9	72.3	36.4	50.0	80.1
550...........	20.9	11.5	10.0	2.8	95.7	38.5	58.1	98.6

(a) In dollars per month.
(b) Percentage of increase or decrease from 1930 to 1934.

of people married and the sex ratio. But the occupants of this area seemed to show a greater amount of mobility, as suggested by the lower percentage of homes owned and the larger percentage of residence under 1 year. Another distinctive feature of this area is the preponderance of Negroes over whites. These two factors were probably not unrelated to the larger number of addicts of this area in our records, but a larger population gives this area a relatively lower addiction rate. But in all essentials, sub-communities 76 and 77, as shown by their addiction rates, may be considered as one area. They may also be thought of as the extension of the Near South Side in relation to the heart of the metropolis.

Sub-community 21. Sub-community 21 is situated north of the central business district, and is often referred to as the Lower North Side. It is surrounded by North Avenue on the North, North State Street and North Michigan Avenue on the East, the Chicago River on the South, and North Wells Street and Sedgwick Street on the West. It includes the notorious North Clark Street, noted for cheap rooming houses and vice resorts. The average adult population of this area for 1930 and 1934 is 29,034, and the yearly average of addicts from this area of whom we had record is a little over 40. The importance of this area as a center of drug traffic is evident, but on account of a relatively large population, the rate per 100,000 for this area is only slightly over 138.   Data on some of the ecological characteristics of this area are presented in Table XVIII.

TABLE XVIII

CHARACTERISTICS OF SUB-COMMUNITY 21

(*Percentages*)

Census Tracts	Median Rental[a]	Homes Owned	Vacant Units	Population[b]	Residence under 1 Yr.	Education 9–12 Yrs.	People Married	Sex Ratio
123..............	19.8	14.5	11.6	−10.9	30.7	23.1	53.6	108.8
124..............	42.8	9.3	9.7	−14.8	42.6	39.3	41.8	102.5
129..............	39.7	2.7	10.3	−13.6	48.6	34.2	41.8	122.9
130..............	61.1	2.0	6.2	−16.4	41.0	34.7	36.0	104.5
135..............	28.4	14.8	20.8	26.1	40.1	17.4	25.5	420.8
136..............	21.0	8.8	7.1	−4.9	55.3	25.8	37.4	209.7
137..............	51.4	3.5	16.3	−22.9	35.4	30.3	33.9	135.2

(a) In dollars per month.
(b) Percentage of increase or decrease from 1930 to 1934.

From the figures presented in Table XVIII, one gets the impression that the 7 tracts included in this area differ from each other rather markedly in more than one respect.   Thus, the median rentals for the tracts situated in the eastern part of the area, along North State Street and North Michigan Avenue,—tracts 124, 130, and 137—are considerably higher than those of other tracts.   In the tracts on the western portion of the area there were also more vacant dwelling units, particularly in tract 135.   This tract is situated directly north of the central business district across the Chicago River, between North Dearborn Street and North Wells, with North Clark Street in the middle.   Besides having the lowest median rental and the largest percentage of vacant dwelling units, this tract is also characterized by the lowest percentage of married people and the highest sex ratio of the whole area.   Here too about half of the residents had not been at their present address for over a year, and the population had increased more than 26 per cent from 1930 to 1934, both facts pointing to a very high degree of mobility.   It was in this tract that we found 91 addicts out of a total of 241 for the sub-community as a whole.   While it is difficult to establish positive correlation between those ecological features just mentioned and the degree of addiction, the fact that considerably more addicts were found in tract 135 than in any other tract in the area is suggestive. On the whole, the characteristics of this area are quite similar to those of the areas we have described, excepting that the former seems to lead in the percentage of residence under 1 year, indicating that probably it had more of a floating population than any of the latter.

Thus far we have briefly described those areas with addiction rates above 100: namely, sub-community 61, which is often referred to as the Near West Side; sub-community 75, the Near South Side; sub-communities 76 and 77, further south of the Loop; sub-community 74, the Loop or the central business district; and sub-community 21, the Lower North Side. As space does not allow us to go further into the ecological features of other areas, let us stop here and see what may be considered as some of common characteristics of those areas so far described, and, in a general way, what kind of social and cultural *milieu* as well as patterns of personal behavior these ecological characteristics may serve to indicate.

First of all, by comparing the areas with high rates of opium addiction with those that had none, we found that, with exceptions in some isolated census tracts, practically all of the former areas were characterized by very low median rentals, relatively large percentages of vacant dwelling units, and considerable decrease of population from 1930 to 1934. These facts may be taken as indices of the low economic status of people living in those areas and of the degree of physical deterioration in the community. The latter phenomenon, it has been found, is mainly due to the invasion of industry and by the consequent increase in land value, so that interest in residential enterprises naturally diminishes,[1] and may, in turn, be taken roughly as an indication of the decline of community organization and of the loosening or absence of effective group control over the individual.

Secondly, in nearly every one of the areas with high addiction rates we found an appreciably low percentage of homes owned, a comparatively low percentage of people married, and a noticeably high sex ratio in favor of men. These facts would seem to indicate that in areas with high addiction rates there were an overwhelming majority of unattached people —more men than women—who have little or no social obligations, and who, in turn, live a more or less isolated existence, without the instinctual

[1] Cavan, *op. cit.*, p. 102.

satisfaction as well as the intimate moral support which only a normal married life can give.

Thirdly, in all of the areas with high addiction rates we found a high degree of mobility, as indicated by the comparatively large percentages of residence under 1 year. Mobility here is taken to mean the movement of people through space. It is generally agreed among sociologists that a high degree of mobility or constant moving in an urban environment has the effect of releasing men from their primary group associations, the family and the neighborhood, and from other affectional bonds that were formed early in life. At the same time, it tends to place men under influences of a most diverse nature, and not infrequently to produce in them mental conflicts of varying degrees.[1] If this were true, our data on mobility alone would lead us to believe that the areas with high addiction rates are areas in which a large amount of personal disorganization is to be expected.

The central business district of Chicago and its nearby communities within a radius of from 2 to 3 miles have been found by previous studies to be the seats of more than one form of social and personal disorganization. In particular may be mentioned the study of family disorganization by Ernest R. Mowrer.[2] In this study the city of Chicago was divided into five types of areas with reference to the type of family life found in each community: namely, the non-family areas, the emancipated family areas, the paternal family areas, the equalitarian family areas, and the maternal family areas. According to this author, the non-family areas, which have more males than females, tend to find a place in or near the central business district, represented in Chicago by the Loop, Chinatown, Hobohemia, and the areas of hotels catering to transients. The emancipated family areas tend to be situated a little beyond the non-family areas, and other family areas still further away from the center of the city. Approximately speaking, our areas with high addiction rates belong mainly to the non-family areas. In these areas the largest amount of family disorganization was found.[3]

Among other studies that have thrown considerable light on the ecological as well as the cultural characteristics of those areas mentioned above

---

[1] G. A. Lundberg and others, *Trends in American Sociology* (New York, 1929), pp. 285 ff.

[2] Ernest R. Mowrer, *Family Disorganization* (Chicago, 1927).

[3] *Ibid.*, Chart XI, p. 121.

and on their relation to personal disorganization, may be mentioned first the study of delinquency and adult crime by Clifford R. Shaw. It was found that the areas with the highest rates of both juvenile delinquents and adult criminals were also located near the central business district, in the Negro area extending south from the Loop, and near Union Stock Yard.[1] This phenomenon was ascribed by the author largely to the lack of homogeneity and continuity of cultural traditions and institutions in those areas, which are essential to social solidarity, neighborhood organization and an effective public opinion. Instead of such constructive forces, young people in those communities are constantly exposed to the influence of adult criminals, and quite naturally take up the patterns of criminal behavior.[2]

Next may be mentioned Ruth S. Cavan's study of suicide. She too found the highest rates of suicide in those areas in which we found the highest rates of opium addiction; namely, the Loop, the Lower North Side, the Near South Side, and the West Madison Area.[3] These areas, according to her findings, were characterized by rooming houses, cheap hotels, pawnshops, houses of prostitution, vendors of alcoholic drinks and dope peddlers, and by a concentration of unsatisfied and disorganized persons.[4] But in the case of the people whom she studied, emotional conflicts sought their solution in the form of suicide.

Finally may be mentioned the ecological study of insanity in Chicago by Robert E. L. Faris. On the basis of the addresses of the patients admitted to the Cook County Psychopathic Hospital in 1930, it was found that the highest rates of insanity were also concentrated in the central business district and its surrounding communities.[5] This was particularly true of schizophrenia rates.[6] According to the findings of this author, one of the principal factors responsible for this concentration was the isolated existence of people living in the hobo areas and in other areas inhabited by isolated national or racial groups.[7]

---

[1] C. R. Shaw and H. D. McKay, "Social Factors in Juvenile Delinquency," *Report on the Causes of Crime*, Vol. II, ed. the National Commission on Law Observation and Enforcement (Washington, 1931), p. 107.
[2] *Ibid.*, pp. 105–07; 110–11; 126 ff.
[3] Cavan, *op. cit.*, p. 81.
[4] *Ibid.*, pp. 100–105.
[5] Faris, *op. cit.*, Fig. 1, p. 5.
[6] *Ibid.*, Fig. 5, p. 20.
[7] *Ibid.*, pp. 130 ff.

Also of interest to us is the distribution of alcoholism in Chicago, as indicated by the deaths from excessive drinking, 1923–24. It was found by Cavan that the highest 5 per cent of rates, i.e., 13–57 deaths from alcoholism per 100,000 population, were also concentrated in the areas in and around the central business district.[1]

Our own findings and those of the previous studies just mentioned, therefore, point conclusively to the existence in those areas in and near the central business district of Chicago of an ecological configuration as well as a social and cultural *milieu* which may be considered as most conducive to various forms of personal disorganization. But in general there is still a great deal to be discovered as to the ways in which an individual is affected by such an urban cultural environment, and in particular we must further inquire how an individual living in such a cultural *milieu*, instead of or in addition to taking up the patterns of an out-and-out criminal, or resorting to suicide, insanity or alcoholism for the solution of their personal problems, comes to be a drug addict. To explore such specific social situations under which the drug habit is formed will be the task of the following chapter.

2. CENTERS OF DRUG TRAFFIC

In describing the areas with high addiction rates in the foregoing pages, we have not mentioned the one ecological feature that is most immediately connected with the welfare of drug addicts, and that is the distribution of the centers of illicit drug traffic in the city. It is needless to say that a knowledge of this distribution is important not only from the point of view of understanding and helping to solve the problems of drug addicts, but from the still more practical angle of controlling the illicit drug traffic in Chicago. Data used in the following consist of the places of offense of 1,591 addicts and peddlers for the years, 1929–1934,— 1,385 cases from the Bureau of Narcotics and 206 cases from the Narcotic Division of the Chicago Police Department. According to the records of the former agency, these are the places where samples of illicit drug were purchased by the government agents as legal evidences against the offender. In the records of the latter agency, they were called the "haunts" of the offender. It was at these places that most of these addicts and peddlers were arrested, either for peddling or possessing

[1] Cavan, *op. cit.*, Map V, p. 99.

drugs, as soon as the evidences against them were secured.   These places, therefore, may be considered as the centers of illicit drug traffic in Chicago, places where addicts generally "hang around" and make their "connections," that is to secure their supply of drug from peddlers.   The distribution of these centers of drug traffic in the ecological organization of Chicago is represented on Map 3, each dot indicating one addict or peddler whose place of offense was known.

In a previous connection, it has been suggested that an area that ranks relatively low in addiction rate may be very important as a center of drug traffic.   This will be clear on inspecting the following table, which is constructed on the basis of the places of offense mentioned above, but in which only those sub-communities which have more than 10 arrests are listed.

TABLE XIX

CENTERS OF ILLICIT DRUG TRAFFIC IN CHICAGO

(1929–34)

Sub-communities	Number of Arrests
61	302
77	181
21	173
76	114
78	92
74	86
75	84
81	70
79	51
7	49
62	48
85	36
82	33
71	26
14	24
83	21
20	18
6	18
13	12
22	12

It will be noticed, on examining both Map 3 and Table XIX, that sub-community 61, or the Near West Side, ranks highest both as an area of addiction and as a center of drug traffic.   "Connections" in this area

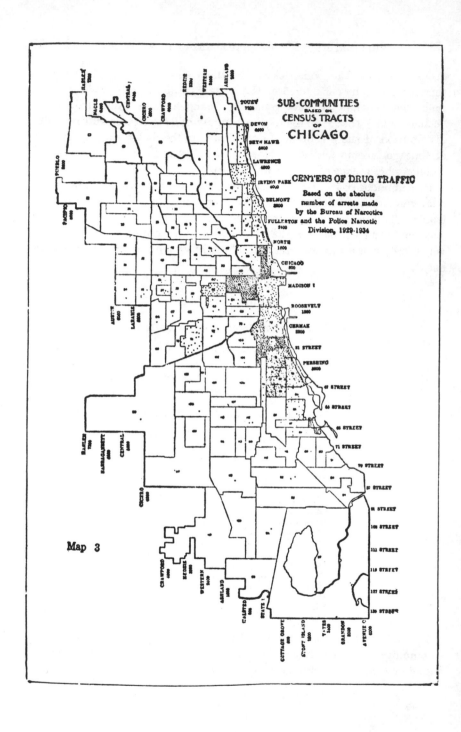

SUB-COMMUNITIES
BASED ON
CENSUS TRACTS
OF
CHICAGO

CENTERS OF DRUG TRAFFIC

Based on the absolute
number of arrests made
by the Bureau of Narcotics
and the Police Narcotic
Division, 1929-1934

Map 3

are usually made in cheap hotels such as the Star, the Legion and MacCoy, and at street corners, mostly along Halstead at Madison and Harrison. Sub-community 77 ranks next highest as a drug-peddling center, although it is fifth in addiction rate. This is mainly a Negro area, and so are a few other sub-communities listed in the above table; namely, 78, 81, 82, 83, and 85. Some of the street corners in this area noted for drug peddling are South State and Thirty-first and Wabash, and State and Twenty-sixth. Sub-community 21 is sixth in addiction rate, but third as a center of drug peddling. "Connections" can be made all along North Clark Street from the river to Division Street. Sub-community 76 is the Chinatown area, Twenty-second and Wabash and Michigan being some of the favorite street corners for the meeting of drug addicts and peddlers. The rest of the areas listed in Table XIX need no special mention.

It is interesting to note that all those areas in which we found the largest amount of drug traffic are also the areas in which we found the highest rates of drug addiction. In order to have a little more precise idea as to the proximity of one kind of area to the other, we must next inquire into the distance between the residence of an addict and the place where he or she was caught selling or possessing drugs. This was done by measuring the distance between the approximate center of the census tract in which an addict lived and that of the tract in which he or she was found guilty. The results of this inquiry are given in Table XX.

TABLE XX

DISTANCE BETWEEN THE RESIDENCES OF DRUG ADDICTS AND THEIR
PLACES OF OFFENSE, 1929–34

Distance in Mile	Number of Addicts	Percentage
Both in same census tract	567	58.1
Less than 1	140	14.3
1, but less than 2	75	7.7
2, but less than 3	66	6.8
3, but less than 4	38	3.9
4, but less than 5	34	2.6
5, and over	56	5.7
TOTAL...	976	100.0

According to Table **XX**, the places of offense of nearly 60 per cent of the addicts under consideration were in the same census tracts in which they lived. In fact, we found a considerable number of cases in which the residence and place of offense were identical. Altogether we may say that more than four-fifths of these addicts lived less then 2 miles away from the centers of drug traffic. This finding is of considerable importance for understanding the peculiar environment of drug addicts and for helping them in any capacity, for, as we shall presently see, unavoidable contact with drug peddlers and accessibility to the illicit source of drug supply is one of the principal factors that undo the repeated efforts of many addicts in quitting their habit.

CHAPTER V

SOCIAL SITUATIONS AND PERSONALITY FACTORS RELATED TO OPIUM ADDICTION

FROM what was said in the foregoing chapter, the general character of the social and cultural environment of the opium addiction areas in Chicago is already evident. It may be restated as an environment in which individuals live mostly by and for themselves, in which the amount of social control is reduced to the minimum, and in which opportunities for unrestrained dissipation and various forms of personal disorganization abound. But such a general characterization of the environment of drug addicts, enlightening as it is, still does not give us sufficient information as to why A instead of B, for example, becomes a drug addict, while both of them may have moved in the same community, and may even have lived in the same lodging house. In order, therefore, to have a fuller understanding of the influence of what are often called "bad associates" to which over two-thirds of the drug addicts under investigation attributed their addiction, we are forced to take up the study of individual cases, and to inquire into the specific social situations in which a person first comes in contact with drugs and drug-users as well as his personality traits that may be said to have predisposed him to their influence, into the sequence of events that finally lead to the formation of the drug habit in the person, and into his subsequent career as an addict with all its pleasures and tribulations. This is the task of the present chapter.

In a previous connection, the nature and the advantages of the prolonged interview method for the purpose of scientific research have been explained. It is this method that we employed in studying most of the cases to be presented in the following. Some of them were interviewed at the Cook County Psychopathic Hospital. Some were located at the shelter houses for men. A few cases were known through the Bureau of Narcotics and the Federal Probation Office. Others were introduced to us by the addicts we had known. Owing to the limited facilities at our disposal for conducting protracted interviews, the cases we studied are probably not numerous or representative enough to yield any conclusive generalization; nor has it been possible to interview every case we came across for a period sufficiently long to secure the kind of information we desired. For these reasons, while our findings in this direction may throw some light on the relation between the addict and his social environment, and help us thereby to understand not only the specific problems of drug addiction but the general problem of the one and the many, or the individual and society, they must be regarded as exploratory and tentative. But it is hoped that they may be suggestive enough to stimulate further research.

The subjectivity of the data secured through interviews is not denied. On the contrary, we want to reëmphasize the fact that what we want to understand about the social situations related to drug addiction is not what they appear to the outsider, but what they mean to the drug addicts. In other words, it is the very subjective world of drug addicts that constitutes our main object of inquiry in this and the following chapters. And we share the conviction of many sociologists, clinical psychologists and psychiatrists that the life-history, written or told spontaneously by a person, is the best available means by which to grasp the significance any given social situation may have for that person.[1]

The reliability or truthfulness of the stories told by drug addicts about themselves is a question that requires careful consideration. First of all, we must understand that the notorious tendency to lie on the part of drug addicts is not without its reason. That this mendacity is a natural reaction to a hostile situation was so penetratingly revealed in the following statement made by an addict of Chicago over a generation ago that it is worth quoting at some length:

> It is due the habitué to say that he has no purpose to injure another when he masquerades with truth; it is only his own protection he is after. If that definition of a lie be accepted which declares it to be a wilful attempt to deceive with a view to injuring another in person or property, then the habitué should be forgiven much that has been said concerning this phase of the slavery. Wounded daily in the thought of his soul's humiliation, feeling hourly the bondage of his judgment and will, yet all the time aspiring to maintain his respectability and sustain his merit before men, he deludes himself that he passes among them as stable and reliable. Conscious of his weakness but most unwilling to give over to it he will not confess to himself, even, that he is mendacious;

E. Mayo, *Human Problems of an Industrial Civilization* (Cambridge, 1933), p. 97.

although, strange paradox, he knows it to be so. It must always be borne in mind that the poor slave constantly fights to hold his position in society, and the confidence and affection of his friends ..... He seeks to deceive that he may protect himself from the shame and reproach of men; he juggles with truth that he may appear before others as his heart desires he actually should be. This is a psychological condition very difficult to portray, and more difficult to be understood by those who have not felt the chastening rod of opium.[1]

What was true of the days before the Harrison Narcotic Act must be more so now. In fact, it may be safely stated that no addict is ever born a liar; nor is falsity a necessary part of the effect of opium. Drug addicts are made liars by a society that condemns them. As the author of the preceding statement said, the tendency to appear truthful and righteous in the eyes of others goes only to show that at heart the drug addict is probably as much a moral being as any of us, and that he may just as naturally tell the truth and enjoy confidence in a situation favorable to him as he lies in a hostile one. It is understandable, therefore, how under a friendly situation an interviewer may get the truth out of an addict; for then, having been assured of sympathy and understanding, the addict's necessity for self-protection will be considerably lessened and his resistance to tell the truth naturally reduced. To be sure, to establish confidence with a drug addict is by no means an easy job; and so the data we secured will naturally show varying degrees of reliability, depending mainly on the circumstances under which the addict was interviewed, the length of time for which the interviews were prolonged, and the extent to which the interviewer succeeded in overcoming resistance. As far as possible, these and other indices of reliability will be stated in connection with every case to be presented in the following, so that the reader may be equipped to form his own judgment in the matter.

As a rule, our interviews with drug addicts were recorded as soon as possible after they were concluded, and in each case an attempt was made to reproduce as accurately as possible the conversation as well as the appearance and gestures of the addict interviewed, together with such other little mannerisms as may serve as indicators of the addict's emotional state during the course of the interview and of his attitude

[1] Cobbe, *op. cit.*, pp. 52–3.

toward the interviewer. As a check on the extent of objectivity with which the interviewer reported his observations, his own attitudes towards the addict interviewed, as far as he was aware of them, were also indicated. The emphasis in these interviews, therefore, was laid not only on the verbal report of an addict about his past, but on his actual reaction to the present interview situation as well, and the attitudes shown by an addict in the interview situation, in turn, are taken to be indicative of his attitudes toward other social situations in life. In some such manner, therefore, the interview situation may be regarded as something of a laboratory of social interaction, and to the extent we refine our technique of observing human behavior in such a situation to that extent our findings will have the same scientific weight as those resulting from an experiment in the physical sciences.[1] It is not implied, however, that this ideal has been in any way approached in our study. But a beginning toward that direction can be noticed in some of the cases to be reported in this and, particularly, in the following chapter.

On the basis of the types of social situation found to be related to drug addiction, the cases we have interviewed may be roughly classified into two principal groups: namely, those in which the drug habit was said to have been formed in the course of medical treatment by a physician either for actual organic diseases or for pain due to accidents or other causes; and those in which the knowledge of opium and the technique of using it was gained through association with confirmed addicts or peddlers. These "bad associates," through whom most of these addicts acquired their habit, may be their relatives in the home, playmates in the neighborhood, friends in school, colleagues in work, fellow-roomers in a lodging house, accomplices in crime, or just acquaintances made at pleasure parties or other chance meetings. In some such order, therefore, the cases we have interviewed will be presented in the following.

I. Cases Whose Addiction Was Primarily Due to Previous Use of Drug in Medical Treatment

Although the cases whose addiction was allegedly due to the previous use of drug in medical treatment is statistically unimportant in our group

---

[1] A. D. Ritchie, *Scientific Method: An Inquiry into the Character and Validity of Natural Laws* (New York, 1923), p. 22.

of addicts, it pays to examine carefully the few we did interview and see in what ways they may differ from those whose addiction was due to the influence of other addicts. Let us first listen to those who claimed that their trouble started from some kind of organic disease. It may be mentioned in this connection that the original records of our interviews are too lengthy to be included in their entirety in this report. In the following only abstracts or summaries from these records will be presented. A certain amount of the reality and spontaneity of the original records is thereby sacrificed for the economy of space.

Case 1. Patient was interviewed two times at the Psychopathic Hospital, where she was being treated for drug addiction. She is about 35, of medium height, but appearing stout. She was coöperative from the start, and told the story of her addiction as follows.

It was in 1922 when she was in the show business in the West that she had to undergo an operation for trouble in her Fallopian tubes. To relieve her suffering from the pain, her doctor gave her morphine, and continued to give her "shots" even after she came out of the hospital. She did not know then that the drug she received was morphine. The doctor came about three times a day for about three months, costing her $3.00 per day. One day a friend of hers told her that he could secure the "stuff" the doctor gave her for a smaller amount of money and explained to her that she had formed a habit. Thereupon this friend supplied her needs until she finished her contract with the show business, and then she went for a cure.

She used only morphine in the beginning, but later used morphine and cocaine together. The effect of this mixture was in her case excitement for about half an hour followed by relaxation, whereas morphine alone would not produce the excitement except during the first few months. She compared this state of feeling with that of getting drunk. She used her drugs three times a day; early in the morning, about midday, and before going to bed. Mostly she used the hypodermic method.

In the last 13 years or so she has had at least five cures. On the average a cure costs her $75 a week and each time she had to stay for 4 or more weeks. Each time after cure it was mixing with her old associates that brought about her relapse. The last time, in the middle of April, she went to a party, and she drank. While in a half-drunken state she accepted a "shot" of morphine that was offered to her, thinking that one "shot" would not do her much harm. But one "shot" led to another, and before long she was back on the drug again.

She said that she came from a good family, her sister-in-law having a good job in the city hall and her brother in some company. They are politicians, and that is why she could get into the hospital. (This was after the hospital had stopped the usual practice of taking voluntary patients for treatment of drug addiction.) Patient was happy over the fact that she was allowed to have visitors in spite of the hospital's rule to the contrary. Food was brought to her by her folks. Her mother was planning to send her away from the city for a while. She was glad, because in that way she could get away from her old associates. If possible, she said emphatically, she would quit the show business, for to be in it would naturally bring her into contact with her old associates.

She also mentioned her desire to open an auto-repair shop again. She had one three years ago and made quite a sum of money, most of which, however, was spent on drugs. She began to be interested in that occupation some years ago, when, being out of job, she worked in an auto-repair shop. When the man died, she bought the shop.

While she was on the drug, she said she did not care for sex, but if she was with a man she cared for she would satisfy him although she might not care for it herself. After the operation mentioned above, she lost the capacity for having a child.

In a sociological analysis of social behavior, three factors are generally considered as of major importance: the nature of the environment or any particular object in the environment to which the behavior under investigation may be considered as a response; the preëxisting attitudes or emotional trends in the personality of the individual which may be said to have predisposed him to respond in a particular manner to the said environment or object; and the actual process of interaction between the individual and his environment, including the specific situation in which the interaction takes place.[1] The environment or object in the environment understood here is not to be taken as something apart from the experience of the individual, but something as conceived by, or as it means to, the individual.[2] The behavior under investigation, therefore, may be thought of as a response to the meaning of the environment or any particular object in the environment for that individual. For the time being, let us use this formulation as our general frame of reference

[1] W. I. Thomas and F. Znaniecki, *The Polish Peasant in Europe and America*, Vol. I, pp. 38, 41–48.

[2] H. Blumer, "Method in Social Psychology" (Unpublished Ph.D. thesis, University of Chicago, 1928), pp. 270–71.

with which to analyze this and other cases in the following, and refine or modify it as we gain more insight from the facts on hand.

The above account of Case 1 is the result of only two brief interviews. Consequently, the data we secured are altogether too meager for a satisfactory analysis. But this much may be pointed out. The patient had been in the show business, and among her associates there were drug users. It is highly improbable, therefore, that she should have been entirely ignorant of the use of drugs before morphine was administered to her during an operation. The part she assigned to the physician for her addiction was probably exaggerated, although the account of her physical difficulty might be true. Even granting that the physician was to blame for her initial habituation to morphine, it is important to note that it was her friend who gave her the suggestion that she had become an addict. This would seem to suggest that one may be habituated to the use of a drug without being addicted to it, but that when one is made to realize that one is addicted one is apt to adopt the rôle of an addict. The use of the hypodermic needle and the spacing of the intervals between injections as related above are some of the common features of this rôle. Again, according to her account, it was her associates who occasioned her repeated relapses.

Attention is called to the psychological effect of opium on the patient, which she described as a feeling of elation followed by relaxation.

About the personality of the patient, our data give very little information. She was divorced by her husband, but the reason given is not complete. However, her boasting of her relatives and their political influence and about the special privilege of having visitors seems to suggest a strong desire for recognition on the part of the patient, which, in turn, may be taken as an effort to overcome her feeling of inferiority in the presence of the interviewer. The desire to run an auto-repair shop, which is a masculine occupation in this culture, might be another indication of the same tendency. The writer remembers in this connection that the patient expressed the desire to write a book about her drug habit, which is beyond her capacity and which clearly shows her tendency to compete with the interviewer. If this inference were tenable, the patient might be expected to maintain the same attitude in other social situations. But how this feeling of inferiority might be related to drug addiction is not sufficiently indicated in this case.

At least we learn one thing from Case 1, and that is, although the physician played a part in her addiction, the influence of her addict-friends was by far more important.

Case 2. The subject was interviewed at the home of another addict, while I was visiting the latter. She appeared with her jaw in bandage. (The interviewer was told first by her woman friend that the subject's infected jaw was due to an automobile accident, but later, on another occasion, he was told that it was due to a beating the subject received from a man with whom she had been staying.) The subject sat on the lap of her woman friend, and talked in a rather buoyant mood. Her hair was cut in the way of a boy's, and she looked boyish too. She danced around the room and appeared restless. She asked her friend to prepare a high-ball, but it was not given her. So the interviewer took the opportunity and offered to take her to a nearby club, where she could have what she wanted. While still at the home of her friend, they talked about a club they went to on the previous night, a club catering exclusively to homosexuals.

The subject is about 23 years old. She is a little above medium height, but slender and somewhat thin. While sipping her highball, she told the following story about herself. She came from New York about three years ago. Her parents are of foreign descent, her father being a physician. They have been divorced, and mother is married again. She herself was born in England and came to this country at six. When her father left her, he put her and her sister in a settlement. For over three years she has lost contact with both of them.

Five years ago she was sick with kidney trouble, and was confined to a hospital for eight months. After her discharge from the hospital, she had to lie in bed and could not walk for four more months. During this period she had so much pain that the doctors gave her morphine, and while at home her father gave her morphine and the needle and let her use the drug whenever she needed it. In this way she acquired the habit. But she constantly fought against it. She would look at the "stuff" and the needle and deliberately postpone taking it, and took it only when she could not stand the withdrawal symptoms any longer. Then she tried milder drugs in the place of morphine, such as pantopon and codeine, and finally stopped using them altogether. The interviewer asked how she did this. She replied that she was then thinking of one person very much, and decided to get rid of the habit in order to be near that person. And that person is a woman she loves. For this reason she stayed off the drug for almost a year. But last November this woman lover of hers left her suddenly. She was so upset that she began to fool around with the drug again. Later, for fear that she might contract the habit again, she resorted to liquor, and she had been drinking almost every day for the past half year.

The subject had been in a hospital for about three months for the treatment of her infected jaw. The pain still bothered her, and she wanted to drink in order to forget it. While in the hospital, she became intimate with one of the women doctors, and while the interviewer said good-bye to her she was heading toward the hospital to see the doctor.

One interview is hardly sufficient to establish confidence in a subject, but the story told by Case 2, however unreliable some part of it may be, is interesting from several points of view. In the first place, she is the product of a broken home, and, having been raised in England, probably had difficulty in adjusting herself in this country. In the second place, for reasons unknown she is homosexual in her love relationship, and her associates seem to be mainly women similarly inclined. The taking of the masculine rôle in relation to women may be interpreted as a possible compensation for her feeling of inferiority as well as an expression of aggression toward her own sex. One indication of her destructiveness to women is seen in her attempt later to betray her addict-friend to the Government in spite of many favors she had received from the latter. Beyond this we have no factual information about her personality. Nor can we prove or disprove her story of the way her addiction started. On the surface, it sounds like one of those stereotyped tales one often hears from drug addicts. But that the subject's attempt to quit the habit and her subsequent relapse were connected with her homosexual relationship is a highly interesting fact. On the basis of our knowledge of other similar cases, this part of her story is not regarded as fictitious. No matter how her addiction was started, it seems to us Case 2 may be safely regarded as one of those in which the use of drugs is closely related to one's love life.

Case 3. The subject was interviewed at one of the shelters for men on three different occasions.[1] He is a white American of German descent. He is about 35 years old and is a physician by profession. When first seen, he had been out of the Federal penitentiary for only a short time after having served time for a narcotic offense.

[1] For data on this case the writer is indebted to Mr. Alfred Lindesmith, one of his colleagues in a separate project.

He has been an addict for the last 12 years or so, and the story he told about his life is as follows.

He was married in 1918. In the following year he developed appendicitis and peritonitis. While being treated in the hospital, he was given morphine and developed a habit. But before he was discharged, the amount of morphine used was reduced and the habit was taken from him.

Around 1925 the gall-stone trouble hit him. He went to a doctor. Morphine was prescribed for him, and he was permitted to administer it to himself. The fact that he had to administer it to himself caused him considerable trepidation, because of his view of addiction and his medical knowledge of the dangers involved. He did so, however, and gradually, as the attacks became more and more frequent, he gave it to himself more and more easily. And after a while he administered it for pains of much less severe character and finally he caught himself taking a "shot" now and then when he had no pain at all. During this period of self-administration, his view of addiction underwent a marked change. He lost his horror of it, and felt that it would be easy to quit. He had to have his gall-stone operation anyway. And so he became addicted.

The period of his life from 1925 to about 1930 was the most successful of his entire career. He concentrated on his work—working 18 hours a day "like a Trojan" and doing his work well, earning the praise of his associates and the loyalty of his patients. He states positively that he knows that the use of drugs had good effects on his practice. He claims that he used only a small quantity—one grain in the morning and one at night—and that the effect was to stimulate him and make him impervious to fatigue.

During this first period of addiction there was, however, a marked change in his personality and in his social relations, brought about by his use of drugs. In the first place, he was constantly afraid that he would be found out that he was an addict, associating as he did with nurses and doctors all acquainted with the use of drugs through their training. He disguised some of the symptoms by using a couple of preparations to keep his eyes in good shape and to dilate the pupil contracted by the drug. In consequence of this fear of being discovered he kept very much to himself and lost his gaiety in company—he was preoccupied. He impressed his associates as "peculiar" and sphinx-like. He noticed one friend after another drop away. His social life, which had previously been quite gay and given to much celebration, lost all interest for him. He had to force himself to go along at all and his interest in women declined. His friends noticed that he was no longer the same and he lost his popularity. His wife noticed the difference. After he got into trouble with the police she finally divorced him.

In the twelve years that he used drugs he had tried to quit the habit at least a dozen times, but always went back to it. He never felt entirely right when he was off the drug, he said, and he is unable to explain this in any other way besides saying that it was a mental craving, inasmuch as his friends would tell him how well he looked and since he put on weight. However, eventually the constant pressure finally would overcome him in a moment of unusual depression or of illness, and he would resume his habit. He went so far as to say that a day of the type on which the interview was held, that is, a dark, dull rainy day, was often enough to cause an addict who was trying to quit to go back to it by causing him to become melancholy and depressed. During the twelve years he had been off drugs once for two years and another time for two and a half years.

The two and a half years occurred just before 1929, and the stock market crash was the occasion for his relapse. He owned two pieces of property and had a good bank account. A friend of his, prominent in business, had given him good tips on the stock market. When the crash came, he had invested all of his money on a margin and he was wiped out. His worries and nervousness became very bad and almost sufficient to spoil his practice, he said. In this situation he resumed his drug habit. The two year period of abstinence was in prison.

The subject at present is reduced to the state of a hobo, and moves between the shelter house and the cheap hotels at West Madison, where he can make "connections." When asked what he intended to do about his habit, he said he was going to try to reestablish himself again, but "of course," he added, "I've done it so many times before."

In Case 3 we have before us the picture of a professional man being reduced to the condition of a bum through the use of drugs. In this case, it seems reliable on the surface that the primary ætiological condition of his addiction was the use of morphine in medical treatment. But, as he himself stated, organic difficulty was not the sole factor, for he continued to use the drug even when he felt no pain and before the habit was formed. One is thus led to ask whether there might not be something in the personality of the subject to which the effect of morphine had such a strong appeal that to resist using it repeatedly was not possible.

Our data, however, throw little light on the personality of the subject, except that the tendency to indulge in pharmaco-erotic pleasure in spite of one's knowledge of the dangers involved may perhaps be taken as an indication of a certain amount of immaturity or infantilism. Again we are told that he often overworked himself and that he treasured the praise of his associates. These facts would seem to suggest a strong tendency on the part of the subject to compete with other men and gain their good opinion at the same time. Besides these rather meager indices of the subject's love of himself and of his aggression toward men, no other inference can be drawn from the data on hand.

Attention is here called to the very interesting account of the effects of his drug habit on his social life, which may be summarily described as self-consciousness, fear of being discovered, isolation and ostracism. It may be pointed out that all of these grow out of society's reproachful attitude toward drug addicts.

We want to point with particular emphasis to the occasion related in the story that brought about one of the subject's relapses, that is, the depression of 1929. The reaction to such a crisis is probably different with different individuals. But the subject's eagerness for praise and recognition would lead us to think that to him loss in the stock market was probably much more than the loss of money; it was the loss of his place in society. Probably it was this emotional component of his reaction to the financial crisis that made unbearable the tension or strain thereby created and forced him to seek the form of release he was most familiar with. In this case, therefore, we see clearly again the close connection between the emotional need of a person as well as the demands of culture and the use of drugs.

We have come across a number of addicts who blamed some kind of accident for their addiction. The following is a case in point.

Case 4. The patient was interviewed 7 times. He is a white American of 45 years, and is a physician by profession. The story he told about himself is as follows.

He was born and brought up on a farm and is the sixth of seven children in the family. He has been very much the baby of the family and a mother's pet. He is the only one in the family to go to colleges. He was so much a pet of his parents that when he first went to college, he became very home-sick, and later had to change college and stay with one of his elder brothers.

He remembers that one day one of his elder brothers teased him and asked him to round up the cow but it was not his turn to do so. So he threw a stone at his brother and it hit the back of the latter's head. He boasted of his ability in throwing rocks at sparrows and hitting them. That was a matter of everyday practice with him when a child.

As a child and an adolescent boy he had no sex habits, such as masturbation, although he said that when he saw a pretty girl he might experience sex desires and have bad dreams. The only form of excitement he had was riding on a sheep. One day he was thrown to the ground by a sheep and he retaliated by getting hold of its horns and strangling it on the spot. There was a priest in the Catholic church who used to talk to him about the evil effects of self-abuse ever since he was 12, saying that it was a sin and that he would become insane if he indulged in it. In his relation with girls he has always been bashful. In fact, while in high school he did not go out with any girl, while other boys had more than one girl to go with. He returned home every week-end and was brought back to school on Monday.

He said that all his elder brothers are taller and bigger than he, although to the interviewer the patient is not small, being about 5'8" in height. He also said that he is by nature reticent, and is apt to be nervous under strain.

After graduation from the medical school, he was married to a girl living next door, and he lived in her home for about 9 years. He claimed that his marital life was satisfactory, including the sexual side of it. He spoke highly of his wife, saying that she is a capable, dependable and ambitious woman, always trying to do too much. Everything had been all right till 1929. His wife had had difficulty in childbirth. In that year she developed heart trouble, sore throat, arthritis and, worst of all, an infection in the ear. And she was laid up in bed.

One day while the attending nurse was away, he acted as a nurse to his wife, and while trying to lift her—a woman of about 180 lbs. —he staggered and his right knee was caught in the bed, and it was hurt so seriously that he had to be sent to the hospital along with his wife,—the latter for ear infection. They stayed in rooms next to each other. The doctor gave him morphine to stop the pain in his knee, but by the end of the first month the use of morphine was stopped altogether. However, he asked one of the nurses to buy him pantopon, mainly because he felt it too much a strain to see his wife in delirium for about three weeks. He repeated more than once that he would not blame the physician, not even the pain in his knee, for his addiction; it was worrying about his wife and his own practice that led him to use pantopon.

Thus by the end of his stay—three months—he had developed a pantopon habit. So instead of resuming his practice, he went to a place for a cure of his pantopon habit. He did so by himself in about three weeks and after 7 weeks' stay he came home and started to work. In the first week he was all right. But in the second week, he began to feel insecure, and was afraid to go out to call on his patients in the night-time. Then he began to try morphine, beginning with $\frac{1}{8}$ of a grain. Morphine gave him a feeling of security; it braced him up. After a few doses the "kick" came. Whenever he had a "shot" of morphine, his feeling of tiredness was gone, and he had "a grip of himself." Then he could think and work. It was an indescribable feeling, he said. The second cure was attempted soon after in a private sanitarium, and at a heavy cost. After six weeks' rest he began to work. But on the third day he went back to the drug, as the same old feeling of insecurity came back and he could hardly meet the situation without the help of the drug. The same process was repeated three more times before he came to the present hospital.

He likes this cure much better. He thinks the medicine does help, but the environment helps more, and by "environment" he means being away from home and the absence of the necessity of putting up a front, whereas at home he had to act to his folks and to his patients in the community as if there were nothing wrong with him. At present he has no craving for the drug, but he cannot be sure that he will not have the craving again when he begins to work.

In perusing the story of Case 4, one cannot help being struck by one personality trait of the patient that can be detected in practically all of his reactions to life-situations before or after his addiction, and that is, to use the patient's own words, the feeling of insecurity. Before his drug habit was established, one sees this trait in his being a mother's pet, enjoying the privileged position in the family, getting homesick, referring to his brothers as being all taller and bigger, and speaking of his schoolmates as having more capacity for mixing with girls. Along with this we notice his strong destructive tendency as manifested in his joy in throwing stones at birds and in hitting his brother for a reason we would consider as trivial. Probably his destructive tendency is a natural sequence to his feeling of insecurity or inferiority in comparison with other people. Then after addiction, the facts on this point are so clear that no elaboration is needed. It seems every one of his relapses was caused by his feeling of inadequacy in facing life-situations, in fulfilling the demands made on him as a physician and as a husband. In fact, we are told explicitly by the patient himself that while the accident he mentioned and the physical pain resulting from it were apparently the starting point of his career as an addict, the really important ætiological factor was his excessive worrying about his wife's illness and his own medical practice. This is not the place, nor do the facts on hand permit us, to go into the psychology of excessive worrying over one's relative, but that his habitual feeling of insecurity had something to do with this extreme anxiety seems more than probable. In this case, therefore, we once more see the very close relation between one's drug habit and one's attitude toward people and other life-situations.

The following is another case in which injury caused by an accident was apparently the principal ætiological factor in his addiction. Let us see what can be found on closer examination.

Case 5. The subject was interviewed at one of the shelter houses for men on five different occasions, first by the writer from April 4–18, 1934, and later by one of his assistants in July, 1935. When first seen, the subject was just out of the Federal penitentiary, and was referred to the Service Bureau for Men by the Probation Office. He is 5' 10" tall and has quite a pleasant and apparently self-sufficient appearance. He was coöperative from the start and told the story of his life as follows.

He was born 44 years ago in a small town in the South, and is the "David of the family." One elder brother died young, and two sisters are living. But contact with his folks has long been lost. Both of his parents were of Irish descent, and his father was something of a politician in his native town. He usually was strict with him and whipped him quite frequently, while his mother was more lenient. He used to like his "dad" a great deal, for he usually took him along wherever he went. Thus in a saloon his father would sit him on a table and give him a big glass of beer. But he was disillusioned about his father later on, particularly in connection with an incident that occurred when he was 12. He and the boys in the neighborhood picked up a piece of iron near the railroad track, which happened to be a torn piece of a cogwheel belonging to a mill. They sold it for a few pennies to buy candy. The mill-owner complained to his father, saying that he had stolen the iron, and his father gave him a severe scolding. Besides, he put him to work with the chain-gang—prisoners—for an entire afternoon, threatening to make him a real prisoner if he attempted escape. He was really scared, but he was not convinced that he actually had done wrong, as he did not steal the iron. They picked it up, not knowing to whom it belonged. He used to think that his father was kind, perfect in every way. But now knowing that his father was not right, he changed his attitude toward him. His mother had an argument with his father about the incident, and the subject was convinced that she was right.

At the age of 13 he ran away from home for the first time. He was not punished, however, for he was sent home by his elder brother. Later he ran away again to his rich uncle's home. This time he was given a severe whipping by his father, for to visit his rich uncle as a runaway was considered by his parents as a sign of ill bringing-up.

He went as far as the second year in high school. His school life on the whole was pleasant except for his relation with an old woman teacher. She had taught his elder brother before him, and whenever he made some mistake she would hold him in ridicule and compare him most unfavorably with his elder brother. But he said this teacher had a bad temperament, and people did not take her seriously.

He used to drink excessively, going on a spree on the average of twice a month. He also learned to smoke as early as he could hold a cigarette. In order to stop him from smoking, the family doctor used to smash the cigarette against his mouth in order to hurt it. His father and aunt both scolded him for smoking, but nothing stopped him.

His ambition as a child was to go into the show business. At 16 he sang for the first time in a theatre, and ever since then he has been "on the road," in the circus and amusement business.

Thus far we learn that Case 5 was something of a problem boy in the family, as shown by the fact that his parents, especially his father, had difficulty in disciplining him. Undoubtedly his life in the home and in the school was made uncomfortable by a strict father and a superior elder brother. His running away from home and later from school may be considered as an escape from such painful situations. On the other hand, his waywardness in learning to smoke and to drink at a tender age points definitely to a strong tendency to emulate the big, strong men he saw around him. Now let us listen to the story of his addiction.

It was while he was in the circus business and was playing the Roman ring in 1909—when he was 19—that he fell and his spine was seriously hurt. The doctor gave him a sedative, the nature of which he did not know then. But when he complained about the pain again, a fellow concessioner in the circus ground, who was a drug-user, told him that what the doctor gave him was morphine, and that he could give him the same "stuff" for a smaller price. So he accepted the offer, and ever since then he continued to receive "shots" from this man whenever he felt the pain, until about four months after the accident he discovered to his surprise that he could not go without the drug. He believes that if he had not met the man in the circus and if he did not know what the doctor gave him, things might have been different.

In short, the above is the story of his addiction we secured as a result of the first few interviews. But in the course of our acquaintance, he volunteered the following additional information concerning his contact with drugs before the period related above, in the form of a short auto-biography.

The first knowledge of drugs was revealed to me as a boy of about fifteen years of age, when I was employed in a drug store in my home town. The former owner's son, being at the head of the pharmaceutical department, was addicted to crude gum opium, which at that time was stored in an open drawer to which all had access. I used to quite frequently see this man go to the drawer, take his knife and cut off a hunk which he would put in his mouth just like a tobacco-chewer does his tobacco. I know I was somewhat curious at my first notice of this and made mention of it at home where I was instructed to refrain from further reference to the matter. Another man, a dentist, I observed often in the store purchasing white pills which I later discovered to be codein. . . . As I view these events in retrospect, I am confident there was very little more than childish curiosity aroused by them.

Two or perhaps three years later, I slipped from Washington, D. C., to Philadelphia to work for the Rapid Transit Company there. Upon arrival, however, I found a strike to be in progress and consequently did not go to work. A few weeks later I procured employment as clerk and houseman in a hotel near 9th and Race Streets in the heart of Philadelphia's Chinatown. Here were people who were foreign to me, although in a short time I became attuned to their mode of existence, and I was liked by most of those with whom I came in contact. In this hotel were a number of women opium smokers who had their lay-outs in their rooms and quite often I would handle a pipe or push the lamp about with never any thought of what it was all about. Here were to be found "Chinatown Whitie," "Butch Turner," "Two Bits," "Peanuts," "Blonde May," "Chinatown Mae," the "Girl in Blue," and Ann Nolan, all of them notorious and known to half the men in the U. S. Navy and Marine Corps—all of them users of opium or its derivatives. Here one could smoke for twenty-five cents. Morphine, heroin, and cocaine could be had for fifty and sixty cents per dram. Never once had I any desire to try any of them, but I was often intoxicated with absinthe and whiskey. While thus intoxicated one night, "Big

Mayme," a smoker, took me to her room where later I was aroused by a smothering sensation brought on by the fumes of opium, and I recall I was ill for sometime after with nausea and vomiting. I had no desire to ever repeat my experience of that night, but I believe that a "subconscious idea," to be later developed, had its inception here; namely, the thought of the impossibility of an addict to ever loose the tentacles of the habit. During the whole time I was connected with this place, I can recall no instance of ever being solicited to try any drug. It is thought, generally, that an addict takes delight in winning converts to the poppy god when to my knowledge such is erroneous. Never have I known an addict who wasn't positive and firm in denouncing the direful effects of drugs to a neophyte. To my mind, plain curiosity and the power of suggestion has been the cause of the great increase in drug addiction, especially in this country. Moreover, thought born of hopelessness and incurability of the habit is one great contributing factor in the influence of these unfortunates that it is futile to attempt to quit. This digression is pardonable as I merely wish to show the state of my mind regarding the possibility of effecting a cure after using the drug for over twenty years.

In accounting for the initial addiction of Case 5, therefore, the environment of his adolescent period as described above must be taken into consideration. While most part of the story just told might be true, judging from his tendency to emulate people superior to him, the statement about his being an abstainer in the midst of well-known opium smokers is open to doubt. As a matter of fact, our suspicion is not without factual support, as evidenced by the following record of the subject's statement in an interview a year later conducted by one of the writer's research assistants: "I began to smoke the pipe when I was about twenty-one. I did not like the habit, but I have done it to be a good fellow. I learned the habit from seeing the best dressed men in town use the drug, and I was determined to try it. I did, and I was hooked. As I did not like the stuff long, I quit it of my own accord. When I was hurt back in 1911, I was getting the stuff in the hospital. I do not say that the doctor gave me the *yen*. I used the stuff of my own free will and like." Here probably we have found the right clue to the way the subject first came to be addicted to opium in spite of the fact that the details of this later statement do not correspond to those of the earlier one, but it is more in line with his tendency to emulate and to compete with the smart people around him. Since in the environment which he described opium smoking was considered as smart, it would be most natural for him to follow suit. Having had some idea of the cultural and personality factors in our subject's initial addiction to drugs, let us next briefly follow his subsequent career as an addict.

When he was 21, he was married to a woman five years his senior, who was a divorcee at the same time. The subject said that it was essentially a business marriage, as the woman was the daughter of a man in the circus with whom he was working. But he claimed that in the course of time they grew to be fond of each other. His wife did not know that he used drugs. One day, while his wife was feeding chickens outside the house, he gave himself a "shot" of morphine in one of the rooms and on finishing the process forgot to wrap up his drug and the needle and to hide them. While he was gone, his wife came in and discovered them. She screamed, for she knew what it meant. He rushed in and tried to explain, but his wife would not let him. She demanded that he had to choose between the two: her or "dope." So he attempted a self-cure, but could endure only for two days. Then he left his wife for good, together with the house and everything he had. Her people later tried to get him back, but he refused to, and never saw her again except once by chance.

He was married again when he was 27. This was more of a romantic marriage. His wife is four years younger, and from the very beginning she knew that he had the drug habit. But soon after marriage he was persuaded to get a cure. He was under the treatment of a private doctor. One day while his wife went out to order a dinner for him, a woman addict in the building came in and offered to give him a "shot" if he wanted it. The temptation was too great, and he gave in. His wife found it out when she was back, and declared that since her husband had no desire to quit the habit she would like to have a "shot" too in order to share the habit with him, otherwise there would always be a gap between her and her husband. In that way his wife too became an addict. But one time he used so much cocaine that he developed hallucinations and accused his wife of infidelity and many other things. She was scared and left him for about three months. Later she came back, but her leaving him in that fashion hurt his pride, and he could never forget it. His means became exhausted, and in order to get his wife the things she used to have and to assure the supply of drug he resorted to stealing, and on account of it he was incarcerated in a reformatory. While there, his wife divorced him. He said he could not blame her for what she did, but he felt hurt and lost every incentive to live. This took place in 1922, when he was thirty-three years old.

Speaking of his sex life, the subject related that when he was 14 his father gave him a talk on the harm of masturbation, pointing out to him men of poor health, warning him that if he masturbated he would become like them. The family physician once talked to him in the same way. Probably it was to prevent him from forming the habit of self-abuse that his parents implicitly condoned his sex relation with a mulatto girl working in the house, which relation he began as early as 13. He claimed that he always enjoyed sex relations with women, but in one of the interviews held with him one year later, he was reported to have said that he could not stick to one woman long, and made the statement: "I get along without them. They are all right for a man, but not for a man like me." When his sex powers were affected by the drug, he indulged in orgiastic appreciation of women without physical relations.

Some of his experiences of the effect of cocaine are interesting. One time he had been on a cocaine spree, having used it for about five days continuously. He had sat in one position for so many days that he developed all kinds of hallucinations. He pulled down the shades, stuffed the window openings, for fear that the police might peep in and discover what he was doing. He heard voices and saw figures. His wife was complaining and said that he should cut off this cocaine habit. Suddenly he got out of bed and looked at himself lying in bed. He was active, while his double in bed was motionless, as if he were dead. He lifted his double up and took him over to the window, opened it, and threw his double out of the window. He saw him fall on the ground and get up and run away. Ever since that time cocaine has not produced in him the same effect as it did before. He added that cocaine never affected his wife in the same manner as it did him. Another time, he ran out to the street while under the influence of cocaine. He was in B.V.D., but his friends—peddlers—brought him back. When he was alone in the room, he saw five or six figures, emaciated, almost lifeless, sitting close to the door, explaining to him the evil effects of cocaine.

His criminal records show that he had been in the County Jail and House of Correction a number of times for disorderly conduct, vagrancy, shop-lifting, and petty larceny besides a term of two years in Kentucky for grand larceny and another of one year in the Federal penitentiary for peddling drugs. For the past two or three weeks since he came out of the penitentiary, he claimed that he had successfully refused the temptation to go back to drugs, although almost as soon as he came out of the prison, people in Kansas City and in Chicago had offered him drugs and asked him to do business —peddling—for them. In all these weeks, he confessed he had received only one "shot" of $\frac{1}{2}$ grain of morphine, but did not feel the satisfaction as he thought he would. But in an interview one year later, he called this first experience of drug after a long period of abstinence the "honey-moon of the stuff," and compared the pleasure he got out of it to that of a sex act after a long period of continence.

One of the most difficult problems of adjustment after his release from the penitentiary seemed to be that of finding a job. He said that he had been looking all over town for a job, but was turned down everywhere because he did not have good references and one time because he gave the shelter house as his address. That he seemed earnest but helpless in finding a job may be seen in a letter he wrote to the probation officer, in which he begged the latter to help, saying in part, "I am completely out of funds and I beg to impress you with my need of work. Please, Respected Sir, do give this plea some consideration, and bear in mind I am not particular. I am willing and anxious to accept anything that will help me fulfil the requirements of my parole and it will greatly lessen the obstacles that daily confront me regarding my former addiction."

A short while after the last interview in April, 1934, the subject left the shelter house, and the interviews were discontinued. After a few weeks the subject called back and asked the interviewer to see him at the Salvation Army Hospital. Before he was interviewed again he left the hospital. It seems evident that he had gone back to the habit. He was seen recently again in one of the shelter houses, and claimed that he was not using drugs. He sent words to the writer, saying, "I will keep my head above water; I am through for good."

What seems most significant about the life of Case 5 after he had formed the drug habit is his unhappy married life. And according to the way he expressed it, what bothers him most is the fact that his pride was wounded, that he should have been rejected by women. Although he repeatedly declared that he could not blame his wives for deserting him, his anger and his feeling of insecurity resulting from these rejections are rather evident. In following his tale of woe, one cannot help inferring that the fault was really his own; his marriage to an older woman for the sake of his own expediency and his unusual emphasis on his own pride all tend to show that his relation with his wives was far from being one of love and of taking responsibilities, but rather one of continuing his favorite rôle of the "David of the family." In fact, the accident of his forgetting to hide his drug and the hypodermic needle that led to the divorce with his first wife and the cocaine spree with its horrifying hallucinations that led to the divorce with his second wife

impress one as deliberate attempts to shun the rôle of a responsible husband.   But emotionally he is dependent on other people's
love; the desertion by his second wife, according to his story, has taken
every incentive to live out of his life and made him resign to his present
mode of existence.   His apparent independence of women and his low
opinion of them, saying that they are no good for a man-like individual
like himself, only reminds one of the story of the sour grapes.   These
observations seem to point to a close relation between the subject's continuing to be an addict after his drug habit was established and his repeated failures in marital adjustment, which failures we found to be
mainly due to his own faulty emotional attitudes.

While the above analysis of Case 5 is by no means complete for lack
of sufficient data, enough probably has been said to show the various
ways in which the drug habit in this case is inseparably related to his
social and cultural *milieu* and to his own emotional tendencies.

Case 6.   Patient is a woman of 34.   Interviews were held first
at the Psychopathic Hospital and later elsewhere in the city on four
different occasions from January to June, 1935.   In the first interview, the nurse had difficulty in getting the patient to come to the
consultation room.   But when the interviewer went to bring her,
she showed no resistance.   Her attitude toward the interviewer from
that time on has been friendly.   In the first interview, patient was
noticed moving her feet constantly from one direction to the other.
She admitted that she has always been nervous.   In the second
interview, while the interviewer was starting to leave, patient asked
for another cigarette and kept on talking, and said she did not know
why she asked for another cigarette.   In the third interview outside
the hospital, patient complained of heart palpitation, and held the
interviewer's hand to her bosom to test it.   On parting, she threw
the interviewer a kiss.   For several times patient expressed her
regret that she could not entertain the interviewer in her room in
the hotel, but hoped that some arrangement could be made whereby
she might have more privacy for interview.   The patient also wrote
to the interviewer several times while she was away from the city.

While recuperating at her home, she dreamed that the interviewer
came to visit her and took her along with him to the Orient.   Another time she dreamed of being in a restaurant and served with the
meat of a rattle-snake.   In association with "a rattle-snake," she recalled that she saw in a movie the other day a small Chinese boy
being frightened by a rattle-snake.   She asked the interviewer if
he knew what her reaction to that scene in the movie was.   To his
question whether she wanted to save the boy, she answered, "Yes."

Patient was born of German parentage, and brought up in a small town. Her parents are Catholic. She is the youngest of four children in the family, the other three being boys. She came to the family as a surprise, for when she was born her mother was past menopause. She remembered that her mother one time teased her by saying that she did not want a girl. Although it was a joke on her mother's part, it meant something to her. Later, however, when she and her mother were living by themselves after the death of her father, her mother said that she then knew why she had a girl. She has had one year of college education and some training in commercial art.

Her girlhood recalls in her mind only pleasant memories, she said. She had a car of her own, and was free to invite her friends to her home. But her relation with boys was very carefully watched. She and her father were "pals." She used to go fishing and playing with him. Her father's death, however, did not create any great crisis in her, for she realized that it is natural for an old man to die. Her mother was more strict with her.

When she was 21, she was married to a man ten years her senior against her will, while in her own heart she loved another man. Her mother persuaded her to marry the former because of his wealth, and objected to her marrying the latter because he was a non-Catholic. Her husband is 6 feet tall and has a heavy build. She had had no sex experience before marriage, and did not enjoy sexual intercourse with her husband until six months after marriage. But her husband is a regular drinker, and when drunk he would abuse her. This was started almost from the very beginning of their married life. She said that while her husband might not know what he was doing while he was drunk, she could not get over the humiliation of being beaten, especially when she had a six months old baby in her. So after one year's stay with her husband, she left him for good. Once she tried to go back to him, but was very unhappy. She thought of getting a divorce, but the Catholic religion forbids it, and her husband would not allow it. She concluded this part of her narrative by saying that the sex issue did not bother her much; what worried her most was how to get rid of her drug habit.

Her first contact with morphine was in connection with her difficulty in menstruation when she was 17. Her menses did not come until she was 16. As nobody had told her anything about it, when her menses first came she was very much shocked. But no drug habit was formed then.

About 8 years ago she had an automobile accident, and she was then staying with a girl, who had been the superintendent of nurses in a hospital. This girl gave her "shots" of morphine, which she did not know to be morphine at that time. For one week she con-

tinued to receive "shots" from her roommate. Then she had to
go to another city for a week end, and when leaving she was advised
by the girl to take some medicine along. She did not understand
why she should. So she went without it. But while away she
grew sick, and had to wire her friend to meet her at a certain railway
station. So she came back to Chicago. From that time on she
was "hooked." Almost immediately she went for a cure and thus
far has had half a dozen cures. But she stressed the fact that in
the past cures she was never sincere; for every time she went to a
hospital she brought with her enough drug to last for sometime.
For then she was not willing to get cured; she was compelled to go
either by relatives or friends. But this time, she said, she was
determined to quit the habit. Before she came to the hospital, she
said she had spent a week in a hotel, trying to decide whether to end
it all or to go to a hospital and get herself cured. Finally she decided to try once again. So she came.

While she was using the drug she took regularly 7 capsules a
day, costing her $5.00. She said that there is something fascinating
about the hypodermic needle, particularly in seeing one's own
blood. She explained that fascination by the hypothesis of a sadis-
tic tendency in her without any suggestion from the interviewer.
She observed that there is not a single addict who does not delight
in seeing his or her own blood. She usually took 3 "shots" a day;
one in the morning when getting up, one around 6 o'clock in the
afternoon, and one before going to bed. The soothing effect of
morphine on her assumed the appearance of a straight line, each
"shot" lasting for about 12 hours. Then the effect wears off, and
the withdrawal symptoms set in. But she would not wait that long
to take the next "shot." So while using the drug she felt contented
all the time.

She recalled her last relapse. For half a year she had been in a
private sanitarium. After she came out she stayed off the drug
for another half year. But some of her girl friends were heroin
users. One time she got drunk, and while she was in that state
she let one of her friends give her a "shot" of heroin. She felt
ashamed, for she said she ought to have had more sense. And that
one "shot," although it made her very sick at that time, was enough
to bring her back to the drug. Remembering this bitter experience,
she thinks now that the best policy for her after leaving the hospital
is to go away from Chicago for at least three years in order to avoid
her old associates.

After her discharge from the hospital she was taken home to her
folks. From her letters to the interviewer, some information is
gathered concerning her state of feeling during the period of recupera-
tion. In one of her letters she said that she thought this time a

complete cure had been effected and appeared rather optimistic. Sometime later she wrote, "Have had a few spells of being melancholic and wishing for deliverance, but they only last for a few hours, and I came out of them and try to interest myself in this rather quiet existence that my family have here. . . . However, I have been having funny dreams, mostly about being out dining and dancing, and I dreamed about you. . . . Have not found that lost incentive for anything constructive as yet." In her third letter later on she informed the interviewer that she was coming back to Chicago. This was only a month since she made up her mind to stay away from Chicago for three years.

While still in the hospital, the patient thought that her major problem in the future was to find a kind of job that would give her real contentment. Later she did find a job that she liked, painting in a summer resort. But when she was seen in April, she reported that she had just quit the job, because she could not stand the boss. He is a young fellow, who seemed to have "picked on" her. One time he attempted to kiss her eyes. He ridiculed her language and her pronunciation. He walked to and fro and came to her place every once a while and asked her all kinds of questions as to what he should do with this or that. Such actions and unkind remarks irritated her. A week before she left him, she went to a city nearby with one of her girl friends and drank. Then she had a quarrel with him and came back to Chicago. Maybe, she said, it was her own fault, because she was nervous and not big enough to stand such a situation. Maybe after a week's rest she would be going back to her work, because the man wanted her to go back, and it would be difficult for him to secure a helper to finish the work in time. She admitted that the man has fine qualities, in spite of his irritating behavior.

When she was seen again in June, she reported that she had not been doing anything. She could not concentrate. She had been drinking constantly, spending $3.00 every day on liquor. Spells of melancholia continued to come from one to two times a week. In one of these melancholic states, she tried to end her life by cutting open the veins on one of her wrists. She felt bad, because she had done too much harm to her family, particularly her mother. She wanted to quit drinking, but did not know how. She realized that her difficulty was mainly mental, as physically she felt perfectly all right, but she did not know why.

Her associates in Chicago are mainly girls, most of whom are commercial artists. She does not like boys, because they generally do not behave. They push her around too much, and she does not like to be pushed around. She mentioned one boy, with whom she had been going for some years. He does not drink and is gentle.

But lately she learned that he has a fiancée; so she has ceased going out with him. She admitted that she had sexual urge at times, but had no way of satisfying it. She denied homosexual practices, and denied masturbation, thinking that it was bad.

The patient asked the interviewer many times whether she had a chance. She argued herself into believing that she had a chance, for in former cures she often dreamed of preparing for a "shot" and woke up just as she was going to give herself one, whereas now she did not dream of that any more. Patient was anxious to have the interviewer call again, but for lack of time interviews with this patient were discontinued.

In Case 6 again we see clearly that while the physical pain resulting from the automobile accident might have been a factor in her addiction, the importance of her associates—most of them are either regular drinkers or drug users—both as an ætiological condition and as a factor in her relapses after cures is much more pronounced.

Further, we found that by the time the patient came in contact with her associates in Chicago she had been separated from her husband for about five years, and that emotionally she was then a very unhappy woman. This unhappy, discontented and restless state of mind, which evidently remains practically unchanged up to the present moment, must be considered, therefore, as an equally important factor in her initial addiction as well as her subsequent relapses.

It is also interesting to note that in this case the purely organic factor, so far as our data go, seems practically nil. Never once in the interviews or letters to the interviewer mentioned above did the patient complain about any organic disturbance, except insomnia, which, in the absence of any serious physical impairment, may safely be regarded as emotional in origin.

Our patient's problems, therefore, resolve themselves into matters of emotional adjustment. We are told by the patient that her unhappy marital life was almost entirely due to her husband's drinking and brutality. It is not safe in a scientific investigation of social interaction between two individuals to accept one party's statement as the whole truth. We must, therefore, inquire into the patient's attitude toward people, men and women, and form our opinion, if possible, as to her part in the breaking up of her home.

We learned from the patient's story that she does not ordinarily enjoy men's company. She likes only those who are gentle and behave, such as, for example, her father, the interviewer, judging from her attitude to him and her dreams about him, and the teetotaler man who occasionally took her out. But as soon as a man gets familiar with her and thereby arouses her passion, she becomes disgusted with him, such as the young boss with whom she worked. These evidences seem to suggest that her relationship with men is most satisfactory when it is divorced of sex. She seems to have the attitude of receiving love from men without giving anything in return. In the current psychological jargon, our patient may be said to have had strong inhibition in her sexual relation with men, and since she enjoys only men of the father-type, her attitude toward heterosexual adjustment may be considered as immature and infantile.

From women the patient evidently has derived more emotional satisfaction, as shown by the fact that she has been associating almost exclusively with her girl friends during the past eight or nine years in the city. In that sense, our patient may be classified as a homosexual, if not in overt sexual act, at least in her affectional inclination. It is interesting to note in this connection that the girl who gave her the first "shot" of morphine, according to our interview records, is one whom she admired. As to the origin of this affectional preference, we do not have sufficient data on the basis of which to form a definite opinion. But if the attitudes formed in one's formative years in the course of one's association with adults are considered important in determining one's attitudes later in life, the patient's feeling of being unwanted by her mother when a child is probably a major factor that inclines her to expect affection more from the surrogates of her mother, that is, her girl friends, than from men.

Some of the verbal communications of the patient show startling flashes of insight into her own state of mind and encourage us to go a little further. Thus, in one interview she stated that there is something fascinating about the hypodermic needle, and that the sight of her own blood delights her. To explain this experience, she supposed that there must have been a destructive tendency in her. In another connection, she reported that she felt that by indulging in the use of drugs she had done too much harm to her mother, and that her sense of guilt was so unbearable that she once actually went to the extent of committing suicide. These communications lead one to infer that if the patient felt that by using drugs she was doing harm to her mother and yet compulsively continued to do so after half a dozen "cures," she must have had some emotional reason for the act besides the disarming influence of her women associates. Recalling that she felt unwanted by her mother when a child and that her mother has always been strict with her and went so far as to dictate her marriage, it is not improbable that a strong hatred toward her mother might have been engendered in that family situation. Granting this, her emotional need for hurting her mother becomes understandable. But to hurt her mother is in conflict not only with the cultural standards with which she has been brought up, but with the other side of her which is emotionally attached to her mother. The result is a deep sense of guilt. It is probably this guilty feeling that plunged her every once in a while into a state of melancholia, as she called it; that, among other factors, compelled her to continue her drug habit as a form of self-punishment; and that actually led her more than once to think of total self-destruction.

From what is said, it seems probable that the patient's homosexual inclination and her highly inhibited attitude toward men must have had their share in her unhappy married life. What is more, as long as the patient remains the victim of the emotional conflicts described above, the chance of her getting happier and more contented than she has been and of quitting the drug habit with all the psychological significance she has apparently attached to it, seems very slight indeed.

In concluding this section on the cases of addicts whose addiction was apparently due to the use of drug in medical treatment either for some organic disease or pain resulting from accidents, it is interesting to observe that in practically every one of those cases we interviewed we found upon closer examination other factors both in their social and cultural environment and in their personality make-up that must be at the same time taken into due consideration. In particular, it may be reiterated that while the physician might in some cases get one habituated to a drug, in practically all of the cases cited thus far, with the exception of cases 3 and 4 and possibly 2, it was through the association with drug users that they learned the properties of the drug they had been given and were initiated into the rôle of a drug addict. The influence of other addicts is also found to be the most common factor leading to relapse after a cure.

Further, in most of the cases thus far reviewed, we found evidences of failure in marital adjustment or inadequacy in their personality make-up, described above as the feeling of inferiority or insecurity, or homosexuality, which states of emotional instability or insecurity seemed to be in these cases irrevocably related to both their initial addiction to drugs and their subsequent relapses after cures.

In other words, in studying the drug habit of these cases, we were led by the facts we gathered to inquire into their whole personality make-up, and into not only the social and cultural environment which was immediately connected with their addiction but that which was. responsible for the formation of their personality traits.[1]

1 The above findings are equally true of some other supposedly medical cases which we have interviewed, but which are not included in the text for lack of space. Thus a woman of 23, interviewed at the Psychopathic Hospital, related that to relieve pain from vaginal infection from an abortion she accepted the suggestion from a friend to smoke opium. She eloped with a man at 14, and has had 5 children by 23. She has been separated from her husband, because he is a regular drinker, but cannot get a divorce on account of her Catholic religion. The cultural and personality factors involved in her addiction are implicit.

Another addict, interviewed at one of the shelter houses, said that his addiction was due to a railroad accident. Upon close examination, it was found that it was from the fellows in one of the pool rooms in the Near West Side of Chicago that he learned all about the drug he had been given in the hospital and received the "shot" of morphine that started him on the road to be a regular addict. Before that he had been a problem boy to her mother and had been in one "racket" after another. The social and psychological factors in this case are also evident.

CHAPTER VI

SOCIAL SITUATIONS AND PERSONALITY FACTORS RELATED TO OPIUM ADDICTION (*Continued*)

II. Cases Whose Addiction Was Primarily Due to the Influence of Drug Addicts and Peddlers

IN the following we shall present a number of the cases we have interviewed whose addiction was admittedly due to the influence of other drug addicts or peddlers. Here again, although for the convenience of presentation the cases are classified according to the ætiological accounts given by the addicts, attention is called to the environmental and personality factors that lie behind these verbal accounts and that may be considered as really responsible for the formation and continuance of their drug habit.

1. *Through going to pleasure parties.* One of the most common social situations in which addicts first come in contact with narcotic drugs is what they call pleasure parties, that is, parties in which two or three or more people smoke opium or use other drugs, especially cocaine, together without restraint. In such parties, men and women usually mingle with the maximum of freedom; and, as their moral inhibitions are made dull by the anæsthetic effect of opium, sex orgies are not seldom indulged in. Those who have gone to such parties are usually impressed by the general liberating atmosphere in which the usual distinctions of sex, race or social position are not emphasized, and in which men and women, generally clothed in pyjamas and reclining on mattresses, leisurely smoke away their secret fears and anxieties. It is not without reason that they are called pleasure parties. The following are some of the cases we have come across who started their drug habit through going to such parties.

    Case 7. Patient was interviewed once at the Psychopathic Hos-pital. He is a white American of 29, being a native of Chicago and raised around the neighborhood of 22nd Street and Wabash Ave.
    The record of the Social Service Department of the hospital—as a rule, however, information is not required of the drug patient

who applies voluntarily for treatment—shows that the patient was educated in a Catholic school till 14; that patient's father died when he was three; and that patient was married five years ago, but is separated from his wife at present. He was brought to the hospital by his stepfather, for as he was restless at home and cried constantly, they were afraid that he might commit suicide.

In the interview with us, patient related that he started his drug habit about ten years ago, when he was 19, by going to pleasure parties, made up of both men and women. They generally smoked the pipe first and then had sexual relations. He went to such parties about once a week and smoked the pipe off and on for about two years without actually forming a habit. But when the habit was formed, he lost interest in women. One night, while he was waiting to be admitted into the party upstairs in a building, a man showed him a hypodermic needle and taught him how to use it, and explained to him that the drug used in this fashion is more effective than smoking. Since then he began to use morphine.

He has tried three times in the last ten years to quit the habit, but he went back on the drug soon after each cure, and he blamed the "environment" for his relapses. For he used to "hang around" the gambling "joints," and one of his last jobs was to play the "shill," which, according to him, is an employed gambler, who gambles with the company's money in order to attract a crowd. Patient was discharged before he was seen again.

Although our information about this case is rather meager, it is included here to show how opium addicts may be recruited from the neighborhood we described as sub-community 75 in a foregoing chapter, noted in those days for its "Levee,"[1] and how by going to what the patient called pleasure parties, where opium-smoking is used primarily to enhance sex pleasure, one may gradually become addicted to the drug. It must also be noted that the same environment that led to this patient's initial addiction later occasioned his relapses. As to the possible predisposing factors in his personality, our information about this case is too limited to provide us a basis for inference.

Case 8. Patient was interviewed two times at the Psychopathic Hospital. She is 26 years old, 5'3" tall and normally weighs 117 lbs. When first seen, patient looked depressed and reticent, but after the interviewer's brief explanation about the scientific purpose

[1] M. S. Mayer, "Corrupt and Discontented?" Social Graphic, October, 1934, pp. 478 ff.

of the interview she coöperated readily. But she remained in her depressed mood and spoke in a quiet and subdued tone.

Patient began her story by relating that her morphine habit started only seven months ago. It was during the last week of the World's Fair in 1933 that one night she went to a club and later to the Fair, and then she had the first contact with morphine. She added with no suggestion from the interviewer that she was then in a very "blue" state of mind; she felt she would not care for anything. If she were not in that state of mind, she said, she possibly would not have degraded herself in this fashion. She was given a "shot" of morphine and for three months she continued to use it hypodermically. Then a friend of hers, a nurse, taught her to use the drug intravenously. Her daily dosage increased to six capsules—two or more grains a capsule—, costing her $6.00 a day.

On the interviewer's questioning why she was "blue" on that night in which she began the habit, she at first hesitated to tell, but gave the following account after some persuasion. She said she was brought up in a family in which the mother was an angel while the father a devil. Her father was well educated and successful as a contractor. He was handsome and attractive. When her mother met him she had been engaged to another man but she broke the engagement and married the father. Things had been all right till the last ten years, during which time her father became a periodic drinker. At least three or four times a year he would go on a spree lasting five or six weeks each. But he kept on working and was killed in an accident six years ago. He fell when showing people some building under construction. When he got drunk he was like a devil and mistreated everybody. Because of this intolerable situation at home, patient consented to marry a man she met only once and left home at 15. Her elder sister left home when she was only 14. The rest of her sisters and brothers all left home early.

She did not love her husband who is 11 years her senior. And she did not enjoy sexual intercourse with him, not only because she was a very young girl when married and suffered pain from physical contact with him, but because she never did care for him. She consented to marry him because of the intolerable situation at home. So she left her husband after having lived with him for two years.

Some years ago she met an artist, who was about 40 and who still cares for her. About three years ago she met another man, who is also 11 years older than she, but who looks young and handsome. He does not smoke or drink. But women are his weakness. She has been in love with him and they are engaged to be married. But more than once she has caught him with other women and he would try to explain things away. That made her furious. But she had too much pride to express her agony. Besides, he is so fascinating that whenever he talks to her for a few minutes she would forget everything. He said he loved her and whenever she did not show up he would look for her. It was in this state of mind that she accepted a "shot" of morphine from her friends at a party, for she said she simply did not care and wanted to forget things. Whenever she took a "shot" she felt all right and got over her blues. One time she ran into her lover after she had taken a "shot" and she passed him by with peace of mind.

Patient repeated in the next interview how handsome her lover is, saying that he is a regular Romeo, that he is always well-dressed, and the way he says things often reminded her of her father. She liked her father; he was a very handsome man, generous and friendly with people. She supposed that he could not help doing the things he did.

She does not like women friends; they do not stick to each other as men do. Except her mother, whom patient said she loves dearly, she has not had a real woman friend. She prefers one man to one hundred women friends.

She stressed the fact that she is that type of woman who cannot go out with many men; she can go with only one man at a time. Her fiancé's attention to other women broke her heart. But now she felt better, because her lover has found out about her condition and is repentant, and is going to take her away for a rest as soon as she leaves the hospital. So she felt fine and was optimistic. She said emphatically that she would not touch drugs again, and that if she should ever be depressed again as before, she would rather kill herself than to resort to drugs.

Patient is of Irish descent and has been educated in Catholic schools. She said that she had not been very religious. And as her husband is a non-Catholic she has automatically dropped out of the church. Her hair used to be black but she dyed it blonde.

In Case 8 we have the rare opportunity of seeing something of the actual process in which the external social situation and the subjective state of mind or feeling worked together to start the patient on the road to being a full-fledged drug addict—the external situation confronting her with the definite suggestion to take a "shot" of morphine and to forget, and the subjective feeling urging her to accept the suggestion without, or in spite of, thoughts of its consequences. In fact, judging from the way the patient reacted to her lover's unfaithfulness and her laying the blame for her habit entirely on the man, one can hardly resist the inference that in this case the use of drugs is not just an effort to forget; it impresses one as if it were a deliberate attempt to punish her lover for his misconduct and to say to him, "See what you have done to me!" As a matter of fact, such feelings were quite explicitly expressed by the patient. Such being the case, the drug habit of this patient may be said to have a symbolic character, and its meaning can be understood only by considering her relation with other people.

The future of the patient is an interesting as well as an important issue, a brief discussion of which perhaps may help to bring out the personality and cultural factors involved in drug addiction. We are told by the patient that her lover has repented and that she is going to quit drugs for good after the cure, for she is going to be happy. The problem, however, does not seem to be as simple as the patient described it. Since her happiness depends a great deal on her lover's attitude toward other women, it seems she can hardly be happy, unless the man ceases to be a Don Juan, which is by no means an easy matter. Besides, we may ask whether there might not be something in her own attitude toward people that perhaps had its share in her earlier failure in marital adjustment and that handicaps her present love relationship. The facts are that she married her husband hastily at the age of fifteen; that she loved her father but detested his drinking habit; that by his age and action her present lover often reminded her of her father; and that she dislikes women in general with the possible exception of her mother. From all these one is led to ask whether her own attitude toward her lover is one of seeking a sex-mate or that of finding a father-substitute and depending on him like an infant. If the latter were nearer to the truth, she can hardly be happy either, unless she changes her own attitude toward people, which again is by no means easy. For such attitudes both on the part of the man and on that of the woman were presumably formed early in their life, especially in the social and cultural *milieu* of the home, a discussion of which problem, however, is not permitted by our limited information about the case.

Case 9. Patient was interviewed three times at the Psychopathic Hospital, in 1934. The hospital record shows that he was 44 years old, widowed, and Protestant in religion.

Patient was quite resistant at first and did not reveal much about his early background except saying that his father died when he was only two years old; that his sister died an infant; and that he has been the only child of his mother all his life until his step-brother came 19 years ago. He has been living in hotels, but used to see his mother everyday in his step-father's home, where his own son also lives. He has two uncles, to one of whom he used to be attached. And as a rule he associates with people older than he on the ground that he has more to learn from them than from younger ones.

He was married at twenty-one and lived with his wife only for five years. When asked the reason for separation, patient showed great reluctance to go into the matter. But finally he revealed that it was on account of infidelity on the part of his wife. She was an actress before marriage and he did some work in the theatre. She was attractive and had beautiful features and he said he was very fond of her. She died six years ago and left him a son nineteen years old. Patient used to drink a lot, particularly after he was married, and at least three times a year he would go on a spree lasting several nights. But when he was on drugs, he did not drink.

Since his separation from his wife, he has had steady women friends. He is particularly fond of one of them, whom he has known for four years. She is different from his wife, for she is several years older than he and cares more for him than his wife did. She is a divorcee but is very sympathetic and understanding. It was through or with this woman that he was addicted to opium four years ago. When she first persuaded him to go to a smoking party, he hesitated. In fact, when he first went to such a party he did not touch the pipe; he just sat around and saw his friend smoke. It was his friend's first time too. But the next time he went he smoked about ten pills—there is one puff in one pill of prepared opium, and there are sixty pills in a *toy*. They first went to the smoking party out of sheer curiosity.

He said his lady friend now was in a private sanitarium, having some money of her own. She used to have a lot of money, but not now. When he leaves the hospital, he plans to live with his mother and to stay away from his old associates, which step he considered as the first essential in getting rid of his habit.

In Case 9 again we found that the immediate social situation leading to his addiction was the smoking party. And we also found that the patient was at the same time confronted by a situation common to those who have been deserted or rejected by their wives on whom they depend for emotional satisfaction. The wound his wife inflicted on his pride by her erratic behavior, granting what he reported to be true, will probably never be healed. Such a discontented state of mind, therefore, is a factor that we must not ignore in accounting for the addiction of this case.

Again we must not be satisfied by a one-sided account of a failure in marital adjustment. We must see what the data we have gathered tell us about the patient's attitude toward women. We are told that he is very much satisfied with his lady friend, because she is older than he, sympathetic and understanding, and cares more for him than his wife did. Judging from his emphasis on what he gets from this woman, and recalling the fact that he has been the only child of his mother all his life until recently, and the further fact that he is emotionally attached to older men, it cannot be far wrong to infer that his relation with women on the whole is passive. With such an attitude toward women and in a culture as ours which makes more demands on men, it is questionable whether the patient would have made a very successful marital adjustment even if his wife had not given him the occasion for separation. That he was ill prepared to play the rôle of a husband seems to find some support also from his increasing tendency to excessive drinking after marriage. As the psychological effect of liquor is similar to that of opium, it may almost be said that the tendency or readiness to use the latter drug on the part of this patient had existed long before he went to the smoking party.

Case 10. Patient was interviewed four times first at the Psychopathic Hospital and two times outside at her residence from April to May, 1934. The hospital record shows that patient is a white woman of 27, Catholic in religion, and a saleslady by profession. Notes on personal history say that patient had a violent temper during adolescence. She is artistic, musical, and always restless. She had been admitted once already for the treatment of drug addiction.

Patient began her story by telling that she started her drug habit by going to smoking parties. It was in Cleveland in 1932. She was with her partner in the dress business. The man took her to a room in the hotel and there she saw a woman cooking opium. She said she was quite shocked by the sight and did not smoke. But later when she was alone in a hotel, a married man placed the smoking outfit in her safe-keeping, because his wife came to town, and she was asked to allow two girls to use the outfit. They came and patient began to smoke opium for the first time in her life. She drank a lot of water to soothe her throat, moved around and became sick. Several days later she was invited by a girl to her sweetheart's apartment, where two other girls and one man were smoking the pipe. She smoked and was sick again. But after she came back to Chicago she kept going to such parties and became used to opium. She had her own smoking outfit and held parties once a week or more often. She claimed that she did not form a habit in this way and that her habit began to show only after she started using morphine.

She was rooming with a nurse and she had insomnia. The nurse advised her to take morphine tablets, but warned her not to use them too often, lest she should develop a drug habit. But gradually she increased the dosage and the frequency. And one day she caught her roommate using the "hypo," and asked her to give her a "shot." She had a "shot," and that "shot," she said, marked the beginning of her morphine habit. It was three months after she had first used morphine tablets.

Last year she came to the hospital for her first cure. But on the third day after discharge from the hospital, she worked from early morning to late at night and was so tired and sick that she could not stand it any longer. So she took a cab to her second husband's apartment and went back on the drug. Now she felt fine and did not believe that she would ever go back to the habit, although she would still like to go to smoking parties.

In the third interview she mentioned her second husband, saying that he was a drug-user, and that they discovered each other to be drug-users on the third day after their marriage. But she flatly refused to speak any more about him, saying that to think of him recalled only very distasteful things.

Patient questioned the use of making investigation of drug addicts and the possibility of arriving at generalizations, for different users react to drugs differently and children from the same family may behave differently. In her case, for example, she said, it was difficult to explain why she should have become a drug addict, while her sister, fifteen years older than she, should have turned out a refined and cultured lady, the wife of a successful business man. Her sister wanted to send her to a state institution. Patient thought her sister was a busy-body and meddled too much with her business, although she thought all was for her good.

Patient went on to mention her mother, who is living and stays by herself in a community away from the Loop. Patient used to telephone her mother everyday, but hesitated to go home for she considered it sacrilegious to take drugs in her mother's house. Her mother, according to the patient, is the sweetest woman she has ever known, but she used to be too strict. She would not allow her to have a drink or to smoke a cigarette or to play with other children on the street while she was at home. Whenever she violated any of the rules of the house, her mother would punish her by not speaking to her, sometimes for two days. That was terrible to her, and she used to appeal to her sister and brother for help, but they asked her to speak to her mother herself. Sometimes she would purposely fall on the stairs in order to obtain her mother's attention.

While her mother has been strict and old-fashioned and even did not allow her to go to movie shows, her father was a "pal" and often sneaked her out to a show. He died when she was 17. She took it quite hard, she said. Three months after her father's death she went to a business college in town and completed the course in a year and a half, and secured a job in a firm in spite of her mother's wish to keep her at home.

It was while working in the firm mentioned above that she met her first husband. He was 19 years older and was sentimental about her, but she did not love him. She consented to marry him because she wanted very badly to get away from home. She used to be proud of herself and indifferent to her husband, and thought it was smart to humiliate her husband before his friends. One time they were due at a dinner party and she was 20 minutes late. Before she entered the dining hall in a hotel, she overheard one of his friends criticizing her, and so from that time on she changed her attitude, and gradually came to like her husband. But all the same she could not live with him, as he could not satisfy her sexually. After three years they were separated and finally divorced. She stressed the fact that she was a virgin when she was first married.

One week after her discharge from the hospital, she called the interviewer, and the interview was held at her residence at 32nd and Ellis, a Negro community. Without much hesitation she confessed that yesterday she went to a doctor and received a "shot" of morphine, because she really could not stand it. All day yesterday, she said, she tore off all her finger nails. She appeared exhausted, dirty and restless, and tried by means of endearing words and manners to get the interviewer's sympathy and money.

In the course of conversation it was spontaneously revealed that she was married to her second husband in the previous year. He is a confidence man, and a cripple, and is thirteen years her senior. He is highly intelligent but has no principles. He never keeps his words and spares no tricks in his dealings with people. She had known him for two years before marriage and never had sexual intercourse with him during the period of courtship. She said he respected her. But in the course of a week after marriage he became bold and showed his perversions. Instead of normal coitus, he preferred cunnilinctus exclusively. She was so shocked the first time that she cried for three days and dared not speak to other people about it. She thought then that it was terrible, and that it sapped her energy and vitality. She much prefers normal coitus and desires to have a baby. But her husband is sterile. He is a drug-user as mentioned above. For these and other reasons she hesitated to go back to him, although he still cares for her, according to her story. The interviewer got the impression that the patient was afraid of her present husband.

Incidents relating to her attitude toward women are grouped in the following. She was educated in a Catholic school. She got along well, but hated to take part in theatrical performances on religious holidays, for she wanted to play in her own way. But the sister in charge often picked her out and asked her to take part, and she would coax the patient whenever the latter showed reluctance in learning her part, saying, "Now,—you don't want to act in such a manner," etc. Then she would feel all right and take her part willingly. She has very few women friends and she never trusts them. They are not like men friends, who could be loyal and faithful to each other. Women are generally "catty" and cut each other's throat. She has always liked men and feels more at home with them.

Patient had told the interviewer that the colored landlady in whose house she was staying is a niece of a colored woman who used to work in her mother's home and used to nurse her, etc. She also gave the interviewer the impression that she was there just for a retreat and then would go home. She continuously asked for money from the interviewer in various ways, and there was no question but that she solicited men for money. But the next time the interviewer called, patient had left the place, and he was told by the landlady that patient had left her without paying the room rent she owed; and furthermore she stole the landlady's underwear and her new sweater. The landlady said that when patient first came to her house, a colored chauffeur accompanied her and said that she was his personal friend. The colored man stayed with her, and later more colored men came and drank a lot of moonshine. The landlady was furious, because she had treated the patient well. She denied the story patient told about her being the niece of a colored woman who used to work in her home.

Patient is red-haired and said that people used to praise the beauty of her hair. She several times referred to it.

Patient addressed the interviewer in a familiar manner from the start and in writing to one of the physicians in the hospital called him her friend.

In Case 10 once more we found that the social situation most immediately connected with her drug habit was the smoking party. It is interesting to note the gradual way in which the patient's initial resistance to smoking opium, which probably was only apparent, was overcome and in which the ways of the "dope world" were assimilated by her. In fact, it must be mentioned with some emphasis that her first experience of opium, as it is with many other addicts, was decidedly unpleasant, and, as she put it, it took her some time to get used to the drug. Pharmacologically, it is understandable how a person's first contact with the depressing effect of opium should be unpleasant and how after a certain degree of tolerance is established to the said depressing effect comes the "kick" or the feeling of well-being so much raved about by drug users. But psychologically the willingness on the part of the neophyte to undergo this initial stage of unpleasant experience until a tolerance is established requires closer examination. Undoubtedly, the anticipation of the "kick" that is coming plays a part in leading the novice on. But the more important incentive seems to come from the desire to be like the other fellow. Case 5, for example, explicitly said that he learned to smoke opium because the best dressed man in town did it; he did it to be a good fellow. The same seems to apply to the present case. She moved in that part of the underworld in which opium-smoking was the fashion. So she learned it in spite of her unpleasant experience in the beginning. Then she had her own "lay-out" and held parties to entertain others. The whole process of acquiring the opium habit in such cases impresses one as similar in many respects to that of learning to smoke cigarettes. Few of us began to use tobacco with any explicit knowledge or anticipation of its effect. In fact, we would be lost if we should try to give any reason for learning to smoke; probably we learned to smoke just because it was the fashion of our group to do so. It seems probable, therefore, that in opium-smoking, just as in tobacco-smoking, the drug is first used by an individual not because of the actual function it serves or the effect it produces; in most cases rather is it resorted to as a symbol of identification with his group, that is, to be like the other fellow.

If the above exposition has some element of truth, in order to understand more fully the drug habit of Case 10, we shall have to find out why she should have the desire to identify herself with opium smokers, or why she should have associated with the underworld at all. To do this it is evident that we must consider such unhappy vicissitudes of her life as her hasty marriage to a man whom she did not love and her disillusion about her second husband because of his sexual perversions. And in order to account for her random matrimonial adventures and failure in obtaining sexual and emotional satisfaction, as has been pointed out in our discussion of other addicts, we must go into her early life at home, where her attitudes toward men and women and life-situations in general were cultivated and given definite shape or direction. There we learn that her father was her "pal," but her mother was something of a despot, extremely religious and old-fashioned. The result was that she never felt that she had had enough of her mother's love, and that she had to play tricks in order to win her mother's attention. It seems only natural that in such a situation the child should develop an intense feeling of inferiority or insecurity along with strong hostility toward her mother. That this attitude of the patient has been carried over to her relation with other women may be seen in her demanding special attention from her school-teacher whenever she wanted her to take part in dramatics, in her disliking women in general, and especially in returning evil for good in her dealing with her landlady.

Whether or not a woman's feeling of inferiority and hostility in relation to other women has anything to do with her heterosexual adjustment is still a question to be studied. But in the case of this patient, her first marriage to a man nineteen years her senior certainly impresses one as if it were a mere repetition of the thing she has always been doing, that is, to escape her mother's domination by running into the arms of her father. That this is far from being the mature attitude toward heterosexual relations is evidenced by her repeated failures in making a marital adjustment.

The patient's attitude toward sex impresses one as of particular interest. She emphasized the fact that she was a virgin before her first marriage, and that she did not have sexual relation with her second husband until they were married, and she considered her second husband's sexual perversion as a way of sapping her vitality. From these one is led to infer that the patient must have had strong inhibition in sexual matters. This might be due to her Catholic bringing-up in the hands of a strict mother. It might also be due to her peculiar way of associating sexual activity with the loss of vitality or power. It is difficult to point out definitely how this conception of sex may have hindered her heterosexual adjustment, but that it must have had its share in her marital difficulties seems probable.

Thus in a rough way we found that in this and other cases presented above the drug habit of a person cannot be understood by itself; it is inseparably connected not only with his or her immediate environment but with the person's emotional attitudes toward people as well as the whole cultural *milieu* in which he or she has been brought up.

2. *Through association with prostitutes and pimps.* Another very common social situation in which addicts first come in contact with drugs and drug-users is the brothel or the house of prostitution. That the pimp in his attempt to entice a girl to his service not seldom "dopes" her and makes her an addict so that she will have to depend on him for her drug and thereby becomes his woman is a matter of common knowledge. It seems less well known that a man may be similarly trapped by a prostitute and thereby becomes her man, as it is called in the underworld. Some of such cases are presented in the following.

Case 11. Patient was interviewed once at the Psychopathic Hospital and once outside in a restaurant. He was a white American of 32, appeared short and slender.

The hospital record shows that patient came from a broken home, but both parents are living. His father is a heavy drinker. According to his mother, the patient had been kind and devoted to his sisters and brother at home and always mixed well with people outside. For the last ten years he complained of stomach trouble and had been weak. Patient was brought to the hospital by the police on the advice of the country doctor who said that patient attempted to jump out of the window, and therefore might be insane. (Later the interviewer learned that this was a means of getting into the hospital for a treatment of drug addiction.)

In the interviews patient related that his morphine habit was started ten years ago. Two women wanted to have him to be their man. One of them secretly put morphine in his coffee. So he felt fine every time he was with her, not knowing why. Finally the girl told him the truth and then he began to use the needle. In about ten days he formed a habit. He finally got so disgusted with the habit that every now and then he would try to quit it. One time he actually stayed away from the drug for three years, and then he went back to it again. To the interviewer's question as to the reason for his relapse, he said that it was mainly because of bad association. Then he added immediately that it was more because he was disgusted with life in general, explaining that when one becomes disgusted with everything one cannot help going back to the habit.

Patient was a pickpocket by profession and had a partner, eighteen years old, who is also an addict. They have been together for a year or so, and have never been apart even for five minutes except when he was in jail. But one day they quarreled over some cocaine. So he decided to quit the habit for good.

Patient was married once about ten years ago. But his wife was too young. After a couple of years they were separated and finally divorced. He said that when he was on the drug he had little sexual desire, except early in the morning before he had a "shot." He now had a steady woman, who is a mulatto, and he kept calling her "my woman."

Patient appeared well-dressed. He said that he had been educated in a military academy for nine years, and learned to dress neatly. He had from 17 to 19 suits and liked always to appear in good clothes.

Before the patient was seen again he was shot by a policeman in his attempt to escape arrest after having run away with a car.

Although our information about this case is too limited for a detailed analysis, several points may be stressed. Besides the fact that his drug habit started through his association with prostitutes, the psychology of his relapses after cures is especially illuminating. Patient spontaneously claimed that bad association alone was not sufficient to cause him to go back to the habit; it was his feeling of disgust with life in general. If we want to know where this feeling of despondency came from, undoubtedly we have to inquire into his previous relations with people, which inquiry, however, is prohibited by our meager information about him. But we are told that he was once married and divorced. This points to his maladjustment in his sexual and emotional life. He appeared unusually intimate with his young partner, and boasted of the fact that they had never been away from each other even for five minutes except when he was in jail or in the hospital. This seems to suggest his homosexual inclination. And that he had had prostitutes supporting him points to his strong dependent attitude toward women and people in general. This is further supported by his profession, which is essentially one of making a living at the expense of others. In the light of these considerations, the patient's feeling of despondency or disgust with life in general may be said to have come from his extreme dependence on others and from his failure in getting what he wanted.

Case 11 may be taken as fairly representative of the whole class of people known in the underworld as "cannons," that is, pickpockets, who generally strive to appear superior to their fellow-beings. An observation of pickpockets in prison, written by an ex-convict who has had a long criminal record, has this to say, "I once asked a 'cannon' why the class as a whole were addicted to narcotics. His answer was, 'For the same reason that men like women—they make 'em happy,'—very ex-

pressively summing up the whole aim and purpose of their existence."[1]
The author's comment on the current sociological conception of criminality as related to the behavior of pickpockets is so much to the point
that it is quoted in part in the following.

> The "cannon" is very evasive in his answers when questioned
> as to the causes of his criminality. Like most other confirmed
> criminals, he is prone to attribute his delinquency to everything that
> does not reflect to his own disadvantage or incrimination. He real-
> izes that criminologists are inclined to regard criminals as victims
> of conditions or circumstances over which they have no control,
> consequently, really not responsible for their actions. The "can-
> non" takes advantage of these theories and plays them to the utmost.
> Many a criminologist, after interviewing a convict, has gone away
> with the impression that he has ascertained the true facts concerning
> the causes of the individual's downfall. In the majority of cases,
> what the criminologist has attained is a choice assortment of bun-
> combe or "bull," to speak plainly. Common sense tells one that a
> person is not going to admit that he alone is responsible for his
> criminality. Such a confession would result in an extended period
> of imprisonment . . . . . When one gets to know and to become in-
> timate with a prisoner serving time, one is told things in direct con-
> tradistinction to those told to the persons in official capacities. One
> soon learns that the confirmed criminal regards his grift as a business
> which yields the maximum amount of profit for a minimum of toil,
> that he deliberately chooses crime in preference to honest labor, and
> that he goes into it with both eyes wide open, so to say. When the
> majority of criminals step out to pull off some illegal act they know
> what they are doing—that they are subject to imprisonment if caught
> and that they themselves and nothing else are prompting them to
> commit acts deemed illegal. The "cannon" is especially conscious
> of this latter fact, confidentially telling that heredity, environment,
> disease, and poverty are a lot of bunk insofar as they are the factors
> that compel them to pursue a criminal career.

In concluding the above statement, the author added, "the 'cannon'
is an egotistical creature and about the last thing he relinquishes in this
life is his conceit and unbounded faith in his ability to wrest an illegal
living from society." What this writer meant to convey is essentially
this: the pickpockets as a class, who are mostly dope addicts at the same
time, have a definite attitude toward life, which may have been due to a

---

[1] An unpublished document written by an ex-convict, entitled, "The Pickpocket
in Prison," loaned to us for use by Mr. Yale Levin, once research assistant in the
Institute for Juvenile Research, Chicago.

certain combination of hereditary and environmental factors, but which is persistent and is little amenable to the ordinary methods of reformation. We have seen something of this attitude in Case 11. To emphasize the more or less persistent personality trends in explaining human behavior is not to say that reformation, in the sense of effecting some change in one's personality organization, is not possible, as seems to be the belief of the writer just quoted. Nor does it discredit the work of current sociology, which gives one the impression of paying exclusive attention to the social factors immediately connected with a given behavior problem. But it does express our conviction that sociological research should be extended to cover those social and cultural situations that give shape to one's personality development early in life.

Fortunately, we were able to get in touch with Case 11's partner in crime. The following is the story he told about himself.

Case 12. The subject was interviewed at his home in an Irish neighborhood near the Union Stock Yard, 1933. He is a lad of 18, being the fourth of eight children of his parents. His father is strict with him, and used to whip him whenever he got into trouble, but his mother always shields him. If it were not for his mother, he said, his father would have killed him. He began to have a police record since 13, and has been twice in St. Charles, a reformatory school for boys.

The subject had been with his "pal"—a pickpocket, a "dope" user and a pimp—for about two years. Last January he contracted gonorrhea and, therefore, could not drink "booze" or have pleasure with women. He was restless. So he asked his "pal" to give him a "shot," saying to him, "I can't drink booze, can't go with women, what shall I do?" His "pal" had refused to give him a "shot" before. But now seeing that the subject could not have a good time because of gonorrhea, his "pal" gave him a "shot," but no more until a couple of weeks had passed. He got sick after the first "shot" and vomited. After two weeks he asked for another "shot" and he had three in one week. In the course of another two weeks he was "hooked."

For about a year he and his "pal" used drugs together and did not try to get cured, for they always had enough money to buy drugs with, except once when they went to another city and there they went without drugs for five days. They suffered and determined to get cured. But as soon as they came back to Chicago, his "pal" used drugs in spite of his persuasion, and so he followed suit.

When his "pal" was in the hospital, he was on a self-cure. He lay in bed for eight days, could not eat, felt pain in the legs and in the muscles.   Then he went on a spree lasting two weeks, in which time he drank and indulged in sex orgies, and forgot all his worries, including the yearning for the drug.   He said he might have suffered a great deal more if he had not been drunk.   Finally he woke up for a couple of days and then again went on a spree.   He said he was now through with drugs but he was going to drink more.

The subject said that he almost always associates with older people.

Last year he proposed to a girl, and the girl rejected the proposal on the ground that he was too young.   He said he was glad that the girl did turn him down, for if he were married he would not be able to support his family.   Now that his "pal" was dead he could not go on with his old profession, for he was still a novice in the art of picking pockets.   He has his meals at home.   His mother will buy him cigarettes.   He supposed he had to take up some job, if he could find one.

In Case 12 the way the drug habit was acquired through association with a pimp and pickpocket is so clear that it requires no further comment.   But it must be pointed out that the subject had been a delinquent before he began to associate with his friend, that he had been an excessive drinker, and that when he asked for the first "shot" of morphine, he was in a restless state of mind.   However limited our information about the case is, both the environmental factor and the subjective state of feeling which we have found to be especially conducive to the formation of the drug habit are sufficiently revealed before us.

Case 13.   The subject was interviewed four times at one of the shelter houses for men.[1]   He is a white American of forty-three, born in Chicago in the neighborhood of Cottage Grove.   His mother died when he was two, and his father passed away when he was eight.   He recalled that his father was quite a handsome man, admired by women who came to their house, but he was a heavy drinker.

Ever since he was about twelve years old, he worked on newspapers and grew to know the underworld characters of that neighborhood, noted in those days for its "Levee," especially the gamblers and the successful prostitutes.   They would hand him coins for the little favors he could do for them, such as running errands and watching for the man while the girl was entertaining some caller that was not too popular with the man who was "running the dump."   And around the neighborhood he saw plenty of "dopes"—addicts—begging from the "sports" the price of a "shot," and was disgusted with them.   He never thought then that one day he would be like

---

[1] For data on this case the writer is indebted to Mr. S. Oreskey, one of the writer's research assistants in a separate project.

them, although even in his present condition he appears neat and well-dressed.

At 12 he had his first sex experience with a prostitute, for which he paid just as the older people did, but he was not potent and took an entirely passive part while with the prostitute. And he felt very much ashamed of having gone to a whore-house.

In the course of time, he said, "I learned when I saw the easy time the whores and the gamblers were having that it does not take brains to make money." He quitted school and had no use for education. At 18 he was picked out by a prostitute as her man. Of this episode in his life he said, "I tell you she got nuts every time she saw me. She used to go for me in a big way, and I was the only one that she had ever loved in her life. Of course, I've done the chores that were to be done around the house. . . . The girls do not keep a man for nothing."

It was when living with the prostitute as a pimp that he first learned to smoke opium. The girl used to go to the "joints" on Wentworth Ave., and asked him to go along with her. His first experience of opium was unpleasant, but the girl insisted on his going with her. So he kept on going and smoking, until he formed a habit. His memories of this period are full of reference to his fear of impotency. For the first two months with the girl, he was not able to perform the normal sex act. But for sometime after going on the pipe he had no difficulty in sexual intercourse, and the girl must have been satisfied.

Then came the crisis of his life. The girl left him. "When the cunt I was living with had gone away with this other fellow and left me alone with but a few bucks in the kicks and me with the *yen*. I felt that the bottom had dropped out of everything. I did not know where to go; the other girls would not have anything to do with me, for I was not their man, and they would not mess with me for fear that the old warhorse would light into them when she would come back. But as time went on and the girl did not come home, I had to nose around . . . . we had funds, but I still felt lost, as if I did not belong to anyone. I did not know what to do. . . . It was as if the world had stopped and all of us were flying around hellbent for some place. . . . There were other girls, some of them made passes at me, but I knew that they were out to make a grub-stake, and that they would not play the game the way that the kid I was with used to play it."

When questioned as to the part women can play in remaking an addict, the subject said, "If all the 'junkers' had mothers to whom they could go, they would not be 'junkers' for long,' cause if a fellow knows that someone cares, he will try his damnedest. But what is the use of bucking the world, when one is lonesome and none of the rest of the world gives a damn if you come or go? Why take the cure? Why live at all, in fact, except to use more of the stuff and wonder what it is all about? If I had a mother I would be a different man to-day."

The above story of Case 13 is a very brief summary of a rather lengthy record. Probably enough has been included to show how in this case the drug habit is connected with his early environment. In that kind of environment where the most fashionable people were the gamblers, the prostitutes, and the pimps, it seems only natural that a boy should strive to be one of them. In that sense, to smoke the pipe may be considered as one of the many signs by which the boy identified himself with his group.

The personality trends in this case are also interesting. In the first place, we are told that the subject has almost always been passive in his sex relation with women, and that opium served to increase his potency, at least in the beginning. More than that, we found that he has been dependent on women all his life both materially and emotionally, and particularly in the latter way. The man was not far wrong when he said that what he needed is a mother. He has been and probably will always be looking for one, but he will never find her and probably will always feel unhappy and despondent. This infantile attitude toward women and anxiety about sexual potency are some of the factors in the personality make-up of Case 13 that we must not ignore in accounting for his enjoying the rôle of a pimp and for his relying on opium in the beginning as an aid in his sexual activity.

What is said about the influence of the underworld environment in giving direction to the ambition and aim in life of a young man who lives in it and the way one may get addicted to drugs through association with prostitutes is made still clearer by what we have found about the following case. Our data are of two kinds: the addict's own story and the records of our interviews with him, which were conducted on nine different occasions. A part of the addict's own story is hereby reproduced, to be supplemented here and there by what we learned through interviews.

Case 14. Experiences at home and in school. I was born in the year 1887, in a small town on an island on the Pacific coast. My father was a sea captain and they had left their homes in the East to come to the Pacific coast to make their fortune. They bought two acres of land on this island and built a large house on it consisting of about twelve rooms.

When I was four years old, my brother was born. The next year I got in the habit of running away from home each morning, and I would go to the school house and tell the teacher that I wanted to attend school. The teachers would send me back home every day and tell me that I was too young to start going to school. They soon got tired of sending me home each morning and finally decided to let me start attending school at the age of five instead of waiting until I was six. I was a very brilliant pupil and passed my examinations with very high marks . . . . and when I was twelve years old I was graduated from grammar school with very high honors.

At that time there was no high school on the island. So my parents decided to sell their property and move to a city, so that I could attend high school. We moved to the city that summer and in the fall I was enrolled in the high school.

My father then took a job as captain of a tug boat which towed logs to the saw mills. From the time that I was born until now he had been the captain of a large sailing vessel that took cargoes all over the world and he would only get home for two or three weeks once or twice a year, so that he was almost a stranger to me. Until this time my mother and I were always together wherever we went. My father was a very heavy drinker, and my mother hated intoxicating liquors, and would not even allow a glass of beer to be drunk in our house.

I was now twelve years old and was attending high school in my freshman year. I was very tall and rangy at this time and I liked all athletic sports and gymnasium work very well. . . . I got very high marks in all subjects but English, and I would just barely skin through in that.

In my sophomore year I started to work in a bakery mornings before school and afternoons after school. The man I worked for was a very heavy drinker and he would send me to a saloon with a note two or three times a day for a quart of whiskey and it was here that I took my first drink of liquor and smoked my first cigarette.

Well, to get on with my story I finished my second and third years in high school and half of the fourth year without any mishap and by this time my parents were making plans to send me to college as soon as I finished high school to study to become a lawyer or a doctor. Everything has gone along smoothly in my life up to this time and I loved my school work and had my heart set on attending college, when out of a clear sky I was accused by a girl of getting her pregnant, and they wanted me to marry her. I had never had anything to do with her and when I was accused of it by the professor of the school I hit him and broke his nose. I went straight home and told my mother the whole story, and she at once swore out a warrant and had the girl arrested. After being locked up for a few days the girl made a confession and completely cleared me, but the damage was already done as far as I was concerned, as everybody in the school had heard about it and about me hitting the professor, and I was ashamed to go back to school and also afraid that if anybody joked about it I might hurt them as I had a very hot temper. So rather than to go back to school and face everybody I became panicky and ran away from home.

In addition to the above information about the subject's life before sixteen, we learned through interviews that his parents did not get along well, as his father was a very heavy drinker; and that his father used to whip him for such small matters as smoking cigarettes, and one time for throwing rotten eggs at a milk boy, which he did not do, but which his younger brother did. His mother always sided with him against his father, and seldom whipped him except several times for masturbation. He denied sex play with boys, but admitted that at fifteen he had the first sex experience with a girl studying in the same high school. He further related that ever since he was eight he began to steal not so much for what he could get as for the fun or satisfaction it gave him, which compulsive tendency to steal has persisted up to the present moment.

From messenger boy to pimp. I was sixteen years old now and I went into Montana. On my way to Montana on a freight train I met two fellows from home and I joined them. They were both older than I and I soon learned to drink and gamble with them. We got into a drunken brawl in Missoula, Montana, and they were both arrested. But I got away, and I was so afraid that I left town at once and went to Butte, Montana. I was nearly out of funds by this time. So when I arrived in Butte I started looking for work . . . . I started working that day on the ·messenger force and I soon found out that the work consisted mostly of carrying trays of food and drinks from restaurants and saloons to the cribs where the sporting women worked and the pay you got was tips and you could always overcharge them each time.

At the time that I started working on the messenger force there were between fifteen and seventeen hundred sporting girls on Galena street which was called "The Board Walk," and a place named the A. B. C. I was the youngest kid working on the messenger force and I made friends with a large number of the girls in a very short time . . . . and when they called the messenger office they always asked for "The Kid," which was the nickname they gave me and it stuck by me for a number of years. . . . .

I worked on the messenger force for about six months before I was able to get a job on the night force and then I started making big money. While working days, the poorest wage I earned per day was about four dollars and it ranged from that up to eight and ten dollars a day, and I worked seven days a week. At this time I had not learned to gamble and I did not care for whiskey, so I was able to save a great deal of what I earned.

There was a large number of boarding houses in the town and almost all of the miners lived in them instead of living at hotels and eating in restaurants. . . . . When I first arrived in Butte almost all of the miners were Irish and they were a wild bunch, but after I had been there for a few years it gradually started changing and a large number of Syrians and Scandinavians started working in the mines.

The first six months that I worked days on the messenger force I saved about twelve hundred dollars. Besides saving this money I had bought four or five suits of clothes. I had ordered them all from a tailor and they cost me from forty to seventy-five dollars a suit. I also bought a good watch and a nugget watch-chain with a twenty dollar gold piece attached to it for a watch charm. I had ordered my clothes and bought the watch and chain, because I wanted to be dressed like the other fellows that worked on the messenger force with me.

Nearly everyone that worked with me had a girl that worked on the line and they were really all "pimps," and they were only working in order to keep from being arrested. I made friends with a great many of these fellows, and being just a kid and not knowing any better, the height of my ambition at once was that I would like to get a girl that worked on the line as the rest of the fellows did. After I had worked a month or two, two or three girls used to call to me every time I passed their cribs, but I was very bashful and I would never stop and talk to them. The other fellows working with me used to kid me about it all the time, and one of them, whom I liked very much, told me that I was a fool, that I ought to make one of the girls that was always calling to me. He explained everything to me and told me just how to go about it to get myself a girl. So shortly after I started working nights I decided that I would try and make one of them. So after that the very first time one of the girls saw me and called to me I stopped and began talking to her. She wasn't busy at the time and after I had talked to her for a few minutes she invited me to come in and sit down for a while. . . . . I went inside with her and sat down and we had quite a talk. . . . . She asked me all about myself and wanted to know if I had a girl. I told her that I didn't have one and she told me that she didn't have a man either and wanted me for her man. I talked to her for nearly an hour, and when I left I promised her that when I finished work in the morning I would come back to her crib and stay with her instead of going to my boarding house to sleep. I was tickled to death about it, and when I got back to the messenger office I called my friend aside and told him her name and he said I couldn't have done any better as she was one of the best money makers on the whole line . . . . Morning finally came and the minute I was relieved from duty at the messenger office I made a bee line straight for her crib . . . . I was just a kid seventeen years old and I had never slept with a woman in my life and I was very bashful and hardly knew what to do . . . . She said she liked me very much and she wasn't long in showing me what to do. . . . .

First experience of opium and its effects. We slept most of the day until late in the afternoon, and when I awoke she got up and got a tray out of the dresser drawer and brought it over and placed it on the bed. I had seen opium pipes two or three different times since I had been working on the messenger force, so I recognized the contents of the tray as an opium layout. She told me that she was a smoker and asked me if I had ever smoked any *hop*. I told her that I never had and she said that I ought to try it once, as she was sure that I would like it. She placed the tray between us in the middle of the bed and lit a small lamp that was on the tray. I soon found out that it was used to cook the opium into pills so that she could smoke it . . . . She told me to put my mouth over the end of the steam and draw back hard. I did this while she held the bowl over the lamp and in that way I smoked my first pill of opium . . . . I suddenly became very nauseated and had to leave the table to vomit. I vomited until there was nothing left in my stomach and I was still sick, so I went back to bed. She wet some towels with cold water and put them on my forehead and after an hour or so I fell to sleep. I slept two hours and when I awoke I felt all right again. . . . .

I went to work that evening as usual. Every time I sat down in the messenger office I would feel drowsy and fall to sleep and my body seemed to itch all over, and when I scratched it, it would feel awfully good. When I got ready to leave her crib to go to work that evening, she gave me thirty-two dollars and told me to be sure to come back when I finished work in the morning. I thought that it was a very easy way of getting money and she was young and very good looking, so it was not very hard for me to promise her that I would be back next morning. . . . .

As soon as I was in bed she brought out the tray with the layout on it and placed it in the center of the bed and then she got into bed. She cooked a few pills and smoked them herself and than asked me if I wanted to smoke. It had made me so sick the night before that when she first started cooking the opium this morning it seemed to nauseate me again. So I declined and told her that I didn't feel very well, and I wanted to get some sleep. She smoked a few more pills and then put the tray away and got back into bed and we went to sleep. I was very tired and I slept like one dead not waking until about the middle of the afternoon. As soon as we were awake, she got up and again got the tray and lit the lamp and got back into bed and started to cook her opium again. She cooked and smoked six or eight pills as I lay there watching her and then she again offered me some. I told her that I was afraid to smoke again for fear that it would make me as sick as I was the night before. She told me that it wouldn't make me sick this time and she coaxed and coaxed, until I finally gave in and said that I would smoke a couple of pills with her just to be sociable. She cooked some more of the raw opium into pills and we both started to smoke again. . . . .

Now, here is the first peculiar thing that I noticed from the effects of smoking opium. We started carrying on our sexual intercourse, and where ordinarily it would have taken me only a few minutes to finish it seemed as though after smoking the opium I would never finish . . . . When I finally finished she threw her arms around me, laughing and seeming very happy. She told me that she had more satisfaction out of our intercourse than she had from anyone in her whole life, and she told me she loved me very much and wanted me to promise never to leave her. She said she would work hard and give me all of her money and supply me with everything that I needed. I promised her that I would stay with her as long as she was on the square and did as I told her to do, and she gladly promised to do it as long as I would live with her, and give her a little loving once in a while . . . . As soon as he—the messenger boy—had left she closed the door and called me into the front room. I went in and she turned her pocketbook upside down and emptied the contents out on the table. She handed me all of the money that was in it and then told me that I had better leave her three dollars in case some one came in to turn a trick, so she would have change for a five dollar gold piece. I gave her the three dollars and we sat down and had our breakfast . . . . She called me back and told me that I didn't have to go to work unless I wanted to, as she would earn all the money I needed. She also told me that she had about eighteen hundred dollars in the bank, and that if I wanted her to she would go down and draw it out for me that day. I told her that I didn't need it then and asked her to leave it in the bank until I wanted it. . . . .

The discovery of being addicted. After I had lived with her for six or seven months she told me that she had a letter from a sister. The letter said that the sister was very sick, so she asked me if it would be all right if she went to see her. I told her to go if she wanted, so I gave her enough money to go and took her to the train. We had smoked just before she left and she had packed the layout in a small handbag and took it with her. I worked that night as usual and everything went along fine, until I went home in the morning, and then I started to get sick. I went to bed, but I couldn't go to sleep. I felt very restless and I rolled and tossed all day. Towards evening I began getting awful cramps in my stomach and also nauseated and started vomiting. I had not eaten any food all that day. So there was nothing in my stomach but a little water, and when I started vomiting nothing came up but green bile and the more I vomited the sicker I got. I finally rang the bell and sent for a messenger, and when he came I told him to tell the boss that I was sick and wouldn't be able to come to work that night. The messenger asked me what was wrong and I told him I didn't know. I told him that I had awful cramps and was vomiting all of the time. He asked me if I had been smoking every day with my girl, and I told him I had. Then he asked me if I had had any opium since she had gone, and I told him that I hadn't. He told me that was the reason why I was so sick . . . . He looked in the drawer and found a jar of opium, so he cooked some of it and gave me three pills. He went to the restaurant and got a pitcher of black coffee and told me to swallow the pills and drink some of the coffee. I did as he told me, and laid down again, and in about ten minutes I began to feel all right again. This was the first time I had missed smoking in the six months that I had lived with this girl. . . . .

We will not reproduce the rest of the story, in which our subject told about his progress as a pimp, such as acquiring more girls to work for him—as much as four at one time and altogether twenty girls in the last thirty years of his life—, and saving more money for himself; and in which he related his first serious police record for killing a man in self-defense in a gambling house and brothel which he ran. His subsequent career as a criminal is too long to go into here. Suffice it to say that most of the offenses he has committed consist of larceny, burglary, drug peddling, and occasionally robbery.

His married life needs a brief mention. The girl he first married was a prostitute, and he married her, he said, in order to protect her, so that she would not be pointed out as a white slave. His second wife used to be a school teacher, and he married her, because she then had two thousand dollars in bank. He did not particularly care for her at first, but as she has proved herself to be a devoted wife he has almost come to what is generally called falling in love with her.   He has never actually fallen in love in his life.

The subject's drug habit, as may be expected, progressed readily from opium smoking to the hypodermic use of morphine and heroin.   He is now using eight capsules or about 16 grains of the latter drug everyday, costing him at least $4.00 per day.   He declared that while in the beginning opium did produce pleasurable feeling in him, now its only effect is to restore him to his normal condition, so that he can eat and beg or steal.   To keep up his expensive habit, he has been working for the Government as an informant or stool pigeon, running a house of prostitution, and has been peddling drugs.   His favorite racket now is to play on the sympathy of good-hearted or simple-minded people—priests, attorneys, bankers, and business executives—by telling them a deplorable story about himself and receiving help from them thereby.   When asked whether he has had desires to quit the habit and what his plan for the future is, he replied that he had never wanted to quit the habit; his previous cures were taken mainly on account of other people, and everytime he came out from a hospital he felt "something lacking." Besides, he said in one interview, "What is to be gained from a cure? There is little in life for me to live for!"

In Case 14 we are privileged to see the actual steps through which the subject—then a lad of seventeen—identified himself with the people he associated with, desired to be like the other fellow, and finally became one of them.   And opium smoking, it must be noted, was not acquired by him as a habit in itself; it was part and parcel of the rôle of a successful pimp.   The connection between his addiction and his environment, therefore, is unquestionable.

In Case 14, too, it seems one single crisis in his adolescent period— the incident in which he hit the professor because of his false accusation —had surprisingly far-reaching consequences.   If the subject's story about this period of his life is reliable, the said episode may be said to have marked the turning point of his whole career.   For it was in connection with this episode that he ran away from the moral control of his home and came under the influence of a new environment, in which he acquired new ambitions, new patterns of behavior, and a new philosophy of life, the philosophy of life that considers the self as the only end and the rest of humanity all means.

However, neither the important episode just mentioned nor the under-world environment the subject was later exposed to, taken alone, is sufficient to explain his subsequent career as a pimp and a drug addict. To have a more complete understanding of the case, it seems we cannot ignore the information we have obtained about his relation with his parents. We learned that he had a strong, strict, and, to him, a very unreasonable father, who whipped him even for such trivial matters as smoking a cigarette. Under such a situation, it seems natural that a child should develop an intense feeling of inferiority together with a strong desire to be as strong as his father. At the same time how could he help hating his father for his mistreatment? The subject one time went as far as to have his big dog bite his father when the latter attempted to whip him. In the light of these childhood experiences, the subject's hitting the school-teacher that created the greatest crisis in his life, his aping the pimps he associated with later, his repeated conflicts with the Government, and his making fools of kind-hearted people at present all become more understandable.

Further, we learned that he has always been his mother's pet, and that his mother always sided with him against his father. Under such a relationship between mother and son, it also seems natural that the son should develop an attitude of excessive dependence on the mother and of using her as a protection against the father. Granting again that a child's attitude toward his mother may be transferred to his relation with other women later in life, we shall be in a position to understand the subject's continual dependence on prostitutes for his living and his unromantic but coldly calculating marriages.

In Case 14, as in the cases cited above, therefore, we found that his drug habit is connected not only with that part of the underworld culture which is characteristic of prostitutes and pimps, but with such emotional trends or attitudes as may be considered as the earmarks of an infantile type of personality.

3. *Through going to pool rooms and gambling houses.* The pool rooms and gambling houses and similar "hangouts" in an urban community constitute another type of social situation in which addicts first come in contact with drugs and drug-users. Some of the cases we have interviewed whose addiction started in this way are presented in the following.

Case 15.[1] I was born in 1894 in a town of about eight hundred population (Illinois).   I had one sister and one brother.   Both of them having married and gone from home before I was born, however, left me as the only child in our family.

From as far back as I can remember anything up to the time I was fourteen or fifteen years of age there were few incidents worth mentioning, which I can recall.   There are, though, some things in regard to our family which stick out very prominently in my memory.   I can remember that my father as a railroad engineer always earned a fairly good salary; yet, even as a child I could gather enough conversation to know that we were always in debt. . . . . Another thing I can remember quite vividly is that my mother was a lodge woman.   She belonged to everything it was possible for her to belong to . . . . Consequently I was left to work out my own problems most of the time, a fact which I considered no hardship at the time. . . . . It was only natural, of course, that I should pick my friends from among those who were about as free as I. . . . .

Before I had reached the eighth grade my father's run had changed which necessitated our moving to Rock Island, Ill.   The move suited me perfectly; for Rock Island was a larger town and, as I still enjoyed the privilege of seeking out my own pleasures and doing a great deal as I pleased, I was able to find many ways to spend my time.   One of the great discoveries I made at this time was the pool rooms.   Then, for the first time in my life, I began to give some serious thought toward learning something.   I was determined to learn all there was to know about kelly pool, rotation and everything else that could be played on a pool table. . . . .

While I was nineteen my folks moved to another town.   I then began to make the new town my headquarters.   In fact, for a few years I did little traveling.   I met a woman there who had been married but had run her husband away from home—at least so she boasted.   For about a year we got along fine.   I would sleep with her nights and play pool days. . . . .

It was while things were going along this way for me that I met Ted.   Ted was about 25 years of age, and just another bum about town.   He was a congenial sort of chap, however, and after a few drinks together we became good friends.   One night while we were drunk I noticed Ted mashing up some little white tablets and snuffing the powder up each nostril.   It was the first time I had ever seen that done and naturally I was curious.   Ted explained to me that the tablets were heroin and that they made one feel good.   But he offered me none.

For a long time, probably six months, I took Ted's word for whatever the effect of the stuff might be.   Everyday we would meet in

[1] An unpublished autobiography loaned to us by Mr. Yale Levin.

the pool room and begin our drinking bouts; Ted at the same time would use his heroin. Altogether on account of fear, however, I stuck to booze alone. I'd watch Ted sniff the stuff and I would wonder just what sort of kick he was getting. There was never much noticeable change in his behavior after he took a dose. . . . .

It was inevitable, of course, that some time that fear was not going to be strong enough. One night we had been on an exceptionally hard drunk and we were both sick. That is, Ted was sick until after he had his heroin. That never failed to bring him out of a drunken sickness. I thought right there that by God I'd take a little of the stuff, if it did kill me. I would have as soon been dead as to feel the way I did. I took one tablet and within ten minutes felt perfectly at ease.

. . . .

After that first shot I began to take a little each day. Everyday we would meet in the pool room and have our heroin. Sometimes Ted would buy it and sometimes I would get it. There was no difficulty in getting it in those days. There was no law against it and anyone could buy any amount from a dime's worth up.

In a short time I became acquainted with other fellows who were using the same stuff. At that time there were about a dozen of us who began to hang around together, all using this junk. None of us were working. We all lived at home with our parents and there was not one among us whose folks could be classed as needy. Therefore, we could all get little money from home now and then when the gambling was slow or when lady luck let us down too hard.

We will not include the rest of the story, in which the subject related how since the Harrison Narcotic Act went into effect in 1915 it has become difficult to buy drugs; the prices of drugs have increased, and therefore illegal means of making money for the support of his habit become necessary. Thus from a rather harmless lad around the neighborhood he became a seasoned criminal.

Our information about the subject's family background is not sufficient for an adequate understanding of his personality development. But the influence of his associates in the pool rooms and the gambling houses in initiating him into the use of drugs is evident. What we want to emphasize here is the psychology of wishing to be like the other fellow that is so characteristic of adolescent boys. On seeing an expert pool player, the subject wanted to be one, and on seeing Ted using heroin he wanted to try it. It is in this sense that we have previously remarked that one's use of drugs is often a symbol of identification with one's group.   In the following case we shall see the same process working, but more data will be available for an understanding of the factors other than the addict's immediate environment.

Case 16.   The subject was interviewed at one of the men's shelters over 15 times from April, 1934 to April, 1935.   He was born in 1875 and in a small town in Iowa, a town of 9,000 population then. He was the only child of his parents.   His father ran a music shop and was not very strict with him except when he played truant, and he did it often.   Mother was always indulgent.

As a rule, he associated with older people.   There are some places in town, where the youngsters generally "hang around."   They are the barber shop, the pool room and gambling houses.   Of all the older people there he admired most the barber for his wit and popularity.   This barber he later found out to be a drug user. While in the company of these older people, he often longed for the day when he would grow up to be a man and be able to do what they did.   He was then only 14, being the only child in town allowed in the gambling houses.   He first learned to drink, because, he said, he wanted to be smart.   He got sick at first after a few drinks, but gradually he learned to tolerate whiskey.   One morning he woke up in a hotel, and he caught sight of two older men drinking in a room.   The door was only half closed.   He edged in and asked if he could have a glass of whiskey.   They looked at each other, realizing that he was a mere child.   Feeling that they had no objection, he helped himself.   Since that day he began to drink whiskey in the morning.   He often went into a spree lasting from one to several weeks.

In order to relieve the ill effect of drinking, he learned to use a little morphine—a ¼ gr. tablet to start with.   This information was given to him by the barber, whom he admired, and who started his own habit in the same manner.   This took place when he was 18.

Ten years later he had an accident.   He fell when drunk and his knees were seriously injured.   He was given morphine for six weeks in the hospital.   Although there was no more pain in his knees, he succeeded in getting morphine through his music students in spite of the fact that he lived at home and was constantly watched by his parents, and began to use the drug regularly as a habit.   At first he was ashamed of it, particularly when the fact of his being an addict was known to people in town through carelessness on his part, for he felt his habit would classify him with the Civil War veterans, who were practically the only users around.   Later on, however, when the Harrison Law went into effect and shortly after, the use of drugs became smart with a certain younger group, both men and women of the sporting type.   The women were mostly hustling "broads" or whores. The popularity of the habit can be seen from the fact that there were around 25 addicts in a town of 9,000. After the drug habit was formed, he stopped drinking, and his mother one time remarked that if he had to use something, she would rather see him use drugs, for with drugs he could at least remain sober.

The subject's father left him some property, from which he used to receive $15.00 every week. But he was ignorant of the whole management of this property; it was entrusted to a man in town. His subsequent career as an addict was marked by constant going in and out of private sanitariums and state hospitals and by speedy relapses. But owing to a steady allowance from home, his criminal record was negligible except for a few sentences for possessing drugs. In about 1928 he read from the newspaper about the easiness in getting "junk" in Chicago. So he came here with his wife.

He was first married to a girl in his home town when he was 21, and the girl 19. He had been going with her for some time. One day he was told that she was going to have a child. So he suggested that they get married. Later he found out that it was all his mother-in-law's trick to get them married. After marriage the girl remained with her mother. He had great difficulty with his mother-in-law, relating how once she prevented him from accepting a job out of town just because she wanted him to stay in town, so that her daughter would remain with her, and how finally she suggested that they get a divorce, although he and his wife still liked each other. He was disgusted with the situation, and hired a lawyer, who made up reasons for his wife to divorce him.

He met his second wife when he was 52. His wife then was a girl of 22, deserted by her former husband. She was homeless and penniless. He gave her food and lived with her, and finally they got married. He said he was in no way sentimental about her, but she seemed crazy about him, possibly just for what he did for her. Since he was so much older than his wife, he expected from the beginning that his wife would some day meet a young man and leave him. But for eight years she followed him wherever he went. His wife finally became addicted to morphine through him. The subject said that his wife was brought up on a farm and was her father's favorite while at home, and added that all of her sisters were married to men considerably older than they. She was also very often dressed in boy's clothes when she went to town with her father.

His wife came to see the subject one time when the subject was talking to the interviewer. She broke in and bitterly attacked the hospital for sending men to get information from her husband, while they refused to take him when he applied for treatment. She was definitely hostile and crude in her manner. She complained of being hungry. When the interviewer offered to give her a meal. she whispered that she could not accept the offer, because her husband was very jealous. She also said that the man at home who managed their property once tried to make love to her, and that an officer in the shelter also once tried to do the same. She is a tall and homely woman, appearing rather masculine and aggressive. Her husband seemed to believe whatever she told him.

The subject and his wife both submitted themselves for a cure in 1933—the man to Bridewell, and the woman to the Reformatory at Dwight—and both came out in the summer. As has been his rule, the subject went back to drugs as soon as he came out of the House of Correction. As his allowance from home had been stopped, to support his habit he resorted to the only thing he could do —panhandling. But as the winter was approaching and as it became increasingly difficult for him to panhandle he tapered the amount of drug he had been using and finally stopped it altogether and came to stay in the shelter house.

While the subject was not using drugs, he drank moonshine whenever he could afford it. One day he was asked by a man to hide a bottle of liquor in the kitchen, and while doing it he was caught by the night watchman as it was against the rule of the shelter house to drink. As a form of punishment he was sent to another shelter. The subject was furious, because he thought it was all a frame-up by the officer who had an eye on his wife, for he was not the only drinker in the shelter. Then his wife had spoken to him a few days ago about a divorce. Although the subject had said before that he expected his wife to leave him from the very beginning, he admitted that he would miss her. She used to come to see him once a while and bring him cigarettes. For these reasons his transfer to another shelter seemed to create a very great crisis in him, for when the interviewer saw him that night he could hardly talk. He kept asking for beer, and wanted to know from the interviewer whether he thought the subject was insane. He said that if he could locate a gun he would shoot himself right away. He said that he did not believe in a God, for if there were a God He would not allow him to suffer as much as he did.

Sometime after this the subject did once attempt to end his life. One night, according to the subject's story, he felt so depressed that he got into a truck in the alley and tried to cut open the veins of his left wrist, but was not successful and was sent to the hospital by the passers-by. When asked what made him depressed, he said that he used to have enough to live by, but now he was a pauper and too old to earn a living. Further, his wife used to stick to him as long as he had money, but now she did not come to see him any more. He felt that nobody cared for him and that life was not worth living.

As the warm weather came the subject again resorted to drugs for solace. Being tired of drinking moonshine and being pointed out as a drunkard, he one day said to himself, "To hell with it. I'm going to go to the Legion and get a pop and get out of this." Legion is the name of a cheap hotel in sub-community 61. So he continued to panhandle and get his "pop" everyday. One night while walking on the street, he stepped off the curb at 25th and Wentworth and was hit by a car traveling about 60 miles an hour and dragged along about 40 feet and instantly killed. That was the end of his life.

In Case 16 we see still more clearly the process of identification with one's group spoken of in previous connections. The one man who did more than others in the neighborhood in initiating this subject into the use of drugs was the barber, who to him was the most admired and most popular man around town. The connection between the addiction of this case and his adolescent environment is so evident that no further comment on this point is needed.

We further found that the subject was the only child and pet of his mother, that he almost always associated with older people, and that he was always nervous as a child, which latter fact was not mentioned in the above summary. These facts betoken an intense feeling of inferiority together with a desperate striving to be as strong, and to use one of the subject's pet words, as smart, as his older associates. It was probably because of this excessive emotional need for being like the other fellow that the subject actually imitated the most popular man in town to the very last detail.

His marriages too serve to bring out some of his personality trends in relief. In his first marriage, he seemed hesitant and passive in his relation with his wife and let his mother-in-law practically run the whole show. And to his second wife too his attitude seems to be one of wishing to get and of never getting enough of her love. Considering this passive and dependent attitude toward women, which was characteristic of him as a child toward his mother, his extreme sensitiveness to his second wife's reports about other men's advances toward her and his very emotional reaction to something he had always expected, i.e., his wife's desertion, become understandable.

The subject's passive attitude toward his own sex and great need for their attention is also seen in his complete reliance on the property left by his father, his leaving the management of the property entirely in the hands of a man at home, and his emotional reaction to being ill thought of by people and to his transfer to another shelter. It is probably this infantile dependent attitude toward people and toward life-situations in general plus their peculiar circumstances that cut them off from normal human relationship that cause many addicts to feel that nobody cares for them and that life is not worth living. And so why should they care?

4. *Through association with co-workers in hotels and restaurants.* Our statistical information about drug addicts has shown that a large number of them were engaged either in domestic and personal service or recreation and amusement work. Some of the cases whose profession was connected with the circus or some other form of commercialized recreation have been discussed in the preceding chapter. The following is a case who acquired his habit in the hotel or restaurant environment. The text reproduced is a short autobiography, and it will be supplemented by what we found through more than five interviews.

Case 17. I was born in 1878 in the central part of New York state of poor but respectable Christian parents. My father died of cancer at the age of thirty-nine when I was two years old. My mother died at the age of forty-one of tuberculosis, when I was seven . . . . My sister, ten years older than I, was married to an artist and moved to the West, and took me with her while I was still a child. . . . .

My sister moved to another city and I followed her. I began working in hotels as a bell boy and later as a waiter, at which I was working when St. Louis had the misfortune of being in the path of a cyclone in 1896 . . . . I went back to work as a bell boy and came to Chicago in that year. . . . .

It was while working at the American restaurant that I started to room with another waiter who was unknown to me and was addicted to the use of opium—of which I knew nothing. But it did not take me long to learn all there was to know about it and I became one of the best cooks (or one who prepares the opium for smoking). . . . . When I left Chicago for New York at the death of my sister, I discontinued the use of the drug after using it for nine or ten months with no ill effects to myself.

In New York I had to make a living, of course. I obtained a position as cook's helper in the M. Hotel, where I served an apprenticeship of five years duration. During this time I again started using opium, which I continued for about ten years. Then I started using morphine, since the opium in smoking form had gone up in price because of the San Francisco earthquake which destroyed the warehouses in which the importers had stored it.

I had returned to Chicago in 1903 and worked at S. Hotel. It was about 1908 that I started using morphine, which I have used intermittently ever since, the lapses being when I went to one institution or another for a so-called cure, of which there is none except through the mind and will-power of the individual.

After I left S. Hotel, where I worked for six or seven months, I traveled to Omaha where I worked in the M. Hotel and then to Denver and worked in the W. Hotel—returning to Chicago about a year later. I obtained work as a waiter in a restaurant on Randolph Street where I met a woman working as a waitress. I lived with her for two years, leaving her once and going to Pittsburgh and returning to Chicago after three months and taking up life where I had left off. I obtained a position in Ashland, Wis., in a restaurant which was connected with a gambling house run by the same man. I stayed six months and again returned to Chicago. From then on I worked in different places . . . . leaving Chicago for New York and Boston and returning in 1907.

While auditing the books in the Chicago Waiters Union with my roommate, an elderly gentleman came into the office and wanted to hire two men to go to Hancock, Michigan . . . . We went to Hancock to work. We rented a room with a woman who had a daughter nineteen years old, whose aunt was visiting there at the time but who lived in a city about one hundred miles away. When she was ready to leave, she asked her sister to let her take the girl home with her for a visit, but the mother refused. They had quite an argument over it. The aunt and I had a talk and she said she would give me a thousand dollars if I could and would get the girl out of the house and send her to her home. So when my partner's girl arrived from Chicago and they were going over to the county seat to be married, the opportunity arrived and I took the girl. The four of us went to the county seat and we were married. We rented rooms, leaving the girls there and returning to work. It was in the afternoon and we were off duty until five, but as soon as we were back, the mother with three friends came up and wanted to know what I had done with her daughter. I told her but did not or would not tell her where she was at that time. So she left and sent her husband, the girl's step-father, to see me—with no results. But they eventually got her in their house and locked her in her room. I had a shooting match with her step-father and was fined fifty dollars. Then I spent $125 on lawyers before I finally got her back. Then the aunt went back on her bargain and I had a wife on my hands whom I did not want. But I felt it my Christian duty to keep and care for her.

I bought furniture from a barber who had sold his shop and was leaving town. His flat, which I took over, was next door to the girl's mother. When my wife became pregnant, after two months, her mother performed an abortion and she was sick. Her mother persuaded her to go back to her house, where she would be cared for properly, so her mother said. So, returning one morning, I found the house cold. After searching for hours, I located my wife in her mother's house and she said that they had threatened to poison both of us if she returned to me. So that was the end, and I do not know where she is now, or if she is alive or not. I have never written to her.

We returned to Chicago again with nine thousand dollars which we invested in a restaurant in Hyde Park on 55th and Lake Park, signing the lease for one year. At the end of the year I signed the place over to G. We had lost nearly everything and I was sick of it. . . . . Since then I have just gone from one job to another and one institution to another for drug cures. In fact, I have spent just about half my time in state hospitals for the last sixteen years, and the jobs I have been able to get have been poorer and poorer until now I am in a city shelter, a pauper with no money and no outlook and no future, unless I am able to go somewhere away from Chicago and start over again. That will not be easy at 56, but I am going to try for I know I am just as quick and able to work as I ever was, although I may not have the endurance I used to have.

I think that covers just about everything.

In Case 17 we see clearly again the influence of addicts in starting a man on the use of drugs, but in an environment that is characteristic of hotels and restaurants, an environment in which contacts are superficial but may have far-reaching consequences.[1] The subject, for example, did not know his roommate in the beginning, but from him he acquired a habit that later proved to be his life-burden.

It is not to be supposed, however, that association with addicts alone is sufficient to account for one's addiction. In this case, there did not seem to be anything in the external situation that compelled the subject to room with an opium-smoker, if he really did not want to. We must, therefore, inquire into his personality make-up and see whether there is something in him that may be considered as a predisposing factor.

[1] Park and Burgess, *The City*, p. 40.

This inquiry, however, is not permitted by our limited information about the case.

But we do have some indications of his personality make-up. His marriage, for example, was almost entirely for a pecuniary purpose. In his interviews with us he also declared that he had never fallen in love with any woman. He may live with some now and then, but sentimental about them he would never be, for he said all women were fickle. His incapacity for love and distrust of women, therefore, is a trait to be taken into account.

Then in his relation with men, he said that he had always been more or less seclusive and unable to make friends. He related too that one time when he was twenty-five years old, he was invited by a man to a theater and then to his home, and he allowed himself to be used by the man for sexual purposes in return for money. He recalled another incident of a similar nature. He said he did not know why men picked him up for that purpose, but thought there must be something in him that appealed to them. These facts seem to suggest a passive homosexual trend in him. It is possible that this factor might have entered into his relation with his roommate mentioned above, if not in overt sexual behavior, then in passive emotional attachment, which we have found to be especially conducive to imitating the other fellow.

What he told about the occasions leading to his relapses after fifteen or more cures in state institutions is quite penetrating. Thus, one time when he came out of an institution, he met one of his old associates—a "dope" user of course—and invited him to live with him. So he saw his friend use the drug and just could not resist the temptation to use it himself. Another time a lady called him from a window and asked him to buy a couple of capsules of morphine for her. In one way or the other he always ran into his old associates and always went back to his habit. In all of these instances, he stressed, it was not so much the desire for the drug as the desire for companionship that brought him into contact with his old associates. He said that a drug addict is a social outcast; nobody cares to associate with him. Naturally he goes to his old acquaintances, and as naturally he relapses into his old habit. This is true at least in his own case, for we learned from reliable sources that while he might not be using drugs when he wrote the above story, he is now definitely back on his habit.

5. *Through the ingenuity of drug peddlers.* It is generally denied by

drug addicts, most of whom are petty peddlers at one time or the other, that they ever try to make proselytes. On the whole, this denial is borne out by our limited experiences with drug users. But occasionally cases of proselyting do occur. The following is a case in point.

Case 18. The patient is a white woman of about 25, appearing well dressed and possessing a certain amount of composure and charm in spite of the fact that she was under treatment for drug addiction in the Psychopathic Hospital.

She related that she began to use heroin last March. It came about this way. One day when she was going out of her apartment, a young lady living in the same building spoke to her and invited patient to visit her at her apartment. Later she did, and as she opened the door she saw the hypodermic needle and the rest. The young lady explained everything and asked if she would like to have a "shot." She accepted the offer out of curiosity, she said, and the lady did not ask her for money. She continued to see the lady and received free "shots" of heroin two more times. Then one day the patient felt "blue." She went to the lady's apartment and asked the lady if she would give her a "shot." The lady then told her that she had a habit and asked for money. For one single "shot" she paid three dollars. In that way her habit began. The patient was convinced that that lady purposely made an addict out of her, so that she could have one more customer.

On being questioned as to what made her "blue" on that day, she first said that she just felt "crabby." But in the course of the interview, she revealed that she was very much hurt by the way she was treated by her husband. She was married to this man eight years ago, when she was 17. She had known him only for three weeks. She was married to him in such a haste, because she wanted to go away from home; she could not stand her step-father any longer. The latter is a heavy drinker, and whenever he got drunk he abused everybody in the house.

She and her husband could not get along. He would not take her out, but fooled around with other women. These women even came to her home, and that hurt her pride. She does not believe in stepping out after one is married. But her husband thinks differently. So they quarreled most of the time when they were together. Finally she came back to her mother, to whom she is very much devoted, hoping that her husband would come and take her back. Instead of that he wrote and told her that he was going to marry another woman. Finally he did marry one, who had some money and bought him a new car. Naturally, she said she was hurt, not because she cared very much for her husband, but because her hope of building a home was frustrated. There is nothing in the world she likes more than to build a home and to work in the home.

She then related that her parents were separated when she was only ten, because her father was a traveling business man and went around with a lot of women, while her mother stayed at home and could not stand his going around with other women. So they were separated. They often quarreled over the patient's education. But she likes her father; he has winsome manners and an attractive personality. She not seldom writes to him for money.

Whenever she thinks about her failure in building a home, she would feel "blue." It hurts her pride, she said. For the first few times she was sick after she took a "shot" of heroin. But that day when she asked for a "shot" she did not get sick. She felt grand. Everything was all right. She forgot her worries. That kind of feeling usually lasts for four or five hours.

One year later the patient wrote to the interviewer and reported that she was in the best of health. She is now in another city. Whether she is actually cured or not it is difficult to ascertain.

However meager our information about Case 18 is, enough evidence is found in support of the hypothesis already advanced in our previous discussions, namely, that for a person to become a drug addict the external situation, however tempting, is not sufficient; there must be some preëxisting attitude or state of feeling which inclines the person to try a "shot," and, having tried once, to keep on using the drug until the habit is firmly established. In Case 18 we see clearly that the emotional strain or tension caused by her thoughts of her failure in marriage or in building a home, as she called it, had already created in her a need for release; what the lady peddler did was to give this very much needed release a definite channel, namely, through the use of drugs. In the light of this consideration, the patient's readiness in accepting the peddler's suggestion to take a "shot," her going to the latter's apartment for more, and her subsequent inability to forego the satisfaction opium gave her all become understandable.

It is also interesting to note that in her married life the patient had almost exactly the same kind of difficulty as her mother had. This might be due to the example set by her mother and the principles of marital conduct her mother taught her. This is a matter of cultural conditioning. It might also be due to her deprivation of her father's love due to her parents' early separation, which might have created in her an excessive desire for her husband's attention. This would be

called the result of inter-personal relationship.   But it is a problem that
cannot be solved with the limited amount of data at hand.

6. *Through homosexual relations.* One of the most talked about
social situations related to drug addiction is homosexual relationship.
A few cases of homosexual addicts we have come across are hereby
included.

Case 19. The subject was interviewed at the Psychopathic
Hospital.   He is a white American of 58 years.   He was sent to
the hospital by one of the shelter houses on account of excessive
drinking and signs of sexual perversion.

Patient related that he was brought up an orphan in an institution in New York and was adopted by a couple in a mid-western
state when he was 11.   They lived on a farm.   He ran away from
his foster home at 16, for he always dreamed of going out and
seeing more of the world.

When 14 he was taught homosexual relations by a man on
the road.   By 17 he lived with prostitutes in a house of ill fame,
where he worked not only as an errand boy but as an inmate
as well, satisfying the sexual needs of both the girls and the men.
His sexual activity takes the oral form.

While living with the prostitutes he had insomnia and he was
advised to take morphine tablets.   In that way his morphine habit
got started.   But he must have the drug while having homosexual
relations with men.   He has made his profession a female impersona-
tor, that is, to use a female vocabulary and mannerisms to solicit
men of similar sexual inclinations for money.   Some men would take
him home and pay him for his service.   But he emphasized that
he could do this only when he is under the influence of the drug;
otherwise that kind of thing does not appeal to him, for it is unnatural.

He kept expressing regrets and lamenting over the fact that all
of his life was gone, that he had not accomplished anything worth-
while, and that he had acted contrary to nature.   He believed in
God and felt that he was a sinner for he had violated all of the Ten
Commandments.   But he said all these things apparently without
emotion and maintained a sense of humor throughout the conversation.   One of his peculiar mannerisms is the constant moving of
his lips and pressing his fingers on them.   He expressed the desire to
quit the drug as well as his old profession and asked the interviewer
to look for a job for him.   When asked his idea of happiness, he
mentioned a state of narcosis and nights in a saloon, where men and
women go free.

In Case 19 we see clearly the psychological function opium may serve
in a homosexual person.   While the patient's ætiological account of his

addiction, including the environment of a brothel and his insomnia, may be true, it is beyond question that the most important subjective factor in the addiction of this case is his homosexual inclination. Judging from what he said, it seems that his greatest difficulty lies in the conflict between his instinctual inclination and the sexual mores of the American society, and the function of opium in such cases mainly consists in dulling the moral senses, so that one's homosexual desires may have an unrestrained satisfaction. On account of our limited information about this case, it is not possible to go any further in our analysis. But in the following case we shall have a chance to see more of the relation between drug addiction and homosexuality.

Case 20. Patient was interviewed mainly at her residence and one time at the Psychopathic Hospital off and on for a period of about two years. She is a white woman of about 32, being about five feet tall, appearing rather ordinary in looks, but intellectually she is brilliant. She is well versed in art and music. Patient was introduced to the interviewer by a mutual friend. So the conditions for interview have been quite favorable. The following is a very brief summary of the case.

Relationship with parents and siblings. Patient came from a middle-class family. She is the baby of the family. Her elder sister, 16 years older than the patient, according to her, was a beautiful lady, and she always loved to watch her sister getting dressed for parties and liked to do things for her, such as handing her slippers, etc. She has two elder brothers, the younger one being 12 years older than the patient. When she was born her mother was in the busiest period of her life, managing a store so that her father could get his education. As a baby, patient was almost always sick and weak. One time she complained to her mother that she was partial to her elder brother, the one who is 12 years older than she, but her mother denied the charge.

Early sex history. Patient used to play almost all the time with boys in the neighborhood, riding bicycles and what not. One of the boys liked her. He was seven then, and she was five. He often took her to a place and liked to take off her clothes and play with her sex organs. Once they were caught by her mother, while the boy was putting his cap on her organ—she could not recall why he did that; and for punishment her mother put red pepper in her vagina and that made her cry for the whole night. Since then she did not dare to play with that boy any more.

When she was 11, her menses came. And on noticing it her mother gave the astonishing warning, "Now, if you keep fooling around with boys, you will have a baby." She was astonished, for she did not know what "fooling around" meant and why just fooling around with boys would bring forth a baby. So from that time on she kept away from boys and mixed more with girls.

It was about the same period that she met her first love object of the same sex. The girl was 18, while patient was 11. Patient became very much attached to the young woman, and the latter often took the patient to the bank of the lake and other places, and kissed her and caressed her, but did not have any actual sexual play with her. This first romance lasted for one summer only.

At 15, she was madly in love with a woman teacher, who was seven years her senior. She brought this woman to a hotel and slept with her.

Marital life. Her husband was nice to her before marriage, but when he proposed to her, she was in love with the teacher mentioned above. It was only after a quarrel with her woman lover that she telegraphed to the man and said that she was coming to marry him. So she was married when she was 16. But she stayed with her husband for only two days, for she could not stand sexual intercourse with him. He was rough, and she suffered a great deal from the first night. She admitted she had sexual intercourse with him only with the intention of having a baby in order to appear normal. From that time on she was with her husband off and on until the latter was killed in an accident.

Patient was later engaged to another man, and she did enjoy sexual intercourse with him to a certain extent, for he was gentle. But finally she gave him up in agreement with a woman lover, who promised to give her man up. She did, but her woman lover did not. This incident proved to be a major crisis in her life, to be related later on.

While her husband was still living, she spent most of her time with her women sweethearts. From an actress she learned the form of homosexual relation which she still indulges in at the present moment, that is, cunnilinctus.

First experiments with opium and subsequent addiction. About ten years ago when she was around 20, patient fell in love with a girl who used drugs. The girl asked her to secure drugs and administered the drug to her. As a rule, they used drugs every time they had sexual relations. She was sick after the first few "shots," but gradually learned to tolerate it. She said that morphine "enhanced" her sexual desire, and lowered her "circumspectness." Under the influence of the drug, she could enjoy homosexual relations with a light heart.

Then she had to move with her family to a distant city, and her woman lover followed. Together they stayed in an apartment and used drugs in connection with their sexual relations everyday for a

period of three months. On account of sickness in the home she
was obliged to stay away from her woman lover. She experienced
discomfort and pain in the legs, but it did not occur to her that she
had a morphine habit. So she simply stopped using drugs until
five years later.

Five years later she was back in Chicago, and fell in love with
another girl, who, patient claimed, was just made for her as a sexual
partner. Morphine was used as usual in connection with their
sexual activities. She sent this girl to school and made plans to support and live with her for life. It was with this girl that patient
made the agreement to give up her fiancé. She did, but the girl
did not; instead she left the patient and got married to a man. That
broke her heart and, she said, marked the real beginning of her use
of drugs as a daily habit.

After a "shot" of morphine, patient said she used to experience
a momentary thrill from head to foot; it is just a matter of an in-
stant. When the interviewer asked how she would compare this
thrill with sexual excitement, she answered immediately that she
had herself for a long time thought that there was only one thing that
could be compared to the thrill from a "shot" of morphine, and that
is, an orgasm. The feeling she used to get from a "shot" of morphine is one of instantaneous excitement followed by complete relaxation. It lasts just for a moment. Furthermore, while under
the influence of the drug her imagination becomes less inhibited; she
thinks more freely and makes all kinds of plans, but does not actually
want to put them into execution. The momentary thrill, however,
will disappear as one increases one's dosage and the frequency of
"shots." Then it becomes only a matter of overcoming withdrawal
symptoms. Besides, she said there is some attraction about the
needle that she could not very decidedly give up. She uses her
drug intravenously. She said she always likes to see and play
with her blood that comes out from her vein, as all addicts do. Then
she also likes to sit on the stool after a "shot" of morphine in order
to have her bowels moved. These are some of the pleasures of opium
she has experienced.

As to the withdrawal symptoms, patient described them as partly
mental, for when one is determined to quit the habit and is ready to
undergo the suffering from withdrawal, one will not suffer as much
as when one is not so prepared. The withdrawal symptoms as she
experienced them are described as follows. There is first an increasing sense of apprehension. Then out of a clear sky something
strikes her larynx and the deadening tickle at her throat commences.
This is followed by waves of tightening all over her body, as if bands
of metal were clutching upon her from her head down to her limbs.
Then a hollow feeling sets in as if her otherwise well connected

system were falling to pieces, and the feeling of collapse possesses her. Excretions become loose, her nose waters, and she feels unable to move.

Cures and relapses. We shall not go into the patient's multiple love affairs with her own sex or her difficulty with the law some years ago. But the situations and states of mind connected with her repeated cures and relapses must be briefly touched upon.

One time after she came out of an institution, patient succeeded in refraining from using drugs for about eight months. Then she went back to her old habit. When asked the reason for this relapse, she at first mentioned the fact that one day she visited one of her old friends, who is a drug-user. Her friend suggested that it would not do her much harm to take just a little morphine. So she did. She then added that it was really not due to her friend's persuasion, for she then was in a very depressive mood and had nobody to talk to. After that she would hesitate before she took another "shot," but there was always the inner voice, saying, "What is the use?" When asked what made her feel depressed, patient said that sometime ago she had the chance of meeting a woman whom she admires and loves. She was ashamed because she felt unworthy of her. Besides, after a short meeting, the woman she admires had to leave her. So patient missed her. It was in such an emotional state that patient accepted her addict-friend's suggestion to take a "shot," that led to her relapse.

Patient felt so helpless and hopeless in fighting the battle all alone that she appealed to the interviewer and asked to be taken to the Psychopathic Hospital for another cure, and it was arranged for her. But before the customary ten days were up, the patient left the hospital. She fought hard against another relapse. But there was work to do in the house and she was weak, and so the easiest way out, she said, was to take a "shot."

Then she went away for another cure, and when she came back, she claimed, she was not using drugs. All this time she had been in love with a married woman, and there had been difficulties of one kind or the other in their relationship. Patient usually takes the active rôle in her relation with women—what is called "Mantee" in the lingo of homosexuals. But she bitterly complained to the interviewer that her present lover is the most selfish person she has ever known. What this woman cares for is physical satisfaction, whereas what the patient wants is love and affection. The result was that every time they were together and had sexual relations, almost as soon as the patient satisfied her lover, the latter would start to go home. This lack of consideration for the patient seemed to her unforgivable. But her lover is physically so attractive that patient could not give her up, although in her heart she often wondered whether she really loved the woman or not. One of the major problems in their relationship came from the man friends of her lover. They objected to the patient's going to her lover's apartment all the time. So one day her lover told her that she could not go on with patient. Patient was so upset that she came home with a gloomy view of life. She felt that everything was gone and that life was not worth living. She started right away to use heroin, expecting to end her life by an overdose. On top of it she applied chloroform to herself. She then shut the windows. She saw herself going away. She thought of the interviewer at that moment, thinking that he might be disappointed in her. And then somehow things in her stomach came up and she vomited. And she came to life, she said.

We shall not go into other suicidal attempts of the patient and her other difficulties in her love life. Enough has been told to illustrate what the patient herself said about her relapses. She concluded from her experiences that practically every one of her relapses was due to two major factors: (1) her difficulty in love relationship; (2) her meeting with friends or acquaintances who are drug users or peddlers.

Relations with men. Patient's relationship with her father, who is still living, is interesting. She likes her father, but complained more than once that he treated her too much as a child; that he could go out any time he wanted to play bridge with his women friends, while she had to be at home; and that he was too nice to her niece. Patient is living with her father and lets him support her.

Patient's attitude toward the interviewer has been of increasing dependence but of decreasing coöperation. Patient did not hesitate to ask the interviewer to do things for her, including such matters as sending her to the hospital, making arrangements for her to go to another institution, and sundry matters in the home which a lady ordinarily would not ask a guest to do. But every time the interviewer went to visit the patient, even though it was by appointment, patient almost always kept the interviewer waiting for hours before she showed signs of coöperation. The interviewer's consciousness of this fact was no doubt partly due to his own desire for the patient's respect and attention, but on the whole this report fairly represents the way the patient acted toward the interviewer. Patient more than once expressed gratitude to the interviewer for being her friend, but regretted that he was not a woman. One time she said she liked the interviewer, because he is small.

In Case 20 the relationship between homosexuality and drug addiction is seen in a much clearer light. As the patient has well expressed it, opium serves to lower her "circumspectness" or inhibitions, and thereby enhances her sexual desire and enables her to enjoy homosexual relations without being reminded constantly what society thinks about it.   The influence of her friend, the drug-user, is no doubt important in accounting for her initial contact with drugs, but the preëxisting homosexual trend in her is no less an important factor.   It was because of the existence of this homosexual trend that she associated with her friend, derived the kind of satisfaction from opium that she did, and kept on using it until the habit was firmly established.

But patient does not seem to be really happy in her homosexual relations.   She seems to be always disappointed by one woman or the other, and judging from what she told about her serious love affairs, her greatest difficulty seems to lie in the fact that the other woman does not love her as much as she expects.   It was such disappointments, we are told, that constituted the principal subjective factor leading to her repeated relapses after cures, the external situations such as meeting a drug addict or peddler only providing the occasion for her emotional need for narcotics to be gratified.

Thus, if we want to have a complete understanding of this case, we must not stop at the obvious environmental factors connected with her addiction.   In other words, we must inquire into the genesis of her homosexual trend.   The patient once remarked that her homosexuality was inborn.   But the episodes she related about her childhood seem to suggest that her feeling of being unwanted or neglected by her mother in preference to her elder brother was probably the most important factor in developing in her an excessive desire for her mother's love, or to use a more technical term, a strong fixation on her mother.   Her mother's rather unwise way of punishing her for playing with boys undoubtedly contributed toward her one-sided emotional development, but that she should have been so obedient and actually stopped going any more with boys from that time on implies a strong desire on her part to please her mother and to get her love and approval.   In some such way perhaps the patient's homosexual trend was given inception and cultivated.   And it is probably her excessive demand on her lover, which, let us assume, is carried over from her original attitude toward her mother, that makes her disappointed every time she thinks she has at last found one who really loves her.

The patient's attitude toward men is also interesting.   The facts are that even at the present moment she is depending on her father's support and is still jealous of his attention to other women and to her niece;

that in her marital relationship she did not show any sign of love for her husband or any consideration of his welfare; and that in her relation with the interviewer the evidences seem to indicate that she was much more ready to get and to exploit him than to give and to coöperate with him. These facts point to a destructive tendency toward men on the part of this patient. It is difficult to trace this trend. Probably the patient's rivalry with her father and especially her elder brother for her mother's love had something to do with it. Our limited data, however, do not permit us to go any further.

If the above analysis is correct, the patient may be said to have the desire to be like other women, as evidenced by her marriage and her desire to have a baby in order to appear normal, and yet is incapable of making a heterosexual adjustment; nor can she be really happy in her homosexual relations, not only because they are socially disapproved, but because it is not likely that her excessive desire for women's love will ever be satisfied. As long as the patient continues to be entangled in such emotional conflicts, her psychological need for narcotics probably will always remain, and, living as she does in such a center of drug traffic as Chicago, she probably will have a lifelong battle to fight against her drug habit.[1]

It is interesting to mention in this connection that one of the patient's lovers, whom she found to be her best sex-partner, did not turn into a drug addict in spite of the fact that this girl used drugs weekly with the patient for about two years and off and on for another seven or more years by herself, and in spite of the further fact that as a nurse she always has access to drugs. The interviewer happened to meet this girl and the story she told about herself is as follows.

Case 21. The subject is a blonde of medium height and appears somewhat stout. She ran away from home at the age of 16, because her father was too strict and would not allow her to marry a man she loved. She came to Chicago as a chorus girl. She saved money and went to a hospital to be trained as a nurse. While there she met Case 20 and was initiated by the latter into homosexual relations as related above. Then instead of coming to live with Case 20 as she had promised, she married a man, who later, however, disappointed her. For he was a jealous man and often beat her for trivial reasons. She married him for his wealth and also out of fear.

---

[1] The author is indebted to Prof. Harold D. Lasswell for a discussion of this case.

In a year she left him, and went to another city and worked there regularly as a nurse, until she was expelled from the hospital on account of excessive drinking. When interviewed, this girl was stopping at the home of Case 20 and asked to be taken back by the latter to live with her. The girl said that she was greatly surprised to find her friend a confirmed drug addict, for she is not, although they began to use drugs practically at the same time. She said that she just could not understand why using opium once in a while for pleasure or using it in medical treatment should cause one to become a drug addict.

To explain why Case 20 became a drug addict while Case 21 did not would require more information than we have about either of them. Case 21 thought that her training as a nurse and her knowledge of the dangers of using drugs too often probably had something to do with her not forming the drug habit, while Case 20 suggested that the fact that her lover did not go in for homosexual relations after the latter left her was probably a more important factor. Undoubtedly there is some difference between the emotional inclination of Case 20 and that of her lover, but then each had her own peculiar problems. We cannot offer any better explanation except by pointing out the fact that Case 21 is a heavy drinker, while Case 20 does not drink at all. It is a question whether there is any great difference between the habitual use of opium and that of liquor, although the one may appear more binding than the other.

In concluding this brief exploration of the social situations and personality factors related to drug addiction, the following points are considered as significant.

We found that practically all of the addicts we have interviewed— over 40 cases altogether—first acquired their information about opium and learned the technique of using it through association with drug users. This we found to be true even of those cases in which medical use of the drug was claimed to be the most important ætiological factor, with only one or two exceptions. In these supposedly medical cases, not so much the actual administration of the drug by the physician but to be told that one had been given morphine or heroin or that one had a habit seemed to be the determining factor in urging one to keep on using it, till it became really a habit.

The social situations in which these addicts first came in contact with drugs and drug users were found to be smoking parties, the houses of ill fame, where either the prostitute or the pimp is a drug user, pool rooms and gambling houses, hotels and restaurants, apartment houses, or any other place where the drug addicts happen to live or frequent. Homosexual relations were also found to be a not uncommon ætiological situation. All these situations may be said to represent an environmental setting, in which either by choice or by circumstances one has left behind one's affectional bonds formed early in life together with the traditions and mores with which one was brought up; and in which an individual's conduct has little or no direction except his or her own personal considerations. This state of affairs has been called by some sociologists social *anomie* or lawlessness.[1]

Just as the man in a Bible story was visited by seven evil spirits because his heart was empty, so the boy on the road or the man or woman living a lonely existence in the big city and divorced of old affectional ties picks up new group affiliations, acquires new patterns of behavior, and learns to enjoy new forms of pleasure. For as Park has well expressed in one place, it is not natural for man to live entirely apart from society; "most human actions are sanctioned in some society."[2] So what becomes of the inexperienced men and women who go with drug users to smoking parties or the house of prostitution is that before they realize it they have gradually assimilated the whole body of habits, slang, traditions, and codes of drug addicts, which, for the sake of convenience, may be referred to as the dope culture. Some examples of it may be given in this connection.

Thus, the paraphernalia of a drug addict almost invariably consist of a hypodermic needle, an eye dropper, a spoon in which to make a solution of the drug, and, in the case of a "vein shooter," an old necktie to be used as a tourniquet. The whole outfit is called a "plant" or "joint." Then the "junk," or the drug, is uniformly used three or more times a day at such intervals: one early in the morning to get up with, one or two times during the day, and one before going to bed. They too have class distinctions among themselves. Thus the "pipe fiend" or the opium smoker generally looks down upon the "skin shooter" or one who uses the drug hypodermically; and the "skin shooter," in turn, may look down upon the "main line" or the "vein shooter," that is, one who uses the drug intravenously. But all of them have this code in common that

---

[1] Mayo, *op. cit.*, pp. 129–31.
[2] R. E. Park, "Personality and Cultural Conflict," *Publication of the Sociologica Society of America*, XXV (1931), p. 98.

no one should betray the other or give away one's "connection," that is, the peddler. For this reason, the stool-pigeon, or the informant for the Government, is the most despised person in the dope world. What are still more interesting are their attitudes toward what they call the "square Johns" or non-users and toward themselves. The drug addicts are all self-conscious in the company of other people and are always afraid of it being discovered that they are "dope fiends." For this reason they tend to associate exclusively with themselves. And yet they do not trust each other, for one can never know when one's friend turns to be a stool-pigeon. Finally, there seems to be a general belief among drug addicts that once an addict always an addict, and that there is no cure for drug addiction; and yet practically all of them keep on hoping that some day they will be cured. In short, these are some of the salient features of what we call the dope culture, and in time all these habits of thought and action are taken over by the newly initiated.

We discovered that the process in which this pattern of opium addiction is taken over by an individual is not very much different from that in which other cultural patterns are transmitted. In a number of cases we found that the drug habit was started less for the effect of the drug than as a sign of identification with the group they happened to be in. In particular may be mentioned cases 5, 7, 10, 12, 13, 14, 15, 16, 17, and 20. This process of identification is found to take place when a young person associates with an older one who uses drugs and who because of the habit or otherwise commands the former's admiration and respect, or when two persons are in some form of love relationship, such as between a prostitute and a pimp, between a husband and a wife, or between two homosexuals, when one of them is a drug user. Such states of emotional rapport are found to be most conducive to the acquisition of the drug habit. In fact, this *esprit de corps* is claimed by Faris to be the essential condition for many forms of effective learning.[1]

In other cases, instead of or besides the desire to be like the other fellow or for group approval, the dominating motive that prompts them to associate with drug users and to take drugs is the desire to forget; and the state of feeling found most susceptible to the suggestions of drug users may be characterized as depression or as one of not caring for any-body or anything. This is especially true of those who have been dis-

[1] E. Faris, "The Primary Group: Essence and Accident," *American Journal of Sociology*, XXXVIII (1932), pp. 45–6.

appointed in love or in marital relationship, or have failed in their career. Speaking only of the cases we have interviewed, the depressive mood caused by maladjustment in sex and love relationship is by far the most common predisposing factor in their addiction to drugs.

The above may be said to be some of the environmental and subjective factors responsible for the addicts' initial contact with drugs and other drug users. The next interesting problem is: after one starts using drugs, when and how one becomes really addicted or "hooked," as the drug users call it, or when and how the use of drugs becomes a compulsive daily habit. We found that the time required for the establishment of the drug habit differs with different individuals, ranging from one week— Case 6 for example—to five years—Case 20 for example. It seems to depend a great deal on the frequency with which one uses the drug. Those who use it daily generally form the habit more quickly than those who use it only periodically. Physiologically, too, one may react to the effect of drugs differently from the other. The difference in emotional satisfaction different individuals derive from the use of drugs is certainly a factor not to be ignored. But the most interesting and important factor we found to be responsible for the addiction of a number of cases is the suggestion of confirmed drug users to the effect that one has had a habit and that one has to do something about it. In the absence of such suggestions, it seems that one may keep on using drugs for a considerable length of time and may even experience what is generally known as the withdrawal symptoms, and yet one may be spared the deadly habit. With reference to this point may be mentioned cases 6 and 20.

Once the habit is established, the life of most addicts seems to consist mainly of series of cures and relapses. In the cases we have interviewed, we found that relapse is the rule, while a permanent or even a relatively lasting cure is a very rare exception. And practically every relapse is found to be due to two major factors: (1) meeting with old associates who are drug users; and (2) incapacity to face life-situations without the help of the drug. And this incapacity to face life-situations, upon close examination, is found in many cases to be characteristic of the addict long before he or she forms the drug habit, and to consist mainly of defective or inadequate emotional attitudes toward people and toward life issues in general. In other words, we found that practically all of the addicts we have interviewed have an infantile type of personality, characterized by excessive dependence on other people and a persistent tendency to withdraw or escape from social responsibilities.[1]

Upon closer examination, it was found that most of the defective or inadequate attitudes toward people that caused the addicts under investigation to shun the demands of culture, and that in the beginning predisposed them to the use of narcotics and in the end made a permanent cure almost impossible, seemed to have definite connection with their childhood life, especially their relation with their parents.

Thus we found that drug addiction is at bottom a symptom of a maladjusted personality; and since the source of an addict's maladjustment either as a child or as an adult is social, drug addiction may also be said to be a product of general social disorganization.

From what is said in the foregoing, it is evident that no single factor, neither the social environment nor the personality trends described above, could be pointed out as the cause of drug addiction. Rather is it in the interplay of social and personal factors that we can expect to find the right clues to an adequate understanding of the problem of drug addiction. Thus, it is a matter of common observation that an individual may live in the areas with high rates of opium addiction described in Chapter IV and may even occasionally go to smoking parties, and yet may be spared the drug habit. On the other hand, persons with the emotional difficulties as we found in most addicts may have nothing to do with drugs whatsoever; they may, for instance, develop neuroses or psychoses, or commit suicide. All of our data point to the fact that it is persons with inadequate emotional attitudes or from a cultural background that has already lost its control over them who are most likely to become drug addicts when exposed to that part of the underworld environment which we call the dope culture, and who, with these ætiological conditions remaining the same, are as likely to remain addicts for life once their drug habit is established.

III. Social Situations Related to the Effective Rehabilitation of Drug Addicts

At this juncture the question inevitably forces itself upon us whether such a thing as an effective and permanent cure of drug addiction is at all possible. To answer such a question requires research on a larger

[1] E. K. Wickman, *Children's Behavior and Teachers' Attitude* (New York, 1928), pp. 131–153.

scale and for a longer period than the present study. But a few cases whose habit on the basis of all available evidences may be said to have been cured—at least for the length of time during which they were under the writer's observation—are presented in the following. They may give us some indications of what from the sociological point of view may be considered as an effective treatment of drug addiction.

Case 22. The subject was introduced to the interviewer by the federal probation officer in Chicago. He is an American male of over 40. The story he told about himself is as follows.

He was brought up in St. Louis as an orphan, for his mother died when he was a mere infant, and his father was then such a poor carpenter that he could not support him and his sister. While in the orphanage he was treated well by the governesses, but none of them could be compared to a real mother. At 15 he began to live on his own resources, and for a period of seven or more consecutive years since that age he worked as a waiter in the then red-light district of Chicago, i.e., around Wabash and 22nd. He mingled constantly with gamblers, "dope fiends" and "hustlers," and began to "fool around" with opium rather early, but, according to his story, he did not get "hooked" until about nineteen years ago, when he got addicted to morphine tablets through medication given by doctors. He joined the War in 1918, and took up opium smoking after the War, for then he was still working in the red-light district. In those days, he said, one could smoke a pipe for 50 cents. He got addicted to opium in five weeks, and since that time on he has been sent to the penitentiary more than once for the possession of opium. This time he was put on probation for two years. He has served one year probation already, and has another to go. He used to smoke opium only, and could not stand what he called the "damned needle," for it gave him a stabbing feeling.

The subject began his promiscuous sexual relations very early in his life. About 18 years ago he fell in love with a girl whom he married after six months' courtship. His wife, he said, is a good and dependable woman, who carried on legitimate business even while her husband was in prison. At the time the interviews were held the subject and his wife were living at that section of South Kedze St., which is dotted with working men's houses, each of which costs around $5,000. And the subject himself was running a store selling eggs, milk and other things. He declared that he was through with opium and was working to save money, so that he could own a house.

The subject repeatedly expressed the conviction that if an addict wants seriously to quit the drug habit, the only way is to live away from drug users. He gave an account of one of his own relapses as follows. Two years ago his wife was running a dress-shop in a hotel, and he was sitting in the hotel lobby. A couple of lads came along and asked him to go upstairs and to "lay down" with them, and there his opium habit returned. He said he could not explain why it was so difficult to resist the temptation to use drugs when he was in the company of other users, but somehow in their company his reason did not work. So he was resolved that he would not go near drug users, and in this he had been successful for the past year.

Our information about Case 22 is too limited to warrant a detailed analysis. Thus his account of his initial addiction as due to medication certainly requires further verification. But the fact that the subject, in spite of the long duration of his drug habit and his rich experience as a drug peddler, has actually abstained from using opium for a complete year is something that is worth our attention. If one were asked to name the factors that made possible his success thus far, one cannot ignore his concern about his wife and home and his interest in his present business. Perhaps the most important factor is the fact that he lived at quite a distance from the Loop and the centers of drug traffic near it. This is both considered as essential by the subject and made obligatory by the terms of probation. While one hesitates to predict how long the subject will remain cured, there seems to be no reason why he should relapse as long as he can stay away from his old associates and persist in his business and home-building activities. The only regrettable thing is that cases of such a hopeful outlook handled by the probation office are few; nor is the policy detailed above consistently applied to every case.

Case 23. The subject is an American male of over 40. He has smoked opium ever since 1909, but we have good reasons to believe that he has not been using drugs for the past three years. When the interviews were held, he was an efficient worker and lived quite contentedly in a kind of home atmosphere, though not far from the Loop. Here we shall not go into the sequence of events or the subjective factors that led to the formation of the opium habit in the subject, but his account for his success thus far in staying away from drugs is highly suggestive.

He used to think that under the influence of the drug he could accomplish more as a professional thief. As a matter of fact, he had experiences of that kind which he could not otherwise account for. But one experience he had in prison disillusioned him. He was then charged with heavy responsibilities as something of a super-intendent of the dining hall in the prison. He took pride in relating how efficiently he used to work at his job when he was not using drugs. By a single glance over the tables he could tell right away if one glass were missing. But owing to the influence of fellow inmates he was "hooked" again, and this time he was using morphine. He became so inefficient in his work that he said to himself, "Hell with it. I did work a lot better without the stuff." And he quit it for good. He explained that he had pride in himself, which he called the Ego, and he wanted to show to others that he alone of all addicts could get rid of his drug habit if he chose.

Another factor which he considered as important is his subsequent contact with university men who not only cultivated in him a genuine interest in research but helped him settle down in his present job. Thus he formed new acquaintances and moved in new social circles. The self-respect gained in this manner apparently has been strong enough to sustain him in his good intention in spite of the fact that the subject has been in constant contact with drug users and lives in the midst of the areas with high opium addiction rates.

In Case 23, if we were to point out any single factor that seems more important than the rest in his successful rehabilitation thus far, it will not be so much the physical separation from drug users as was emphasized and carried into effect by Case 22 as the social distance gained through contact with respectable society and a new outlet for his narcissism gained through interest in research work that has apparently kept the subject psychologically aloof from his old associates.

Case 24. The subject is an American woman of 56. She is a home missionary, and the interviews were held at the Moody Bible Institute, where she was the speaker of the day. The story she told about herself is as follows.

She is the youngest of fourteen children of her parents. Her father died when she was very young. Due to poverty of her home she was brought up by her uncle and as a child she was always delicate. Her parents were Christians working in a mission. At the age of 15, she was married to her god-father who was then 63, and a child was born who died an infant. At 20 she fell in love with a man of 30 and by this man she bore seven children, all of whom died except a girl. When her second husband died, she got married for the third time to a man, who, she later discovered, already had a wife. So she left him. She did not get married again. She declared she now is married to Jesus.

Up to the age of 32 she was a spotless woman. She did not play bridge, smoke or dance. But at 32 she had a nervous breakdown due to the heavy work at home and in the mission, and what the doctor gave her turned out to be morphine, which she discovered only when the habit was firmly established. She has had at least five cures and none was effective. While she was using drugs, she ran a house of prostitution, keeping nine girls and having a great deal of difficulty with the law.

Ever since she began to use drugs and left home, her parents would not allow her to come home or to see her own daughter. The thought of her girl finally gave her the incentive for the last cure. She went to the Bellevue Hospital and after the cure went home, expecting to see her daughter. But she was again turned away. She was so utterly discouraged that within three days she was back on morphine again, in order to forget her worries, she said. Finally, however, her daughter came to her and she was then 13 years old. As the girl lived among prostitutes she naturally picked up smoking and drinking, which the subject tried to prevent but in vain. For fear that her own girl might turn wild and become a drug addict, she thought of committing suicide, so that her folks would come and take the girl back. So one night she took an overdose of morphine. The next thing she remembered was that she was brought to a mission. A missionary woman took care of her and tried to read the Bible to her and talked to her about Jesus Christ. She was sick and dirty and refused to listen to the missionary, saying that she did not believe in the Bible. But finally the tenderness and love of that missionary woman won her and she let the latter pray for her. This contact with the missionary woman, however, produced little effect on her, for she kept using drugs and went back to her sporting girls several times a day. In fact, the Christian mission and her house of prostitution were situated on the same street. The missionary woman apparently did not lose hope in her and even came to the brothel to call her back.

But one night while she was with her sporting girls, the missionary woman called and said that she had been discharged by the mission authorities because they did not approve of her visiting the subject at the house of prostitution. On hearing this the subject was furious and immediately went back to the mission with the missionary woman and gave the mission authorities—a man and his woman assistant—a severe scolding and told them that they were not real Christians while her missionary friend was a real one. She gave the missionary woman a protecting hand, and while the latter was sleeping inside the room the subject sat outside at the door and kept watch, so that no one could throw her missionary friend out. On the next day she left her sporting girls and took the missionary woman to live with her in a separate place. She started to give herself a cure at home by the method of gradual reduction. Four days had gone by, but on the fifth night she could not stand it any longer. Her missionary friend, however, threw her on the bed and sat on top of her and would not let her get up. She fought hard but could not get away. Then she fell asleep. While she was sleeping, the missionary woman prayed for her, so that the Lord might save her. In the next morning she woke up a different woman and the desire for the drug was gone. And from that time on she and her missionary friend have been living together for the past 17 years. Once only, she admitted, she experienced the temptation to try drugs, but the thought of Jesus kept her back.

She said that before this all the doctors she had seen told her that she was hopeless, but the Lord saved her. One time—it was in 1925—she appeared in a physicians' conference and was given different kinds of medical tests. While the doctors were talking about her blood, she stood up and testified that it was the wrong blood that they were talking about; it was the blood of Christ that saved her.

The genuineness of the story as a whole seems to admit of no doubt, but the explanation offered by the subject for her successful rehabilitation requires further scrutiny. If one were to ascribe her success entirely to the Christian religion as the subject has done, one is up against the difficulty of explaining why in the first place the religion had failed to prevent the subject from becoming an addict. What brought about the miracle, so to speak, does not seem to lie so much in the religion as it is as in the subject's later attitude toward it, and the subject's later attitude toward Christianity seemed to be conditioned entirely by her relation to her missionary friend. And the occasion that brought about this transformation was one that called forth from the subject what may be called "holy indignation" against a male authority and his assistant and the powerful urge to protect the weak of her own sex. What these emotions mean to the subject may not be manifest owing to the lack of pertinent information, but that they did bring about a total affectional reorganization in her is a fact that is worth our notice. Apparently she now is quite contented emotionally with a homosexual attachment to a woman four years her senior, her sublimated heterosexual love of Jesus, and her ego-elevating work among the downcast and the poor. She was right in a way when she told the physicians that her own blood had little to do with her cure, for medical men who are interested only in locating some physical agent in the soma of a drug addict in accounting for his or her behavior before or after cure generally overlook the problem of the addict's emotional and social adjustment. What actually cured this case, to borrow a term from psycho-analysis, seemed to be a new libidinal organization and a plan of life that is made spontaneous by her upbringing.

Case 25. The patient is a white woman of over 40. She was first seen at the Psychopathic Hospital and then at her residence off and on for seven months. Correspondence kept up the contact to the time of writing. Certain facts about her life pertinent to our present topic are summarized in the following.

She is the second child of a large family. Her father was very religious and strict in dealing with his children, while her mother is more lenient and good-natured. But her father also liked the light side of life, such as music and dancing. She has been told and is convinced herself that she takes after her father. Ordinarily she is always restless. She had asthma since ten. At 14 she began to go around with people in the show business and had her first sex experience, which she characterized as "being ruined." At 17, she ran away from home and lived with a man many years her senior. He was a "big shot" in the underworld and peddled opium but not other drugs. To this man she was formally married when she was 22. She confessed that she did not love him, but he had money.

Her husband would not allow her to touch the pipe, although he himself was an opium smoker. But he was in and out of prison most of the time. So during his absence the patient learned to smoke opium, and through a lodger in the same building she also acquired the morphine habit. Her husband died of general paresis and left her a widow at 30. Ever since she used drugs she has not been bothered by asthma.

Her present husband is a Negro, whom she consented to marry after a brief acquaintance. He was then making good money and married her in spite of her drug habit. He had spent a large sum of money on her cures, but none was effective. For after a cure she invariably became restless and first took to whisky and before long was back on drugs. For a period of six years, however, she hid her habit so successfully that her husband thought she was cured; only since he was not making much money recently did he begin to be inquisitive about the way she spent her money and thereby about her habit.

Repeatedly she emphasized the fact that socially she was ostracized, for although she lived with her husband in the Black Belt she did not want to associate much with colored people; nor could she mingle with whites with a colored husband. On the other hand, she has great respect for her husband, for she has observed that whereas most other white women who live with colored men have to support them—pimps in other words,—she has been well taken care of. But to be in the home all the time with nothing to do and no friends to associate with has been too much a strain for her, and it was because of this, she stressed, that she had to drink after every cure, and that when drinking failed to relieve her she resorted to drugs. While under the influence of the drug she was seldom restless and was contented in being alone in the home while her husband was away working.

Upon discharge from the hospital, the patient declared that this time she was not going to touch even whisky, to say nothing of drugs. In a week's time, however, her drinking habit returned, and the interviewer found it necessary in the following months to bring her a bottle of gin once in a while in order to gain her coöperation. But drugs she did not touch. This was rather difficult on the part of the patient, for almost all of her women associates are "hustlers" and drug users, and the place where they lived is surrounded by drug peddlers. The patient gradually grew dependent on the interviewer and would not hesitate to call him to her aid whenever she felt "blue."

The patient's sexual relation with her husband seemed to be one of indifference. She said that she enjoyed it in the beginning because of novelty, but did not care much for sexual intercourse while she was using drugs. But when she was out of drug supply and grew restless, she might find some release in coitus and then would become still more restless. When asked to compare the feeling of contentment after coitus and that after receiving a "shot" of morphine, she described the latter feeling as much more intense than the former. She said that she often compared the suffering that comes from yearning for the drug to the agony a woman experiences when yearning for her lover. When she yearned for the drug she was extremely restless, had no appetite and no interest in anything, but as soon as she had it she would ask for food and drink and become a different woman all at once.

The crisis came when her husband was unemployed and they were asked to leave the place where they lived. The patient became very much upset and declared that if she had the money to buy drugs she would use them again, for she knew exactly what she wanted now. She confessed that all along she had the craving, but the hardship she had gone through in the past on account of her drug habit taught her not to take a wrong step. Soon after this the patient was sent to another city and since then correspondence has taken the place of interviews. At the time of writing it is exactly one year since the patient left the hospital, and we are positive that she has not touched the drug during all this period. As time went on the patient definitely became more optimistic. What took place was a new love affair with prospects of a home more satisfying than the one she had, the details of which, however, cannot be entered into here.

Case 25 is interesting in more than one respect. What call for special emphasis are the influence of the underworld environment upon her initial addiction to drugs about twenty-five years ago, although her temperament or constitution as a possible ætiological factor, as indicated by her being always restless, is not to be ignored; the close relation between her social isolation and her repeated relapses; and the possible relation between her difficulty in heterosexual adjustment and the erotic feelings she attached to the use of drugs. Evidently what might help her achieve a permanent rehabilitation is some substitute for opium whenever her restlessness needs a relief, which she has found in alcohol; and, better still, a readjustment in her sexual life, which, due to the happy turn of events, seems to be within her reach now, although a person's sexual adjustment is such a complicated matter that a mere change of love-object may not make much difference. The information up to date, however, inclines us to consider the prognosis of this case as hopeful.

Our information about those cases cited above is far from being sufficient to warrant a generalization about the factors that are essential in the effective rehabilitation of drug addicts. But the experiences of these cases seem to suggest that for an addict to achieve an effective cure he must place himself in a new social situation in which relapse through contact with other drug users is made difficult. Most important of all, he must be helped to bring about an emotional reorientation or a total reorganization of his personality, acquiring new interests in life and setting up new goals to live for. This may be accomplished through interesting work, religion, or love, as shown in the cases cited above. Once this is achieved, the giving up of the drug habit does not seem to be such a hopeless task as it is generally thought. In other words, according to our limited observation, the rehabilitation of drug addicts turns out to be essentially a problem of their social adjustment. This finding is in line with our previous observation that almost every relapse of drug addicts is occasioned by their failure to face life-situations, especially emotional problems. To help effect a satisfactory social adjustment amounts to eliminating that feeling of insecurity, inferiority or isolation in the face of straining social situations that sends an addict back to his drug as quickly and naturally as a disappointment in life sends an ordinary neurotic person back to his favorite ailment. All these considerations point to the one conclusion that for the effective rehabilitation of drug addicts, medical treatment alone is not sufficient; nor can legislation or penal measures accomplish much; international agreements to limit the production and manufacture of opium and other narcotic drugs, in such a lawless world as it is, are still less reliable; and the only intelligent and humane way is to understand each and every drug addict as a member of society and to help him or her achieve a satisfactory social adjustment.

CHAPTER VII

SUMMARY

HERE we come to the end of our exploratory study of opium addiction in Chicago. The following are some of the significant findings that call for emphasis and that may serve as a basis for further study.

1. THE PHARMACOLOGICAL EFFECTS OF OPIUM AND THE OBJECT OF THIS STUDY

The study of the physiological effects of opium belongs to the field of pharmacology. But a cursory excursion into this field brought to light the fact relevant to our inquiry that the pharmacological effects of opium are both stimulating and depressing, although the stimulating effect is more apparent than real and is only transitory; and that its depressing effect first reaches the highest layer of the human brain, which is the seat of associative reasoning and moral control, before it spreads to the entire organism. These facts suggest to us that our main line of inquiry is to find out how the stimulating and depressing effects of opium are utilized to satisfy the needs peculiar to human beings. The crux of the whole problem lies in the fact that after one uses the drug for a certain period, one is apt to be addicted, that is to say, one must keep on using it, otherwise one is likely to suffer from the functional disturbances generally known as withdrawal symptoms. The nature of these withdrawal symptoms is still a very much debated question in pharmacology. But the consensus of opinion among serious students of the problem seems to be that the basic nature of these withdrawal symptoms is more emotional or psychological than organic or physiological. In particular, we have mentioned the clinical studies of drug addicts made by Light and others at the Philadelphia General Hospital. Our task in this study is to begin just where these pharmacologists and physiologists stopped, and to find out what the emotional basis of these withdrawal symptoms is and where the addict's troubles really come from. Looking at the problem from the sociological point of view, we began with the hypothesis that the addict's troubles mainly come from his relation with other people and from his failure to fulfill the requirements made on him by culture as a member of society.

2. THE NATURAL HISTORY OF OPIUM ADDICTION

We first approached the problem of opium addiction from a point of view that is familiar to cultural anthropology, and found that the euphoric use of opium has a natural history, that is to say, it grew and spread under certain ascertainable historical, social, and cultural conditions. Both the knowledge and the euphoric use of opium spread from the West to the East since very early times, but it was not until the nineteenth century that it became a world-wide problem. Conditions favorable to the increase in the euphoric use of opium are found to be the rapid industrial development of the nineteenth century and the consequent breaking down of the previous social order in the West accompanied by the individualization of conduct. Once mainly for therapeutic purposes, the use of opium now became more and more a form of self-indulgence. One of the principal factors favorable for the increase in the opium traffic is found to be the psychology of exploitation, resulting from the ascendency of commercial and pecuniary interest in highly industrialized cultures. And the points of diffusion where this pattern of using opium for euphoria passed from one culture to the other are invariably found to be urban centers, while the social stratum within a culture that serves best as medium for its spread, particularly in this country, is found to be the illegitimate and lawless group popularly known as the underworld. By looking at the problem of opium addiction from this broad historical and cultural perspective, it becomes clear that the opium habit cannot be adequately understood by studying the individual addict alone, less by laying the blame entirely on him for his habit; for the origin, the spread and the present forms of the drug habit all lie outside the individual. He acquires it from others. The psychological mechanisms as well as the social conditions by and under which this pattern of using opium for euphoria passes from one individual to the other, therefore, emerge as a highly interesting and important problem.

3. CHARACTERISTICS OF OPIUM ADDICTS IN CHICAGO

We next studied the characteristics of over 2,000 drug addicts in Chicago by means of the statistical procedure, and the following are some of the significant findings.

Race and nationality. We found that about four-fifths of our group of addicts were white, about one-fifth Negroes, and the rest other races. This finding seems to discredit the popular notion shared by many that opium addiction is a vicious habit peculiar to a certain race or nationality.

Nativity. With the exception of a little over six per cent, all of our group of addicts were native-born. But only two-fifths of them were born in the city of Chicago. Most of them were brought up in other urban communities and came to live in the city for various lengths of time.

Education. The educational status of drug addicts in Chicago was found to be not particularly deficient compared with that of the general population. While the percentage of addicts receiving secondary and higher education is somewhat lower than that of the general population, more of them had elementary education. Nor is the extent of illiteracy much higher among our group of addicts than among the general population.

Occupation. It is an interesting fact that compared with the general population, the addicts in Chicago led in two occupational groups: domestic and personal service, and commercialized recreation and amusement. It was found that their employment was most irregular. This finding is significant in that employment in occupations like a waiter or a circus man, besides being irregular, involves constant moving and, thereby, frequent contact with new people and new influences.

Marital status. Over a half of our group of addicts were single, a little more than one-third married, and the rest widowed, separated or divorced. This finding suggests that most of these addicts were free of the social responsibilities usually borne by married people, but at the same time were denied the kind of instinctual as well as other emotional satisfactions that can be obtained only in a normal married life.

The drug habit. About their drug habit, the following points may be reviewed. During the years for which we have data, about half of these addicts used morphine alone. But recently heroin has been more widely used. The most common dosage used varies from five to nine grains a day, and the most popular method of using these drugs has been hypodermic injection. About two-thirds of these addicts formed their drug habit between the age of 20 and 29, and about an equal proportion of them have had their habit for from five to thirty or more years. The most significant finding of all about their drug habit is the fact that about two-thirds of them gave as their reason for addiction bad associates or the influence of other addicts.

The drug habit and physical well-being. The chronic use of drugs did not seem to have much deteriorating effect on the physical well-being of our group of addicts. Four-fifths of the federal cases were reported as having no physical ailment or deformity at the time of their arrest. Although this finding was not the result of exact medical examination, that such a large proportion of them made no mention or complaint of any ailment is significant, considering the fact that most of them had used drugs for five or more years.

Drug addiction and crime. There seems to be some positive relation between the chronic use of opium and criminality, as shown by the fact that four-fifths of the federal cases had had no known criminal record prior to their addiction. But the crimes they committed after addiction are mostly connected with the maintenance of their drug habit. Very few of these addicts committed crimes of violence, still fewer sex offenses. These findings are quite contrary to the popular view that identifies the "dope fiend" with a heartless criminal.

While these statistical findings do not give us a complete picture of the drug addicts in Chicago, they do clarify our notions about them to a considerable extent. More than that, they give us useful clues for further investigation. Thus, if two-thirds of these addicts attributed their addition to the influence of other addicts, in order to have an adequate understanding of the ætiology of the drug habit, it is clear that we must have a thoroughgoing exploration of the social situations in which the influence of drug addicts is said to be contagious. This is exactly what we have done, and the following are some of the results of this attempt.

4. THE DISTRIBUTION OF DRUG ADDICTS IN CHICAGO

We began the exploration of the social situations related to drug addiction by finding out the places where these addicts lived and frequented. This was done by what we call the ecological approach. The addresses of over 2,600 addicts were sorted according to 120 sub-communities, and on the basis of the number of addicts in these sub-communities and their average population 20 years and over for 1930 and 1934, opium addiction rates per 100,000 population were calculated for each of them. From this procedure we found that the areas with the highest rates of addiction are either in or near the Loop or the central business district; namely, the West Madison area or the Near West Side, the South State and Twenty-Second area or the Near South Side, and the North Clark area or the Lower North Side.

By studying carefully the ecological characteristics of these areas as shown by the census data of 1934, it was further found that practically all of these areas, compared with those with no addiction rates, are characterized by small percentages of privately owned homes, low median rentals, large percentages of vacant dwelling units, and decrease of population, with the exception of sub-community 61 or the Near West Side, where the influx of transients seemed to have kept the population trend of the area as a whole stable between 1930 and 1934. These characteristics are taken to be indications of a considerable degree of physical deterioration as well as the lack of what may be called the neighborhood spirit. These areas are also characterized by high sex ratios, low percentages of married people, and large percentages of residence under one year. These characteristics seem to indicate that most of the occupants of these areas are unattached men and that they are constantly moving from one place to the other.

What the ecological features mentioned above indicate with respect to the social and cultural environment peculiar to these areas is that here the control of traditional mores and of what are ordinarily called primary-group associations, such as the family and local community, is practically nil, and the individual's life, thereby, often lacks organization or direction. It is in this sense that the environment of these areas may be said to be one that is most conducive to personal disorganization. As a matter of fact, these areas have been found by previous studies to be the centers of family disorganization, crime, vice, alcoholism, insanity, and suicide. And it was in this environment too that our group of drug addicts lived.

5. SOCIAL SITUATIONS AND PERSONALITY FACTORS
RELATED TO DRUG ADDICTION

To know the social environment of drug users in a general way is not sufficient to understand why and how a particular individual in that environment and not others becomes a drug addict. As we have stated in the beginning of this resumé, our object is to discover the specific social situations and the psychological mechanisms in and by which the pattern of using drugs for euphoria passes from one individual to the other and the nature and source of the suffering that follows the withdrawal of the drug after one has used it for some time. To reach this goal, we undertook the study of individual drug addicts by means of what we call the prolonged interview method.

The social situations in which the addicts we have interviewed first began to use drugs were found to be smoking parties; houses of prostitution, where either the prostitute or the pimp is a drug user; pool rooms and gambling houses, hotels and restaurants, apartment houses, or any place where drug users live or frequent. The one common and obvious characteristic of all these situations is the persuasive influence of drug users, either intentional or not. Another characteristic common to these situations, if we look at the wider environmental setting in which these specific situations were found, is the marked absence of social control in the sense explained above.

By exploring further these addicts' previous experiences, especially their relation with other people, we further discovered that when they were first in the company of drug users and learned to use drugs themselves, they either had admiration for the drug users or were in some form of affectional relationship with them. In such states of emotional rapport, the non-users were found inclined to identify themselves with the users, who might be the formers' heroes, intimate friends, or lovers, and to do what the other did. Other cases revealed that when they were first in the company of drug users, they were "blue" or depressed, and wanted to forget; so they did not care and followed the drug users' suggestion to take a "shot." In some other cases, the drug was taken to increase their sexual potency. In all these cases, their state of mind, when they were first in the company of drug addicts, may be said to be one of feeling inferior, inadequate, or insecure, either in relation to their immediate company or to people outside the immediate situation. If one were emotionally self-sufficient, it seems very unlikely that one would readily accept the suggestion of a drug user and to enchain one's self to a practically lifelong habit. By whatever name we may call it, the feeling of inferiority or inadequacy, this predisposing factor found in all of the addicts we have interviewed when they first began the drug habit must not be ignored.

Granting this feeling of inferiority or inadequacy and the accompanying attitude of dependence on others and of withdrawal from difficult life-situations, it becomes understandable why drug users, once having tasted the narcotic effect of opium, find it difficult to face reality again without the help of the drug. In fact, this incapacity to face life-situations or to fulfill the demands of culture was found to be the principal subjective factor in every case of relapse among these addicts. It is probably this fear of facing reality and of bearing responsibility that intensifies the purely physiological suffering or discomfort following the withdrawal of the drug.

By exploring still further the early experiences of drug addicts, it was found that this feeling of inferiority or inadequacy and the attitude of dependence and withdrawal seemed to have their inception in the addict's relation with parents and other members in the family during his or her childhood. For example, one of the pimps we have studied, when a child, was his mother's pet, but had a father who was a heavy drinker, strict and unreasonable. And a prostitute we have studied was her father's pet when a child, but had a mother who was extremely religious and unusually dominating. The attitudes engendered in such family situations are found to have a direct influence upon the later behavior of drug addicts and their mode of adjusting themselves to society.

In the light of foregoing considerations, opium addiction cannot be considered as a purely physical disease or a vice that is inherent in the individual or race; it is essentially a symptom of a maladjusted personality, a personality whose capacity for meeting cultural demands has been handicapped by inadequate emotional and social development, for which, as shown by our case materials, the general cultural chaos and social disorganization that is characteristic of modern society is mainly responsible. From this point of view effective rehabilitation of drug addicts can come only from sincere attempts at assisting drug addicts to achieve a satisfactory emotional and social adjustment, and the prevention of drug addiction becomes a matter of emotional education and general social reorganization.

APPENDIX I

TABLE XXI

OPIUM ADDICTION RATES FOR THE CITY OF CHICAGO, 1928–34

Number of Sub-Communities	Average Population of 1930 and 1934, 20 Years and Over			Annual Average Number of Addicts, 1928–34			Rate per 100,000 Population, 20 Years and Over		
	Total	Male	Female	Total	Male	Female	Total	Male	Female
1.................	22,004	10,029	11,975	.....	......	.....	.....	......	.....
2.................	22,205	9,951	12,254	.3	.3	.....	1.5	3.3	.....
3.................	28,049	13,333	14,716	.8	.8	.....	3.0	6.2	.....
4.................	16,640	8,067	8,573	.6	.5	.1	4.0	6.2	1.9
5.................	24,643	11,190	13,453	2.6	1.8	8	10.8	16.4	6.1
6.................	24,855	11,374	13,481	5.5	3.5	2.0	22.1	30.8	14.8
7.................	33,050	16,361	16,689	14.0	9.0	5.0	42.4	55.0	29.9
8.................	13,666	6,472	7,194	.5	.2	.3	3.7	2.6	4.6
9.................	20,373	9,697	10,676	.6	.6	.....	3.3	6.9	.....
10.................	19,164	9,445	9,719	.1	.1	.....	.9	1.8	.....
11.................	14,547	7,368	7,179	.3	.3	.....	2.3	4.5	.....
12.................	23,957	11,657	12,300	1.8	1.2	.6	7.6	10.0	5.4
13.................	24,436	12,416	12,020	7.1	3.1	4.0	29.3	25.5	33.2
14.................	19,657	8,237	11,420	4.3	2.7	1.6	22.0	32.4	14.5
15.................	18,721	9,646	9,075	1.1	.6	.5	6.2	6.9	5.5
16.................	17,116	9,091	8,025	1.6	1.6	.....	6.8	12.8	.....
17.................	16,275	8,261	8,014	2.3	1.0	1.3	14.3	12.1	16.6
18.................	20,689	10,235	10,454	8.0	5.2	2.8	38.7	50.5	27.1
19.................	13,246	6,819	6,427	.6	.5	.1	5.0	7.3	2.5
20.................	16,789	9,197	7,592	5.0	2.8	2.2	29.8	30.8	28.5
21.................	29,034	17,520	11,514	40.1	25.6	14.5	138.3	146.5	125.9
22.................	14,344	6,276	8,068	3.0	1.8	1.2	20.9	29.2	14.4
23.................	12,757	6,252	6,505	.....	......	.....	.....	......	.....
24.................	12,813	6,437	6,376	.1	.....	.1	1.3	.....	2.6
25.................	17,808	8,672	9,136	.....	.....	.....	.....	.....	.....
26.................	30,970	14,827	16,143	.1	.....	.1	.5	.....	1.0
27.................	25,421	12,675	12,746	.3	.....	.3	1.3	.....	2.6
28.................	17,357	8,700	8,657	.3	.3	.....	1.9	3.8	.....
29.................	13,061	6,427	6,634	.3	.2	.1	2.5	2.6	2.5
30.................	17,081	8,249	8,832	.5	.3	.2	2.9	4.0	1.8
31.................	16,043	7,966	8,077	.1	.1	.....	1.0	2.0	.....
32.................	17,387	8,865	8,522	.....	......	.....	.....	......	.....
33..	20,857	10,764	10,093	.8	.3	.5	3.9	3.1	4.9

TABLE XXI (*Continued*)

Number of Sub-Communities	Average Population of 1930 and 1934, 20 Years and Over			Annual Average Number of Addicts, 1928–34			Rates per 100,000 Population, 20 Years and Over		
	Tota	Male	Female	Total	Male	Fe-male	Total	Male	Fe-male
34................	17,135	8,600	8,535	.....	.....	.....	.....	.....	.....
35................	16,049	8,033	8,016	.1	.....	.1	1.4	.....	2.0
36................	18,239	9,004	9,235	.....	.....	.....	.....	.....	.....
37................	13,375	6,667	6,708	.....	.....	.....	.....	.....	.....
38................	20,837	10,373	10,363	.1	.1	.....	.7	1.6	.....
39................	24,196	11,770	12,426	.8	.8	.....	3.4	7.0	.....
40................	14,834	7,496	7,338	.6	.3	.3	4.5	4.4	4.5
41................	13,945	7,200	6,745	.5	.2	.3	3.5	2.3	4.9
42................	12,806	6,506	6,299	.3	.2	.1	2.6	2.6	2.6
43................	17,501	8,883	8,618	.6	.6	.....	3.8	7.5	.....
44................	21,774	11,091	10,683	.1	.1	.....	.7	1.5	.....
45................	28,256	14,439	13,817	.5	.5	.....	1.7	3.4	.....
46................	20,518	10,636	9,882	1.6	1.3	.3	8.1	12.5	3.3
47................	18,867	9,881	8,986	.3	.2	.1	1.7	1.6	1.8
48................	6,545	3,504	3,041	.3	.3	.....	5.0	9.5	.....
49................	9,365	5,632	3,733	1.1	.8	.3	12.4	14.8	8.9
50................	22,112	11,875	10,237	.5	.5	.....	2.2	4.2	.....
51................	18,210	8,963	9,247	.....	.....	.....	.....	.....	.....
52................	16,978	8,468	8,510	.1	.1	.....	1.0	1.9	.....
53................	17,847	8,495	9,352	.3	.3	.....	1.8	3.9	.....
54................	23,640	10,825	12,815	.3	.3	.....	1.4	3.1	.....
55................	16,852	8,018	8,834	.8	.8	.....	4.9	10.3	.....
56................	20,070	10,020	10,050	1.6	1.5	.1	8.3	14.9	1.6
57................	14,375	6,932	7,443	1.0	.8	.2	6.9	12.0	2.2
58................	23,002	11,587	11,415	1.6	1.5	.1	7.2	12.9	1.4
59................	19,270	9,969	9,300	1.5	.8	.7	7.7	8.3	7.1
60................	8,177	4,075	4,102	1.3	1.2	.1	16.3	28.6	4.0
61................	20,284	16,029	4,255	60.8	53.0	7.8	299.9	330.6	184.0
62................	20,090	10,833	9,257	9.8	6.0	3.8	48.9	55.3	41.4
63................	19,069	10,433	8,636	2.1	1.5	.6	11.3	14.3	7.7
64................	16,467	9,050	7,417	2.5	1.8	.7	15.1	20.2	8.9
65................	12,948	7,399	5,549	1.5	1.3	.2	11.5	18.0	3.0
66................	16,631	8,406	8,225	.8	.8	.....	5.0	9.9	.....
67................	30,564	15,377	15,187	1.8	1.8	.....	6.0	11.9	.....
68................	22,148	11,416	10,732	1.0	.7	.3	4.5	5.8	3.1
69................	18,851	9,601	9,250	.....	.....	.....	.....	.....	.....
70................	13,750	6,997	6,753	.3	.3	.....	2.4	4.7	.....
71................	16,167	9,179	6,988	.5	.5	.....	3.0	5.4	.....
72................	27,644	11,564	10,080	.8	.6	.2	3.8	5.7	1.6
73................	15,534	8,466	7,068	.3	.3	.....	2.1	3.9	.....
74................	5,435	4,411	1,024	12.8	10.8	2.0	236.1	245.5	195.4
75................	7,508	3,518	3,990	21.0	15.0	6.0	279.6	426.3	150.3
76................	10,080	6,172	3,908	17.8	17.6	.2	176.9	286.2	4.2
77................	13,052	6,894	6,158	22.5	14.5	8.0	172.3	210.3	129.9

TABLE XXI (*Continued*)

Number of Sub-Communities	Average Population of 1930 and 1934, 20 Years and Over			Annual Average Number of Addicts, 1928–34			Rate per 100,000 Population, 20 Years and Over		
	Total	Male	Female	Total	Male	Fe-male	Total	Male	Fe-male
78.................	25,081	12,692	12,389	15.3	10.6	4.7	61.1	84.0	37.6
79.................	18,371	8,890	9,481	13.8	7.3	6.5	75.3	82.4	68.5
80.................	13,502	6,753	6,749	.8	−.3	.5	6.1	4.9	7.4
81.................	26,844	13,240	13,604	10.6	8.3	2.3	39.7	62.9	17.1
82.................	19,514	9,490	10,024	6.3	3.5	2.8	32.4	36 8	28.2
83.................	15,158	7,146	8,012	3.8	3.0	.8	25.2	41.9	10.4
84.................	23,146	9,710	13,436	1.3	.8	.5	5.7	8.5	3.7
85.................	36,775	17,848	18,927	7.0	5.0	2.0	19.0	28.0	10.5
86.................	23,967	11,024	12,943	3.0	2.3	.7	12.5	21.1	5.1
87....••.........	20,427	10,013	10,414	4.0	2.5	1.5	19.5	24.9	4.4
88.................	21,295	10,294	11,001	3.8	2.5	1.3	18.0	24.2	12.1
89.................	26,408	12,145	14,263	.6	.3	.3	2.5	2.7	2.3
90.................	17,670	7,838	9,832	.5	.3	.2	2 8	4.2	1.6
91.................	14,369	6,676	7,720	.1	.1	.....	1.1	2.4	.....
92.................	26,990	13,006	13,984	.8	.6	.2	3.0	5.1	1.1
93.................	18,098	9,127	8,971	.3	.3	.....	1.8	3.6	.....
94.................	14,683	8,615	6,068	1.3	.6	.7	9.0	7.7	10.9
95.................	13,216	6,911	6,305	.....	.....	.....	.....	.....	....
96.................	22,876	11,896	10,980	.....	.....	.....	.....	.....	..
97.................	23,004	12,797	10,207	.5	.2	-.3	2.1	1.3	3.2
98.................	16,612	8,824	7,788	.3	.2	.1	2.0	1.8	2.1
99.................	17,448	9,306	8,142	.1	.....	.1	.9	.....	2.0
100.................	12,437	6,461	5,976	.....	.....	.....	.....	.....	.....
101.................	14,171	7,544	6,627	.1	.1	.....	1.1	2 2	.....
102.................	12,277	6,344	5,933	.6	.5	.....	5.4	7.8	.....
103.................	13,673	7,125	6,548	1.1	.8	.3	8.5	11.0	5.0
104.................	16,139	8,616	7,523	.5	.3	.2	3.0	3.8	2.2
105.................	14,009	7,710	6,299	.1	.1	.....	1.1	2.1	.....
106.................	22,749	12,315	10,434	.6	.6	.....	2.9	5.4	.....
107........••.....	18,495	9,375	9,120	.1	.....	.1	.9	.....	1.8
108.................	19,263	9,925	9,338	.....	.....	.....	.....	....	.....
109.................	21,354	10,559	10,795	.3	.3	.....	1.5	3.1	.....
110.................	18,032	9,112	8,920	.1	.1	.....	.9	1.8	.....
111.................	22,672	11,433	11,239	.1	.....	.1	.7	.....	1.4
112.................	26,215	13,318	12,897	.6	.3	.3	4.0	2.5	2.5
113.................	15,400	7,704	7,696	.3	.2	.1	2.1	2.1	2.1
114.................	16,905	7,297	9,608	.8	.7	.1	4.9	9.1	1.7
115.................	18,093	8,757	9,336	.3	.1	.2	1.8	1.9	1.7
116.................	23,070	11,562	11,508	1.0	.7	.3	4.3	5.7	2.8
117.................	10,912	5,560	5,352	.8	.5	.3	7.6	8.9	6.2
118.................	39,474	19,220	20,254	1.0	.8	.2	2.5	4.3	.8
119.................	19,932	9,424	10,508	.3	.2	.1	1.6	1.7	1.5
120.................	15,316	7,529	7,787	.3	.3	.....	2.1	4.4	.....

APPENDIX II

A GLOSSARY OF SLANG USED BY DRUG ADDICTS IN CHICAGO[1]

Abb.	Abcesses caused by bad drugs or dirty needles.
Bamboo.	Opium pipe. See also *Gonger*.
Bandhouse.	The workhouse.
Beef.	Any sort of charge, as in "They gave me the beef for it," meaning "They charged me with it." See also *Rap*.
Belt.	The sensation derived from the use of drugs. Also called *kick, boot, drive*.
Big House.	The penitentiary. Also called *stir*.
Big shot connection.	A large peddler.
Bindle.	A very small quantity of drugs done up in paper. Sometimes referred to as *a paper of stuff, a bird's-eye, a deck, a go*, or *a cap*.
Bing, Bingo, Bang.	A shot of drugs. Also called *Jabpopp, Jabpoppo*.
Bird-cage hyps.	The poorer class of addict. Also called *boots* or *boot and shoe dope-fiends*.
Bird's-eye.	See *Bindle*.
Bit.	A sentence in the penitentiary. Also called *time* or *a jolt*.
Block.	A cube of morphine. A term used in some localities.
Blow a shot.	To lose a shot. If a hypodermic outfit leaks, the user will lose his drug through lack of sufficient pressure to force it through the needle.
Blowing.	Taking drugs via the nostrils. Also called *sniffing*.
Boob.	The jail. Also called *the can* or *the bucket*.
Boost, the.	Shoplifters. Also called *boosters* or *the clout*.
Boosters.	See *Boost*.
Boot and shoe dope-fiends.	See *Bird-cage hyps*.

---

[1] Compiled by one of the writer's research assistants, who has been a drug addict.

Boots.	See *Bird-cage hyps*.
Brick gum.	Raw opium. Also called *leaf gum* or *mud*.
Buck.	A paper dollar. Also called *a slug*.
Bucket.	See *boob*.
Bug.	An insane person. Also called *a crack-pot, daffy, dingy, junk simple, rum-dum, stir simple*.
Bull-horrors.	When an addict is full of cocaine, he thinks the police are watching him. This is called *bull-horrors*. Cocaine does not affect everyone in this way.
Bunk-habit.	One who likes to lie around a lay-out is said to have a *bunk-habit*.
Business.	The entire paraphernalia used for smoking opium or for taking drugs hypodermically. Also called *the joint, factory, machinery,* or *the works,* or *the engine,* or *outfit*.
C.	Cocaine.
Can.	See *Boob*.
Canned stuff.	Commercial smoking opium. Sometime called by the name: *Lem Kee, Li Young,* etc.
Cannons.	Pickpockets. Also called *whizz, P. P., guns*.
Cap.	See *Bindle*. A *cap*, or capsule, is of varying size.
Chef.	The person who prepares the opium for smoking. Also called *cook*.
Chuck-horrors.	When an addict is breaking the habit, he develops what is called the chuck-horrors. He is always hungry; he will eat anything at any time and in any amount. This develops after the first sickness has passed—usually after about a week of abstinence, depending upon how bad a habit the patient has, his health, etc.
Clout, the.	See *Boost*.
C-note.	A paper bill for $100.00. Also called *a yard*.
Coke.	Cocaine.
Cokies.	Users of cocaine. Also called *snow birds*. (In the East the term cokie refers to all users except smokers.)
Collar.	An arrest. Also called *nailed, a pinch, a sneeze*.
Connect.	To make a purchase of drugs. Also called *to score*.
Connection.	A drug peddler. Also called *a pusher* or *a shover*.
Cook.	See *Chef*.

Cop and blow.   An expression meaning "Take it and go quickly." This expression is generally applied to drugs, but it may be applied to anything.

Crack-pot.   See *Bug.*

Croaker.   A doctor.

Cutered pill.   When an opium bowl becomes too hot or too full of *yen-shee*, we get a *cutered pill.* It is very strong and unpalatable.

Cutter.   A silver quarter-dollar. Also called *a shilling.*

Cut them.   To dilute drugs. Morphine cannot be cut as it comes in cube form, but heroin, being a powder, is *cut* by using sugar or milk. Cocaine can be *cut;* that is, flake cocaine can, but crystal cocaine cannot.

Cut up old scores.   To talk about incidents in one's past life. Also called *to cut up old touches.*

Daffy.   See *Bug.*

Deck.   See *Bindle.*

Deuce.   A paper bill for $2.00.

D., F., and L.   An expression meaning dirty, filthy, and lousy.

Dimmer.   A ten-cent piece.

Dingus.   An eye dropper; it is composed of the bulb and the barrel. Also called *a dripper.*

Dingy.   See *Bug.*

Dog.   The residue left from gum when making smoking opium.

Dope-fiend.   A hypodermic needle user. Also called *hypos, hyps, dopey,* and *old dopey.*

Dope-pop.   A drug addict.

Dopey.   See *Dope-fiend.*

Double saw-buck.   A twenty-dollar bill.

Dram.   An eighth of an ounce of drugs.

Dripper.   See *Dingus.*

Drive.   See *Belt.*

Dropper.   See *Dingus.*

Dynamite.   Very strong drugs.

Eighth.   See *Dram.*

Engine.   See *Business.*

Factory.   See *Business.*

Fin.   A five-dollar bill.

Finger of stuff. A quantity of drugs which is smuggled into prison in a rubber finger. The reason for this is to keep the drugs dry.

Fire plug.   A large pill of smoking opium. Also called *high hat*.

Fix.   To use drugs. Also called *to take a shot, a pop, a prod, a fix,* or *to get one's yen off*.

Full of poison. Filled with drugs. Also called *high* ("*higher than a Georgia pine*"), *geed up, loaded,* or *polluted*.

G.   The Government. Also called *whiskers*.

Gate money.   The money given to a prisoner upon release.

Gee.   Drugs in general. Also called *stuff, junk, gow, hocus,* or *smeck*.

Geed up.   See *Full of poison*.

Gee fat.   The lining of an opium pipe.

Gee rags.   Rags used to make the shank of the opium bowl tight where it fits into the shank.

Geeser.   A shot of drugs.

Getting one's   The act of smoking opium. See also *Fix*. Also called
  yen off.   *lying on the hip, kicking it around, puffing,* or *kicking the gong around,* or *rolling the log around*.

Go.   See *Bindle*.

Go into the   To inject drugs intravenously. Also called *to go in the
  sewer.   line* or *in a vein*.

Go into the   To inject drugs subcutaneously.
  skin.

Gonger.   Pipe for smoking opium. Also called *the stick* or *log* — usually *the stick*.

Goods.   Drugs in large quantities. Also called *merchandise*. Big dealers always use this term when speaking of drugs.

Gow.   See *Gee*.

Gow heads.   Addicts who use hypodermic needles. Also called *junkies, needle fiends, hypo smeckers*.

Gow it out.   To clean out the inside of the bowl of an opium pipe.

Gowster: One who smokes opium. Also called *smoker, pipe fiend, pipies*.

Grease.   Smoking opium.   Also called *gow, hop, skamas, tar*.

Guns.   See *Cannons*.

H.	Heroin.
Habit.	Addiction to drugs. Also called *monkey* as in "I have a monkey on my back," usually used when one is sick.
Half a buck.	Fifty cents. Also called *half a slug*.
Half a C.	$50.00 in paper money. Also called *half a yard*.
Half a Grand.	$500.00 in paper money. Also called *half a G*.
Half a slug.	See *Half a buck*.
Half a yard.	See *Half a C*.
High hat.	See *Fire plug*.
Hitch up the reindeers.	An expression sometimes used when one is going to use cocaine.
Hop.	See *Grease*.
Hop-toy.	Any opium container regardless of size.
Humming-gee bowl.	An opium bowl, the top of which is made from a piece of human skull.
Hypos.	See *Dope-fiend*.
Hyps.	See *Dope-fiend*.
Hypo-smeckers.	See *Dope-fiend*.
Japbopp, Jabpoppo.	See *Bing, Bingo, Bang*.
Joint.	See *Business*.
Jolt.	See *Bit*.
Junk.	See *Gee*.
Junkies.	See *Gow heads*.
Junk simple.	See *Bug*.
Kick.	See *Belt*.
Kicking it around.	See *Getting one's yen off*.
Kicking the gong around.	See *Getting One's yen off*.
Kick the habit.	To get off drugs. The expression "I am off" means "I no longer use drugs."
Knocker.	A person opposed to the use of drugs.
Lamp-habit.	One who likes to see the lamp lit all the time is said to have a *lamp-habit*.

Lay-down joint.	A place where one can go and smoke opium. These places supply one with everything needed for a price.
Lay-out.	The paraphernalia used to smoke opium. See also *Business*.
Leaf gum.	See *Brick gum*.
Leaping.	A person who is excessively filled with drugs is said to be leaping.
Lice.	Informers. Also called *mice, rats, stool pigeons, stools,* etc.
Lipping it.	The method by which a hypodermic or smoking outfit is tested to determine if it is air-tight.
Loaded.	See *Full of poison*.
Lobb.	A person who hangs around and runs errands. Also called *Lobby-gow*.
Lobby-gow.	See *Lobb*.
Log.	See *Gonger*.
Lying on the hip.	See *Getting one's yen off*.
M.	Morphine.
Machinery.	See *Business*.
Main-liners.	Addicts who inject drugs intravenously. Also called *vein-shooters*, and *main-line shooters*.
Make a meet.	To make an engagement, as in "I have a meet with a connection to score."
Margin men.	Dealers or runners that have no money invested in the goods; they use some other person's bank-roll. They will make a trip with goods on a short-margin, and they have nothing at stake except their liberty.
Merchandise.	See *Goods*.
Monkey.	See *Habit*.
Mooch.	To beg on the street. Also called *the pling*.
Mouth habit.	To take any drug orally. Also called *scoffing*.
Mud.	See *Brick gum*.
Nailed.	See *Collar*.
Needle fiends.	See *Gow heads*.
Narcotic bulls.	Narcotic officers. Also called *narcotic coppers*.
O.	An ounce of drugs. Also called *a piece*.
Off.	See *Kick the habit*.

Old dopey.	See *Dope-fiend*.
Outfit.	See *Business*.
Panic on.	When drugs are scarce, there is said to be a *panic on*
Paper of stuff.	See *Bindle*. Also called simply *a paper*.
Pick-up.	A shot. A term used in prison, as in "I will pick you up."
Piddle.	Hospital. Also called *poggy*.
Piece.	See *O*. Also there is ½ *piece*, ¼ *piece*, etc.
Pill.	Opium as it is consumed on the bowl. Also called *yen-pok*.
Pinch.	See *Collar*.
Pin shot.	To take a shot without a needle. In prison a point is made from the needle of a power sewing machine; it is called a *Tom-cat*.
Pipe fiend.	See *Gowster*.
Pipies.	See *Gowster*.
Plant.	A place where drugs are kept. Also called *stasch*.
Playing the nod.	To go to sleep from over-indulgence.
Pleasure-smoker.	One who smokes the pipe once in a while, but has no habit.
Pling.	See *Mooch*.
Poggy.	See *Piddle*.
Point.	A hypodermic needle. Also called a *spike*.
Polluted.	See *Full of poison*.
Pop.	See *Fix*.
P. P.	See *Cannons*.
Prod.	See *Fix*.
Puffing.	See *Getting one's yen off*.
Pusher.	See *Connection*. As in "So-and-so is pushing."
Push-shorts.	To peddle drugs in small quantities. Also called *to shove shorts*.
Raise a plant.	An expression which may mean (1) to find a plant, (2) to open a plant, or (3) to rob a plant. See also *To spring a plant*.
Rap.	Same as *Beef*; as in "I will take the rap," meaning "It's my responsibility."
Rats.	See *Lice*.

Rolling the log.	See *Getting one's yen off*.
Route.	The means by which drugs are smuggled inside a prison.
Rum-dum.	See *Bug*.
Sacht.	Any article that is impregnated with drugs is said to be sacht. The word is derived from saturated. The drug is put in solution, the article saturated with the solution and then dried. Any article that will absorb the solution is used: sometimes a handkerchief is concealed in their shoes or in the lining and seams of clothing. When the medium used is nearly dry, a hot iron is applied to iron out the wrinkles. It can be chewed or shot. When shot the procedure is reversed. A piece of the sacht is put in a cup or spoon, water put on it, heat applied, and the drug goes back in solution.
Saw-buck.	$10.00 in paper money.
Schive.	A knife is always called this, both in prison and out.
Scoffing.	See *Mouth habit*.
Score.	See *Connect*.
Score-dough.	Money necessary to purchase drugs.
Shilling.	See *Cutter*.
Short go.	A small amount of drugs for the money.
Shover.	See *Connection;* as in "So-and-so is shoving."
Shove shorts.	See *Push shorts*.
Skamas.	See *Grease*.
Skin-shooters.	Addicts who inject drugs subcutaneously. This is called *going in the skin*.
Slug.	See *Buck*.
Smeck.	See *Gee*.
Smeckers.	Addicts who use hypodermic needles. See *Gow heads*.
Smoker.	See *Gowster*.
Sneeze.	See *Collar*.
Sniffing.	See *Blowing*.
Snow birds.	See *Cokies*.
Speed-ball.	A combination of cocaine and morphine.
Spike.	See *Point*.
Spread the joint.	To get ready the paraphernalia for smoking opium.

Spring.	To produce any article as in "I spring my plant" or "They sprung my plant." This latter may mean either "I opened my plant" or "They found my plant."
Square-John.	A non-user. May be called simply *a square*.
Stasch.	See *Plant*.
Stick.	See *Gonger*.
Stir.	See *Big House*.
Stir simple.	See *Bug*.
Stool pigeons.	See *Lice*.
Stuff.	See *Gee*.
Suey-pow.	A wet sponge used to cool an opium bowl. Sometimes a powder-puff is used.
Take a shot.	See *Fix*.
Tar.	See *Grease*.
Time.	See *Bit*.
Tom-cat.	See *Pin shot*.
Touches.	See *Cut up old scores*.
Toy.	Smoking opium is sold by the *toy;* any opium container, large or small, is called a *toy*.
Vein-shooters.	See *Main-liners*.
Whiskers.	See *G*.
Whizz.	See *Cannons*.
Yard.	See *C-note*.
Yen.	Sickness caused by lack of drugs. See *Getting one's yen off*.
Yen-hok.	A large needle used to prepare opium for smoking.
Yen-pok.	See *Pill*.
Yen-shee.	The residue or ash that forms inside the bowl when opium is smoked. It may be recooked and smoked. It is usually mixed with fresh opium. Yen-shee gives the opium added strength. It can be smoked by itself, but is bitter and hard to prepare, as it becomes very brittle.
Yen-shee-gow.	An instrument used to clean out the inside of the opium bowl. See *Gow it out*.

BIBLIOGRAPHY

Armstrong, C. P. *660 Runaway Boys*. Boston, 1932.

Baily, M. D. "Drug Peddling, Addiction and Criminals," *Journal of Criminal Law and Criminology*, XXII (1932).

Bills, A. G. *General Experimental Psychology*. New York, 1934.

Bishop, E. S. *The Narcotic Drug Problem*. New York, 1920.

Blumer, Herbert. "Method in Social Psychology." Unpublished Ph.D. thesis, University of Chicago, 1928.

Burgess, E. W. and Newcomb, C. (ed.). *Census Data of the City of Chicago*. Chicago, 1930.

Cavan, Ruth S. *Suicide*. Chicago, 1928.

Cobbe, William R. *Doctor Judas: a Portrayal of the Opium Habit*. Chicago, 1895.

Cooley, Charles H. *Human Nature and the Social Order*. New York, 1920.

Cusack, W. J. "The Narcotic Situation in Chicago." Unpublished report of the Narcotic Division, Chicago Police Department, 1934.

Cushny, A. R. *Pharmacology and Therapeutics*. 10th ed., 1934.

Dewey, John. *Human Nature and Conduct*. New York, 1922.

Dunn, W. T. *The Opium Traffic in the International Aspect*. New York, 1920.

Emerson, H. (ed.). *Alcohol and Man*. New York, 1932.

Fernald, M. C. *A Study of Women Delinquents in New York State*. New York, 1920.

Faris, E. "The Primary Group: Essence and Accident," *American Journal of Sociology*, XXXVIII (1932).

Faris, R. E. L. "An Ecological Study of Insanity in the City." Unpublished Ph.D. thesis, University of Chicago, 1931.

Feldman, W. M. "Racial Aspects of Alcoholism," *British Journal of Inebriety*, XXI (1923).

Fishman, J. F. and Perlman, V. T. "The Real Narcotic Addict," *American Mercury*, XXV (1932), 100 ff.

Gillespie, R. D. "Insomnia and Drug Addiction," *British Journal of Inebriety*, XXVIII (1930), 9.

Glueck, S. and E. T. *One Thousand Juvenile Delinquents*. Cambridge, 1934.

Groves, E. R. and Ogburn, W. F. *American Marriage and Family Relationships.* New York, 1928.

Gunn, J. A. *An Introduction to Pharmacology and Therapeutics.* London, 1929.

Henderson, D. K. and Gillespie, R. D. *A Text Book of Psychiatry.* London, 1932.

House of Correction of the City of Chicago. *A Retrospect Covering a Half Century of Endeavor, 1871–1921.*

Howell, W. H. *A Text Book of Physiology for Medical Students and Physicians.* Philadelphia and London, 1929.

Hunt, J. R. and others. *The Biology of the Individual.* Baltimore, 1934.

Illinois Revised Statutes, 1933. Chapter 91: sections 134–56.

International Anti-Opium Association. *The War against Opium.* 1922.

Kolb, L. and DuMez, A. G. *The Prevalence and Trend of Drug Addiction in the United States and Factors Influencing It.* Washington, 1924.

Laufer, B. *Tobacco and Its Use in Asia.* Chicago: Field Museum of Natural History, 1924.

Lewin, L. *Phantastica: Narcotics and Stimulating Drugs.* New York and London, 1931.

Light, A. B. and others. *Opium Addiction.* Chicago, 1929–30.

Lowie, R. H. *Culture and Ethnology.* New York, 1917.

Lundberg, C. A. *Trends in American Sociology.* New York, 1929.

Lyall, L. A. *China.* New York, 1934.

Macht, D. I. "The History of Opium and Some of Its Preparations and Alkaloids," *Journal of American Medical Association,* February, 1915.

Marks, J. "The Opium Habit," *Social Science.* Edited by Leroy Allen, 1929.

Mayer, M. S. "Correct and Discontented?" *Social Graphic,* October, 1934.

Mayo, E. *Human Problems of an Industrial Civilization.* Cambridge, 1933.

McDougall, William. *The Effects of Alcohol and Some Other Drugs During Normal and Fatigued Conditions.* London, 1920.

——. *The Energies of Men.* New York, Chicago, 1933.

Mendenhall, Walter L. *Tobacco.* Cambridge: Harvard University Press, 1930.

Menninger, Karl A. *The Human Mind.* New York, 1930.

Morse, H. B. *The Trade and Administration of the Chinese Empire.* Shanghai, 1908.

Mowrer, Ernest R. *Family Disorganization.* Chicago, 1927.

National Anti-Opium Association. *Opium: a World Problem.* Edited by Bingham Dai. (Shanghai, 1927–29), I-II.

Newcomb, C. S. and Lang, R. O. *The Census Data of the City of Chicago,* Chicago, 1934.

Norwood, E. W. "Mental Defectiveness and Alcoholism and Drug Addiction," *British Journal of Inebriety,* XXIX (1932).

Ogburn, W. F. "The Family and Its Functions," *Recent Social Trends in the United States.* New York, 1933.

Owen, D. E. *British Opium Policy in China and India.* New Haven: Yale University Press, 1934.

Park, R. E., Burgess, E. W. and McKenzie, R. D. *The City.* Chicago, 1925.

—— and Burgess, E. W. *Introduction to the Science of Sociology.* 2d. ed. Chicago, 1924.

——. "Sociology," *Research in the Social Sciences.* Edited by Wilson Gee. New York, 1929.

——. "Personality and Cultural Conflict," *Publication of the Sociological Society of America,* XXV (1931).

Payne, E. H. (ed.). *The Menace of Narcotic Drugs.* New York, 1931.

Petrullo, V. *The Diabolic Root.* Philadelphia: University of Pennsylvania Press, 1934.

Rado, Sandor. "The Psychic Effects of Intoxication," *Psychoanalytic Review,* XVIII (1931), 69 ff.

Reckless, W. C. *Vice in Chicago.* Chicago, 1933.

Reitman, Ben L. *The Second Oldest Profession.* New York, 1931.

——. "The Underworld the Most Common Road to Drug Addiction." Unpublished statement prepared for this study, 1935.

Ritchie, A. D. *Scientific Method: an Inquiry into the Character and Validity of Natural Laws.* New York, 1923.

Rosanoff, A. J. (ed.). *Manual of Psychiatry.* 6th ed. New York and London, 1927.

Sceleth, C. E. "A Rational Treatment of the Morphine Habit," *Journal of American Medical Association,* March, 1916.

——. "Drug Addiction," *Journal of American Medical Association,* March, 1924.

Schilder, Paul. "Personality in the Light of Psychoanalysis," *The Biology of the Individual.* Edited by J. R. Hunt and others. 1934.

Severs, M. H. "Acute and Chronic Narcotic Drug Poisoning." Unpublished Ph. D. thesis, University of Chicago, 1928.

Shaw, C. R. *Delinquency Areas.* Chicago, 1930.

—— and McKay, H. D. "Social Factors in Juvenile Delinquency," *Report on the Causes of Crime.* Vol. II. Edited by the National Commission on Law Observation and Enforcement. Washington, 1931.

Sigerist, H. E. *Man and Medicine.* New York, 1932.

Sutherland, E. H. *Criminology.* Philadelphia and London, 1924.

Terman, L. M. *The Measurement of Intelligence.* New York, 1916.

Terry, C. E. "The Development and Causes of Opium Addiction as a Social Problem," *Journal of Educational Sociology,* February, 1931.

—— and Pellens, M. *The Opium Problem.* New York: Bureau of Social Hygiene, 1928.

Thomas, W. I. and D. S. *The Child in America.* New York, 1928.

—— and Znaniecki, F. *The Polish Peasant in Europe and America.* Vol. I. Boston, 1919.

Thorndike, L. *A Short History of Civilization.* New York, 1926.

Treadway, W. L. "Drug Addiction and Measures for the Prevention in the United States," *The Journal of American Medical Association,* July, 1932.

——. "Some Epidemiological Features of Drug Addiction," *British Journal of Inebriety,* October, 1930.

——. *Further Observations on the Epidemiology of Narcotic Drug Addiction.* Washington, 1930.

U. S. Bureau of Narcotics. *Traffic in Opium and Other Narcotic Drugs,* 1930, 1931, 1932, 1933.

U. S. Bureau of Prisons. *Federal Offenders,* 1932–33.

——. *Federal Penal and Correctional Institutions,* 1930.

U. S. Public Health Service. *Chemistry of the Opium Alkaloids.* Washington, 1932.

Wickman, E. K. *Children's Behavior and Teachers' Attitude.* New York, 1928.

Willcox, Sir W. H. "The Prevention and Arrest of Drug Addiction," *British Journal of Inebriety,* XXIV (1926).

——. "Medico-legal Aspects of Alcohol and Drug Addiction," *British Journal of Inebriety,* XXXI (1934).

Willoughby, W. W. *Opium as an International Problem.* Baltimore, 1925.

Wu, W. T. *The Chinese Opium Question in British Opinion and Action.* New York, 1928.

Young, K. *Social Psychology.* New York, 1930.

INDEX

PATTERSON SMITH REPRINT SERIES IN
CRIMINOLOGY, LAW ENFORCEMENT, AND SOCIAL PROBLEMS